THE TASTY SIDE OF NEW ENGLAND

A Guide to Great Food by Mail

BETH HILLSON

· THE STEPHEN GREENE PRESS ·
LEXINGTON, MASSACHUSETTS

THE STEPHEN GREENE PRESS, INC.
Published by the Penguin Group
Viking Penguin Inc., 40 West 23rd Street, New York, New York 10010, U.S.A.
Penguin Books Ltd, 27 Wrights Lane, London W8 5TZ, England
Penguin Books Australia Ltd, Ringwood, Victoria, Australia
Penguin Books Canada Ltd, 2801 John Street, Markham, Ontario,
Canada L3R 1B4
Penguin Books (N.Z.) Ltd, 182-190 Wairau Road, Auckland 10, New Zealand

Penguin Books Ltd, Registered Offices: Harmondsworth, Middlesex, England

First published in 1988 by The Stephen Greene Press, Inc.
Published simultaneously in Canada
Distributed by Viking Penguin Inc.

10 9 8 7 6 5 4 3 2

The recipes and logos appearing in this book are reproduced by
arrangement with their respective proprietors.
Photographs by Tony Dugal

Library of Congress Cataloging-in-Publication Data
Hillson, Beth.
    The tasty side of New England: a guide to great food by mail / by
Beth Hillson.
        p.   cm.
    ISBN 0-8289-0664-5
    1. Groceries — New England — Catalogs.   2. Mail-order business —
New England.   3. Cookery, American — New England style.   I. Title.
TX354.5.H55 1989
380.1′41′029474--dc19   88-19894
                                                                    CIP

Designed by Schneider & Company
Printed in the United States of America
Set in Garamond by AccuComp Typographers
Produced by Unicorn Production Services, Inc.

To Joel and Jeremy
for their love, support, and "tasty" comments

❧ CONTENTS ❧

✤ ACKNOWLEDGMENTS ✤

A book that's this diverse would not be possible without the help of a number of enthusiastic people.

I am particularly indebted to my research assistant Barbara Kreminski who spent untold hours helping me track down material for this book; photographer Tony Dugal for reproducing the logos included here; and Jeremy's babysitter, Fran Weigand, who shouldered many mothering responsibilities while I was working.

For invaluable resources, a debt of gratitude goes to Susan Peery and Polly Bannister, *Yankee* Magazine; John Lazenby, *Vermont Life* magazine; Chefs Chris Pardue, Steve Krantrowitz, and Susan Coughlin; and all the people at the New England states' Departments of Agriculture and Economic Development.

In the category of "just doing their job but doing it with a little extra," thanks goes to our UPS delivery man and letter carrier who brought the tasty side of New England to my doorstep; and New England Telephone Operator #432 for helping to find Molunkus, Maine.

A big thank you to my parents for giving me an appreciation of New England and its fine cuisine at an early age. A resounding "thanks" goes to others of the "royal we" for their tasting, comments, and help in every way: Suzanne Flake, Jennifer and Karen Fish, Lorna Godsill, Elizabeth Hillson, Sarah Holzman, Jennifer Hudner, Marjie Manter, Betty Ann and Sara Rubinow, Susan Stillman, and Lynn Weigand (It is this author's belief that food is not meant to be eaten or even sampled alone, but rather, savored with friends.)

Thank you also goes to Tom Begner without whom this book would not be possible and to Lary Bloom and Judith Haynes Hochberg at the Hartford *Courant*'s *Northeast Magazine*, for giving me my first and many subsequent opportunities to write about my favorite subject—food.

Lastly, we should not overlook the entrepreneurs—innovative and pioneering folks—who are responsible for bringing us all the *Tasty Side of New England*.

Not so long ago, food in New England was as predictable as the changing tide. Friday was fish day; Saturday meant baked beans; Wednesday was spaghetti day; and boiled dinner—corned beef or plain boiled beef, potatoes, and cabbage—showed up at least once a week. Like Yankee tradition, this food was wholesome and honest, and it was filling. But it could hardly be called "exciting."

Then, about 10 years ago, Americans began to realize that we did not have to travel abroad to have good food. We started looking in our own backyards and found them rich with our own natural bounty. New England, with a cornucopia of land and seafood unparalleled elsewhere in our nation, quickly became a star in the world of cuisine. And in the weeks and months that followed, these six northeastern states attracted many fine chefs, food enthusiasts, and a burgeoning specialty cottage foods industry. This book is about the cottage foods industry—the suppliers of the many wonderful products that embody a new and exciting New England cuisine.

These suppliers have taken the best that Yankee tradition has to offer—rich and creamy fish and seafood chowders, Indian pudding, johnny cake, mussels, and Belon oysters, and, certainly, the lobster—and added a lot more.

They are purveyors of shiitake mushrooms and operate smokehouses producing delectable smoked bluefish, pheasant, and hams. They are raising pheasants and selling quail eggs. Others are turning the native cranberry crop into chutneys and sauces. Still others are busy restoring old traditions such as grist mills and sugar houses or renewing natural resources such as our supply of trout and sturgeon. Many more are improving on tradition by introducing French cultures to domestic cheeses, producing a local supply of chèvre, or developing a breed of lamb that stands up very well in international competition.

Thanks to them, names such as Vermont cheddar, Putney Chutney, and Aroostook potatoes now evoke the same approval that was once reserved for foods with French-sounding names.

This guide is also about the men and women behind these businesses, some of whom gave up lucrative careers to find a cozy corner in rural New England where they might join the culinary movement and some who returned to the land to carry on century-old family traditions.

They are entrepreneurs for they see the marketing wisdom of a "Made in New England" label and the image of green rolling hills, clean air, and nature that it evokes. But they are, first and foremost, people who love New England. They are drawn to preserve its Yankee traditions of hard work, excellence, and quality control that are only possible when a business is kept intentionally small. And many favor century-old methods of production and doing things "by hand," even though it may take longer.

We've included listings for all six New England states, and we've divided each chapter by state to help cooks in locating the closest source for products. We've picked our favorite sources. But if a company is not mentioned, that doesn't mean that their product is not good. We may not know about them or simply have not tried their foods.

We've provided information on how to mail order from these companies (note, however, that prices may vary on some products). We've also offered recipes and cooking hints on ways we've enjoyed using their products. All the recipes here have been tested, and all the ingredients mentioned here can be shipped to any place in the United States.

Directions are given for those businesses that have retail stores on the premises. Many are glad to have visitors and offer tours, but most operate on very demanding schedules, so understand that their time is valuable and that they may be able to spend only a few minutes with you.

Finally, we've tried to select people and products that tell some of the story that is New England, its heritage, and the exciting new direction in New England fare.

We are grateful to this booming cottage industry. For no matter where we live, it allows us all to taste a little bit of New England.

APIARIES & SUGAR HOUSES

CONNECTICUT

Maple Syrup

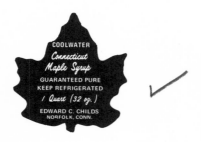

COOLWATER SUGAR HOUSE. Great Mountain Forest, Windrow Road, Norfolk, Connecticut 06058. 203/542-5202 or 5201 (Sugar House).

In the 6,500-acre Great Mountain Forest in the sparsely populated northwestern corner of Connecticut is a sugar operation. And it takes place just about like any traditional sugaring operation in any of the six New England states. But that's where the similarity with most syrup businesses stops.

The main objective of the Great Mountain Forest is to practice good forestry and good land and water use, says Darrell Russ, who's been the head forester for more than 30 years. Maple syrup is one phase of the work being done in this carefully controlled environment.

Owned by Edward (Ted) Childs, professional forester and miner, Coolwater has been in the Childs family for nearly 80 years. It was founded by Ted's grandfather, who also started General Electric many years ago.

Childs and company started making maple syrup in 1940 after Russ got the idea when he visited a sugar house while attending a forestry meeting in Vermont. Since the Coolwater property has many sugar maples, and syrup making would take place in the late winter and early spring when other work is at a low ebb, Childs and Russ thought it would be worth a try. Childs built a small sugar house and purchased an evaporator, sap buckets, and other necessary equipment, and the very next spring, the folks at Coolwater were making maple syrup.

Although the principal sugaring expert is Ernest Smith, "most everyone gets involved in sugaring come spring," says Russ. People stop to buy Coolwater maple syrup which is sold at the sugar house. But there's also a thriving mail order business, and syrup is sent to people all over the world. One well-known customer was Eleanor Roosevelt, who used to buy her maple syrup from Coolwater every year.

HOW TO PURCHASE: Coolwater grade A (light and medium amber) maple syrup is available in gallons for $30; half gallons for $16; quarts, $10; and pints, $6. Shipment is via Parcel Post and postage is extra. To order, send check or money order payable to Coolwater Maple Syrup, c/o Ernest Smith at the address above.

TO VISIT: Coolwater Sugar House welcomes visitors, especially during sugaring time. From Norfolk's only blinking light (junction of U.S. Route 44 and Conn Route 272), go south on Route 272 one block to Mountain Road and turn west. Go to the first intersection (about ⅓ mile), Westside Road, and take a left. Go 1 mile to Windrow Road and turn right. Go up the hill about ⅛ mile, and the Sugar House is on the right.

Maple Walnut Sour Cream Cake with Maple Butter Cream Frosting

This light, rich cake has the subtle taste of maple. Frost it with the maple cream frosting on page 10.

> ½ lb. unsalted butter, softened
> ⅔ cup lightly packed light brown sugar
> 3 eggs, yolks separated from whites, whites stiffly beaten
> ⅔ cup Coolwater maple syrup
> 2 cups all-purpose flour
> 1 teaspoon baking powder
> 1 teaspoon baking soda
> ⅛ teaspoon salt
> 1 cup sour cream
> ½ cup walnuts, chopped

1. Preheat oven to 350°F. Grease two 9-inch round cake pans. Cream the butter with the sugar until light and fluffy. Add the yolks and beat; then add the syrup and beat to combine. Sift the flour, baking powder, soda, and salt together. Add the flour mixture to the butter mixture, alternating with the sour cream. Beat just until combined. Stir in the walnuts. Fold in the whites. Divide the batter between the 2 cake pans. Bake 25 minutes or until a cake tester comes out clean when inserted into the center of the cakes.

2. Remove from the oven and run a kitchen knife around the edges to loosen the cakes from the pans. Turn onto a baking rack and cool completely before frosting. If the cakes are not used right away, wrap them in plastic wrap and store at room temperature.

Yields two 9-inch round cakes.

Maple Syrup/Maple Taffy

LAMOTHE'S SUGAR HOUSE. 89 Stone Road, R.F.D. #3, Burlington, Connecticut 06013. 203/582-6135.

Although maple sugaring is not customarily associated with Connecticut, there are more than 400 producers in the state, says Rob Lamothe, who has his own thriving sugar house and helps others in the state who want to tap their maple trees for profit or hobby.

His is a family affair. Rob and wife Jean, daughter Jessica, son Andrew, and Rob's brother Leonard all pitch in. The business was originally Leonard's idea. He wanted to make "just a little syrup," so Lamothe agreed to let him tap a few of his trees. (He has several acres of sugarbush on his property and manages 147 acres of hardwood for a neighbor.) They liked the results.

At first they made just enough for family and friends, but spurred on by their initial success, they tried sugaring for a second year, this time making a little more. Soon this homespun operation was a bona fide business. With the help of some neighbors, the Lamothe family built a sugar house. They purchased an evaporator, outgrew it, and bought an even larger one. Where they once collected sap-filled buckets by hand, yards of plastic tubing now connect the taps and automatically fill giant holding tanks.

Still strictly a mom and pop operation, Lamothe's is also trying to be self-sufficient. A few pigs, some chickens and turkeys, a few head of beef cattle, and a large vegetable garden help in the effort. In addition, by day, Lamothe is an experimental machinist with a nearby aerospace company. Jean operates a flourishing cake-decorating and bread-baking business. And the children are active 4-H'ers but still find time to help with the sugaring after school and in between tending their blue ribbon livestock.

The Lamothes have been operating their sugar house since 1982. The syrup is made daily during the maple sugar season (from late February to mid April). "The sooner you boil the sap, the fresher and better tasting your maple syrup will be," says Lamothe.

In 1985, the family added maple candy, maple cream, and maple taffy to their line of products. Jean makes the candy by an intricate process that includes molding the sugar after it's boiled. The taffy is a favorite from Rob's childhood in Quebec, Canada. It's known to local patrons as "Sugar on Snow," but Rob has many Canadian customers who call it by the French Canadian name, *La Tire*.

All of this goes on within the little space in the kitchen that's left over from the family's other enterprises, but the Lamothes are planning a new sugar house to hold all their businesses, including a growing mail order business that serves customers from all over the world.

People frequently stop in just to pick up a pint of syrup, despite the out-of-the-way location of the sugar house. And often these customers will request that a pint of syrup be sent to relatives who cannot get the pure version in their locale. Part of their success, says Lamothe, is the demand for a locally made, high-quality product that's available all year round.

HOW TO PURCHASE: Syrup is sold on the premises and by mail. A half-gallon container is $20; a quart is $12.50; a pint is $7; and ½ pint is $5. A 3-oz. gift box of maple sugar candy is $4.50, and the maple cream is $6 for ½ lb. The taffy, $8 for a 10-oz. container, must be kept frozen, so it's sent overnight express. The other items are mailed U.P.S., and postage is between $2 and $8 depending on location and weight. Prices tend to fluctuate based on the current maple crop. It's best to write or call for current prices. However, an order that's accompanied by a check (to Lamothe's Sugar House) will be filled, and Rob Lamothe will either refund an overcharge or bill you for the difference. They do not accept credit cards.

Maple Pecan Mousse

This rich, airy treat is difficult for even a non-mousse lover to resist.

> *1½ envelopes unflavored gelatin*
> *¼ cup water*
> *4 eggs*
> *½ cup firmly packed dark brown sugar*
> *1 cup medium or dark amber maple syrup*
> *2 cups cold heavy cream*
> *¾ cup chopped toasted pecans*

1. In a small saucepan, combine gelatin with water and let sit until firm, about 5 minutes. Set over low heat until melted. Reserve.
2. Beat the eggs with the sugar until foamy. Add the syrup and beat to combine. Transfer to a double boiler and whisk over medium heat until mixture becomes very warm and thick (8–10 minutes). Whisk in the melted gelatin and transfer to a large mixing bowl. Continue whisking for 2 minutes or until slightly cooled. Let cool at room temperature for 30 minutes.
3. Beat the heavy cream until stiff. Fold the cream into the maple mixture. Refrigerate for 30–40 minutes or until mousse begins to set. Fold in ½ cup of the pecans and turn into an 8-cup souffle dish or 12 individual dishes. Sprinkle top with remaining pecans. Refrigerate at least 2 hours before serving.

Serves 12.

MAINE

Maine Blueberry/Raspberry Honey

ELLIS ENTERPRISES. 419 North Main Street, Brewer, Maine 04412. 207/989-6565.

Dave Ellis started beekeeping with a friend as a hobby when the two were in high school. He went on to college where he majored in life biology. But his interest in beekeeping continued, and eventually he moved to Minnesota to serve a 3-year apprenticeship with an expert beekeeper.

Today he's back home in Maine where he operates his own apiary with between 800 and 900 hives. The bees live in Georgia for the winter. But come May, they return to Maine where Ellis rents them out to blueberry growers to pollinate the blueberry crop. A by-product of this arrangement is a delicate and slightly fruity blueberry honey.

After a few weeks among the wild blueberries, the bees move farther north to raspberry country. Raspberry bushes pop up profusely in the clearings left by loggers and then exposed to the late spring sunshine. The honey produced from the wild raspberry blossoms is rich-bodied, light colored, and has a mild, delicious flavor.

When the wild raspberry crop is finished, most of the bees move on to the clover. But Ellis sends some to fields in Aroostook County (near the Canadian border), where the potato farmers have rotated the crop and planted buckwheat that produces a very dark, distinctly flavored honey. This particular product doesn't have universal appeal, so Ellis sells most of his buckwheat honey to a wholesale producer in New Hampshire who blends it with other honey for commercial use.

All Ellis's honey is collected in northern Maine, where the sparse population and rural setting contribute to an environment that guarantees a pure product. "Honey is a bit like wine," says Ellis. The taste varies according to the predominate flower on which the bees have been feeding. "We're fortunate that Maine has so many wild flowers available to produce so many types of honey," he says.

His is a symbiotic relationship with the bees and another beekeeper—Swan Apiary—that's just down the street (and included in this book). Ellis, who's been working for himself since 1980, also worked for a short time for his neighbor before starting out. He buys bees from Swan and sells them honey and vice versa at different stages of their businesses. Since both have a thriving mail order business, it doesn't seem to matter that their businesses are a stone's throw away.

HOW TO PURCHASE: Ellis Enterprises offers a rustic wooden box with three 8-oz. jars of honey (raspberry, blueberry, clover) and a maple honey dipper for $9.95. Individual 8-oz. jars of honey capped with a gingham cloth cover and packed in cedar shavings (your choice of flavors) are $2.95. A 2½-lb. jar of any flavor of Ellis honey is $6.95. Shipping, by U.P.S., is an additional charge: $3 for an order up to $14.99; $4 for an order between $15 and $29.99; a value of $30 to $44.99 is $5 and so on. Ellis will send orders to others for you for $1 extra per address. Checks should be made payable to Ellis Enterprises; Ellis accepts Visa and MasterCard.

Citrus Salad with Raspberry Honey Dressing

Tart and sweet at the same time, this salad finds its way to every brunch we've ever had. But don't stop there. It's great with any meal.

> *4 large seedless oranges (or a mixture of oranges*
> *and grapefruit)*
> *1 small red onion*
> *Freshly ground black pepper*

Dressing

> *3 tablespoons raspberry vinegar*
> *2 tablespoons Dijon mustard*
> *4 tablespoons Ellis raspberry honey*
> *½ cup olive oil*
> *1 tablespoon poppy seeds*

1. Peel the oranges (and the grapefruit) and scrape away any pith that remains on the fruit. Cut the fruit and the onion into thin slices. In a shallow serving dish, alternate fruit and onion slices and grind some black pepper over each layer.

2. Whisk the vinegar with the mustard; then add the honey and mix until combined. Add the olive oil and whisk well. Then stir in the poppy seeds. Pour over the fruit slices. Chill and serve.

Serves 6–8.

Raspberry/Blueberry Honey

R. B. SWAN & SON, INC. 25 Prospect Street, Brewer, Maine 04412. 207/989-3622.

Seated at the chrome and Formica table of a farmhouse-style kitchen, Hilda and Harold Swan pull out every imaginable article about beekeeping and an endless collection of recipes for cooking with honey. The house and garage are fairly well stocked with jars of raspberry, blueberry, and wildflower honey. But there's not a bee to be found.

These honey experts, together with their sons, operate R. B. Swan Apiary, one of the largest honey producers in the state of Maine. Started in 1942 and now run by the third and fourth generation of Swans, it's one of the oldest cottage industries in New England. The key players, the bees, however, are never at home. Most of the week from May to the fall, they are out pollinating crops. These little creatures play an even more important role in the state's economy than making honey. They maintain the existence of some essential products such as the Maine blueberry.

In May the bees are rented to the blueberry growers. While in the blueberry barrens, the bees gather an amber honey with a distinctive, tangy flavor. As spring moves into summer, the bees move on to the wilderness area near Moosehead Lake in northern Maine, where raspberry bushes spring up in the clearings left by logging operations. The raspberry honey is somewhat lighter in color and fruitier in taste. In August and September, and until the first heavy frost, the bees make honey from goldenrod and asters that grow in fields and along the roadsides. Along with the clover and other summer flowers, this produces the smooth-tasting wildflower honey.

The beehives are transported by forklift from one large open field to another throughout the state. The honey is extracted after the bees have pollinated each type of crop. And the product is labeled for the predominant flower in the field or area that they've just worked.

The Swan family began beekeeping with 150 beehives. In 1982, they had increased to 800 or 900 hives, but it left them with little time for the honey-gathering side of the business.

An apprentice, Dave Ellis (also listed in this book), set up his own apiary just down the road. Since 1982, Harold Swan has been buying more and more honey from Ellis and selling him some of the beehives.

Cutting back on the number of hives he needs to transport and maintain leaves Swan more time to do marketing for his business and try out new specialties such as a wild raspberry honeycomb that's a natural, unstrained honey with a piece of honeycomb. A delicacy that was easy to come by 30 years ago, Swan and other apiaries are trying to bring it back. "Once people have put it on their toast, I've got them for life," says Swan.

HOW TO PURCHASE: Swan honey is sold by mail. A 17-oz. plastic jar of wildflower, wild raspberry, or wild blueberry honey is $3; 3-lb. containers are $7. Shipping is $1 extra west of the Mississippi River. Two pieces of wild raspberry honeycomb (9 oz.) sell for $6, including postage. To order, send for a brochure or mail a check or money order to R. B. Swan & Son, Inc.

Moist and Spicy Applesauce Cake

This blue ribbon recipe from Hilda Swan is a honey of a cake. Top it with your favorite cream cheese frosting or use ours on page 61.

¼ lb. butter or margarine
1 cup Swan's blueberry honey
1 egg
1 teaspoon vanilla
1 cup whole wheat flour
1¼ cups all-purpose flour
1 teaspoon baking soda
½ teaspoon salt
1 teaspoon cinnamon
½ teaspoon nutmeg
¼ teaspoon allspice
½ cup chopped walnuts (or other nuts)
½ cup raisins
1 cup unsweetened applesauce

1. Preheat oven to 325°F. Grease and flour a 9x9-inch pan. In a large mixing bowl, cream the butter. Add the honey in a steady stream and beat until mixture is light and fluffy. Add the egg and vanilla and mix well.
2. In a medium bowl, combine both kinds of flour, baking soda, salt, and spices. Mix well. In another bowl, combine the nuts and raisins and mix with 2 tablespoons of the flour mixture.
3. Alternate adding flour and applesauce to the butter mixture, beginning and ending with the flour. Fold in the nuts and raisins. Pour into prepared pan and bake 55 minutes or until cake tests done in the center.
4. Cool 10 minutes in pan. Turn cake onto a cake rack and cool completely.

Pure Maple Syrup

DAN JOHNSON'S SUGAR HOUSE. 70 Ingalls Road, Jaffrey, New Hampshire 03452. 603/532-7379.

A visit to Dan Johnson's Sugar House is a trip back in the history of maple sugaring. Heading down the dirt road to Johnson's farm, the traveler is lured to a rustic-looking building by the delicate, sweet aroma of boiling sap and the sharp, clean smell of burning wood. Standing at the door, Johnson is holding a bottle of his latest product up to the light. He swirls it and samples it with the élan of a professional wine taster. Although he's not a native of New Hampshire, the retired school teacher has been making maple syrup in these parts for more than 30 years. He thinks he has the formula for making the best product, and most folks tend to agree.

As a youngster, the Worcester, Massachusetts, native spent vacations at his grandfather's farm (not far from the farm he now owns). During one visit, he happened on a steaming, bubbling cast iron cauldron, and beneath the rising vapor, a man was making maple syrup the "old-fashioned" way. That was all Johnson needed to see. He was hooked.

Johnson tries to retain some of the past in his own sugaring operation. He talks about centuries back when everyone in "this part of the world" had a sugarbush or maple orchard and depended on the maple tap for their only source of sugar. He recounts how wood choppers would go into the woods, tap a maple tree in the morning, then cut their wood and return to drink the sap for lunch. Half his sugar house is set up to make syrup the nonmechanized, wood-burning way so people can see the old-time process. (The rest of the system is a state-of-the-art network of plastic tubing and holding tanks.)

Johnson enjoys telling visitors about the art of making pure maple products. He claims to be able to tell his from any other maple syrup, and he probably can. While most start with 30 gallons of sap to produce one of sugar, Johnson uses 40 gallons. After his sap is boiled down in the spring, it's stored in wooden casks like a fine wine and fired a second time in the fall, a trick he learned from locals who always heated their syrup before they used it. The result is an intensely maple-flavored syrup that's at once reminiscent of a crisp New England winter and caramelized sugar.

HOW TO PURCHASE: Dan Johnson's pure maple syrup is sold at his sugar house and by mail. It comes three ways: light amber (delicate maple flavor); medium amber (regular); and dark amber (strong maple flavor and deep carmel color). Light amber, the first run, is prized for having the best maple flavor, so the cost is 10 percent higher than prices given here. Cost is $7.70 for ½ pint; $10.50 for a pint container; $15 for a quart; and $23.50 for ½ gallon. Prices include shipping and are higher south of Virginia and west of Ohio. Johnson also sells packages of six (a "good buy," he says) and 12 (the "best buy") of any size container. Write or call for the latest catalog.

TO VISIT: Dan Johnson's Sugar House is open all year, but the best time to visit is when the syrup is being made from March to mid April. To get to the sugar house, take Route 124 to Jaffrey Center. At the center, take South Hill Road and follow posted signs for the sugar house.

Maple Pecan Pie

This New England version is just as rich and gooey as its southern cousin!

> *9-inch pie crust*
> *4 eggs, lightly beaten*
> *Pinch salt*
> *⅔ cup loosely packed brown sugar*
> *6 tablespoons unsalted butter, melted*
> *1 cup Dan Johnson's pure medium or dark amber maple syrup*
> *1 cup pecan halves*
> *1 cup whipped cream for topping*

1. Preheat an oven to 425 °F. Prick the bottom of a 9-inch pie crust and bake blind for 10 minutes. Remove weights and foil or pie plate. Brush the bottom and sides of the crust with a little of the beaten eggs. Return to the oven and bake 3 minutes. Remove and cool on a wire rack while making the filling for the pie. Lower the oven temperature to 350 °F.
2. Beat the eggs with the salt, using an electric mixer on low speed. Add the sugar while beating the mixture. Then add the butter and the maple syrup and beat well, but do not allow the mixture to become too frothy. Set pie plate on a baking sheet. Sprinkle pecans over the bottom of the prepared pie shell and pour the mixture over it. Bake 40 – 45 minutes or until a stainless steel knife inserted in the filling comes out clean. Cool on a wire rack. Serve at room temperature with whipped cream.

Serves 8.

RHODE ISLAND

Rhode Island Honey

RHODE ISLAND

HONEY

WICKFORD APIARIES. 107 Chatworth Road, North Kingstown, Rhode Island 02852. 401/295-5383.

Beekeeper Charlie ("Mac") McKellar has bee psychology all figured out. The key is to handle them gently, explains the hobbyist turned honey businessman.

"For the most part, they are very gentle, themselves," says McKellar, who also says he knows better than to try to handle his bees on a cloudy or rainy day, after dark, or when they're riled. "If I do, I can count on stings," explains the man who's as feisty as his bees. "You can't make marmalade without counting the oranges," he says of his occupational hazards.

A British Columbia native, McKellar was raised on a farm and attended a one-room school until the eighth grade when he came to the United States with his father. At age 17, McKellar joined the Marine Corps and retired 22 years later in Rhode Island. Now in his sixties, he started keeping bees as a hobby in 1984 while continuing to work in a second career in data processing. He began with just one hive but quickly grew to twenty-five, then added more. Before he knew it, he was on his way to a thriving business.

Until 1987, however, beekeeping was just a sideline for McKellar. Now retired for a second time, he makes the Wickford Apiaries label his primary interest. In addition to a lucrative honey business, McKellar also sells beekeeping supplies, and it's McKellar who new beekeepers come to see when advice is needed.

McKellar enjoys what he does far too much to watch the proverbial bottom line. Although he works hard, his bees work even harder. For him, the harmonious bee colonies are a source of constant fascination. "We humans could learn a lot from honeybees," says the enthusiastic McKellar.

McKellar's honey is not of any specific blossom. Due to its size, Rhode Island doesn't generally produce honey from a single floral source. But the mixture of nectars through the various blossoming seasons provides a delightful product—clover, raspberry, and orange blossoms in the spring; locust in late May; and goldenrod and daisies in the fall.

If that sounds like just plain old honey, think again. McKellar's product has received blue ribbons and top honors all up and down the Atlantic seaboard. For those who still doubt that a man from Rhode Island can produce the best honey on the East Coast, McKellar sums it up. "You can't tell quality until you taste it," says the grandaddy of Rhode Island beekeepers.

HOW TO PURCHASE: McKellar will sell you some of his prize-winning honey under the Wickford Apiaries label if you send him a check for $6.50 payable to Wickford Apiaries. For that price, he'll send a 2-lb. bottle or a 1-lb. bottle and a 12-oz. squeezable plastic bear. Please specify. Price includes shipping to anywhere in the United States.

Elaine's Honey Whole Wheat Bread

When my friend Elaine Larkin brought me two loaves of this bread as a gift, I was hooked forever. When you try it, you will be, too.

> *2 cups boiling water*
> *1 cup uncooked oatmeal*
> *2 packages active dry yeast*
> *⅓ cup lukewarm water*
> *½ tablespoon sugar*
> *⅛ teaspoon salt*
> *½ cup Wickford Apiaries honey*
> *2 tablespoons butter, softened*
> *2½ – 3 cups unbleached flour*
> *1¾ cups whole wheat flour*
> *¼ cup sesame seeds*
> *1 egg yolk, beaten*

1. In a large bowl, pour boiling water over oatmeal and let stand until soft and cool (about 30 minutes). Proof the yeast by combining the yeast, lukewarm water, and sugar and allowing to stand 10 minutes or until yeast begins to bubble.

2. Add salt, honey, and butter to the cooled oatmeal; then add the yeast mixture. Add the flour a little at a time, mixing after each addition. (Use the smallest amount of unbleached flour and add the remainder as the dough is worked.) Knead 10 minutes by hand or 5 minutes with a machine that has a dough hook attachment. Put into an oiled bowl, cover with a towel or oiled plastic wrap, and let rise 1 hour or until doubled in size.

3. Punch down and divide into two. Place in 2 greased 9x5-inch loaf pans. Cover with a towel or sheets of oiled plastic wrap and set in a warm spot away from a draft. Let rise until the dough comes up to the top of the pans (about 30–40 minutes). Preheat oven to 350°F. Brush the tops of the loaves with egg yolk and sprinkle with sesame seeds. Bake 30–40 minutes or until breads sound hollow when tapped.

4. Turn onto rack and cool thoroughly.

Makes 2 loaves.

VERMONT

Crystallized Honey

CHAMPLAIN VALLEY APIARIES

CHAMPLAIN VALLEY APIARIES. P.O. Box 127, Middlebury, Vermont 05753. 802/388-7724.

Of all the products we sampled for this book, Champlain Valley Apiaries' spirit-lifting crystallized honey is the treat that steals the show. Its subtle, sweet taste and chewy texture make for an orbit-launching spread!

One fan of this honey is Susan Peery, a senior editor of *Yankee Magazine*. And it was her endorsement—"I put the crystallized honey on toast and could eat 10 pieces!"—that sent us looking for the apiary.

Perhaps the most extraordinary thing about this wonderful honey product is that it comes straight from nature. Champlain Valley merely helps it to our tables by simply extracting it from the honeycombs, then packing it without heating or filtering the honey first. This ensures that it retains its original delicate flavor and all the nutrients.

As basic as this sounds, crystallized honey is not commonly available because it cannot be made with low-grade honey. So, we should say a resounding "thank you" to Charles and William Mraz, who own Champlain Valley Apiaries, raise the bees, and oversee the production of the top-grade honey that's used in making such a rare delicacy.

Champlain Valley Apiaries was started in 1931 by Charles, who's now well into his eighties. His son William has taken over much of the family business in recent years, but the patriarch of this operation still comes in every day, collects some of the honey, and keeps up with the mound of correspondence that accumulates from a loyal following of customers. The senior Mraz also conducts research into honey and its effect on arthritis. And both father and son have a wealth of information on the nutritional value of honey.

Champlain Valley Apiaries has about 1,000 beehives situated in the hinterlands of Addison County in northwestern Vermont, bordering on Lake Champlain. The bees make their honey primarily from blossoms of clover and alfalfa. The honey is light in color and delicately flavored.

Because of the high grade of the Mrazs' honey, it doesn't usually spoil. Low moisture and high-sugar content prevent that. (Their clear honey is also spared any filtering and is carefully processed at temperatures that do not exceed 140 degrees.)

Champlain Valley Apiaries has been providing its customers with the same good honey for nearly 60 years via several means, including a small retail store on the property that's worth a visit. Infused with the slightly sweet fragrance of honey, a visitor could not miss the fact that this is the outlet for Champlain Valley Apiaries' clear honey, crystallized honey, and beeswax. The honey is also sold to other stores and by mail in 5-pound pails.

HOW TO PURCHASE: A 5-lb. pail of clear or crystallized honey is from $11 to $12.50 including shipping via U.P.S. Gift packs are also available. Price varies depending on destination. To order, send cash, check, or money order payable to Champlain Valley Apiaries.

Vermont Pumpkin Pie

How can a recipe miss when it has both honey and pumpkin in it? This New England favorite is easy to make—and that's fortunate since it'll disappear before your eyes.

> *1 deep-dish, 9-inch pie shell, unbaked*
> *⅔ cup Champlain Valley Apiaries honey*
> *½ teaspoon salt*
> *1½ teaspoons cinnamon*
> *½ teaspoon ground ginger*
> *½ teaspoon nutmeg*
> *½ teaspoon allspice*
> *½ teaspoon ground cloves*
> *1 tablespoon cornstarch*
> *1½ cups cooked and puréed fresh pumpkin (or one 15-oz. can)*
> *1⅔ cups heavy cream*
> *2 eggs, lightly beaten*

1. Preheat oven to 425°F. Chill the pie shell for several hours. Combine honey, salt, cinnamon, ginger, nutmeg, allspice, cloves, cornstarch, and pumpkin and blend. Beat the cream with the eggs and mix with the pumpkin until well blended.

2. Set the pie shell on a baking sheet. Prick the bottom several times with a fork. Pour the filling into the shell. Bake 15 minutes. Reduce heat to 350°F. and bake 35 minutes or until custard is set. Remove and chill. Serve with whipped cream or vanilla ice cream if desired.

Serves 8.

Maple Nut Brittle

GREEN MOUNTAIN SUGAR HOUSE. R.F.D. #1, Route 100 North, Ludlow, Vermont 05149. 802/228-7151.

It all started more than 40 years ago when David Harlow first boiled sap in an iron kettle over an open wood fire. Every year he'd continue the tradition, making syrup for family and friends. Then in 1968, Harlow and wife Marjorie decided to start selling their maple syrup and maple products.

In the meantime, daughter Ann went away to nursing school but soon returned to work in the family business, which by then included a gift shop and a mail order business. Her husband, Douglas Rose, was also lured into the business. A carpenter by trade, he'd work at Green Mountain Sugar House during his slow times, which happened to coincide with the peak sugaring months.

Together, the Roses took over the family business in 1985, with the Harlows helping out during the busiest seasons. It must have been "something in the blood" that drew the Roses to carry on, speculates Ann, who hopes to pass along the operation to their two children one day.

Green Mountain Sugar House makes a wide range of pure maple products, in addition to a large syrup production. Two spin-offs are maple candies and maple cream. Made weekly to ensure freshness is the house specialty, and our favorite, maple nut brittle. Without the cloyingly sweet taste that's usually associated with brittle candy, this one is subtle with a light maple sweetness. A new product for the Green Mountain Sugar House, Maple Nut Brittle requires reducing the maple syrup to a point beyond that needed for regular maple candy. Then the thick syrup concentrate is poured into a generous heap of nuts—cashews, pecans, walnuts, almonds, peanuts, and sunflower seeds.

The Green Mountain Sugar House now publishes an impressive mail order brochure that includes a number of non-maple products. Jams, smoked products, and cheeses are also featured, along with other Vermont-made items. Next door is the sugar house, and nearby is a cider mill that's active in the fall. The Harlows and Roses gladly offer tours of both.

Do they ever tire of maple syrup? Apparently not. Both families use syrup as their principal sweetener. "Fortunately we all still love it (maple syrup)," says Ann Rose.

HOW TO PURCHASE: All products may be ordered via mail. An 8-oz. bar of maple nut brittle is $7.50 and $7.95. A ½-lb. box of maple candy hearts or leaves is $11.50 or $11.95. An 8-oz. jar of maple cream is $7.95 or $8.50. A quart of medium or dark amber maple syrup is $16.95 or $17.75, and pints of either cost $11.25 or $11.75. The first price is for delivery east of the Mississippi River, and the second is for points farther west. Check, money order, and all major credit cards are accepted.

MAPLE GROVE FARMS OF VERMONT. 167 Portland Street, St. Johnsbury, Vermont 05819. 802/748-5141.

Maple Grove was started in 1915 by a mother and daughter team on a farm near St. Johnsbury. Katherine Gray and her daughter Helen made candies from maple syrup and Jersey cream produced right on the Gray farm. Their products were made in the family kitchen, and they were sold on the front porch and the farmhouse lawn. Customers were chiefly tourists who were summering in Vermont. When the summer ended, the ladies expected the candy business would be over, too. But soon they were receiving letters requesting candies for Christmas gifts. So Maple Grove became a mail order business as well.

When their confection operation outgrew the farmhouse, the Grays bought the old Governor Fairbank's mansion in St. Johnsbury. In addition to larger quarters for the candy business, the two operated a tea room and overnight guest accommodations. That was a little much even for these two energetic ladies, and in 1929, they sold the maple candy business to a large company, Cary Maple Sugar, which moved it to a building at the edge of town. It has remained here ever since. But ownership has changed twice in the ensuing years.

In 1975, the current owner William Callahan bought the company and expanded the product line to include salad dressings, barbecue sauces, maple spreads, and fruit syrups, all using Vermont maple syrup. The Callahans have concocted a delightful sweet and sour barbecue sauce and a salad dressing using maple syrup and maple vinegar. A very healthy mail order business sends these and other Maple Grove products all over the country.

Maple Grove continues to make maple sugar candies the way Mrs. Gray and her daughter did many years ago, with 100 percent pure maple syrup. They have also introduced the less-sweet Cabin Candy, a blend of maple and cane sugars and fresh cream. And they make mint, cranberry, and blueberry candies as well. Maple Grove, of course, sells pure maple syrup, and it comes in an array of sizes. They also carry maple cream (also called maple butter) that's merely an intensely flavored syrup that's been boiled until it's very thick.

To supply Maple Grove and its production line requires well over 100,000 maple trees. (One mature maple produces about 8 gallons of sap in a good season, and that yields about a quart of syrup.) Maple Grove makes all its own products, and they buy the syrup they need from several thousand area farmers. What's left of the "sugaring" part of Maple Grove is a replica Sugar House and Maple Cabin Museum dedicated to explaining the process and open to visitors the year round.

HOW TO PURCHASE: Maple syrup is $10.95 for a pint and $15.95 for a quart. A half gallon of Grade A dark amber syrup is $31.25 per tin and $30.50 in a jug. Maple cream is sold in a 1-lb. jar for $13.75 or three 8-oz. jars for $19.50. Granulated maple sugar comes in a 1-lb. bag for $12.65. Dressings are sold in sets of four 8-oz. bottles for $14.50. Flavors include Sweet 'N Sour, Chunky Blue Cheese, Cheddar 'N Bacon, and Herb 'N Buttermilk. Shipping is extra. Add $1.75 for orders up to $5; $2.25 for orders from $5.01 to $10; $2.75 for orders from $10.01 to $15. Write or call for the complete chart of fees and latest catalog. Payment is by check, money order, or major credit card.

Maple Butter Cream Frosting

Use this frosting with the maple walnut cake included in the entry for Coolwater Sugar House on page 2 of this book. Garnish with walnut halves for a dessert that has Vermont written all over it.

> *1½ cups Maple Grove maple cream*
> *¾ cup sour cream*
> *1 teaspoon pure vanilla extract*
> *4 tablespoons unsalted butter, softened*
> *¾ cup coarsely ground walnuts*
> *½ cup walnut halves, for garnish*

In a saucepan, combine the maple cream and the sour cream. Heat until blended and cook until mixture reaches 234°F. on a candy thermometer (soft ball stage). Remove from heat. Beat until light, creamy, and cool to the touch. Add the butter and beat well. Frost cake immediately. Sprinkle ground nuts around the sides of the cake and garnish the top with walnut halves.

Yields enough frosting for a 2-layered, 9-inch round cake.

Maple Syrup/Maple Cream

Palmer's Maple Syrup

PALMER'S MAPLE SYRUP. Box 246, Waitsfield, Vermont 05673. 802/496-3696.

When the temperature drops below freezing at night and rises to 40 or 50 degrees during the day, Kathryn and Everett Palmer head for the woods—their woods. The maple sugaring season has begun.

Everett, a retired dairy farmer, has been been doing this most of his life. In fact, he and his wife tap the same 32 acres of trees that his father and grandfather tapped before him. Everett, now in his 80s, and his wife go by "instincts, urges, and feelings" to determine when the sugaring season will begin. Those same instincts are what help them produce some of the best syrup in the state.

To make their syrup, they filter the sap into a storage tank, from which it then flows into another tank in the sugar house, a wooden structure that sits on the edge of the woods. The steam rising from the sugar house on almost any day during sugaring season tells people across the valley that the Palmers are making syrup. An evaporator built by Everett's grandfather takes up most of the sugar house. And a constantly fed wood fire produces a fierce heat that keeps the sap at a rolling boil until it reaches just the right density.

That density is determined by a method known as "sheeting off." Kathryn or Everett scoops a ladle of boiling sap and watches it as it flows off the bottom edge. If it has reached the correct density, it should flow in a sheet rather than in drops. A hydrometer is the sure method of testing, but the Palmers have been doing this for so long, they most often rely on their eyes and their instincts.

The syrup is strained and immediately canned to preserve the clear, golden product. The Palmers work day and night during the maple sugaring season and most of the time during the rest of the year to prepare for the time when the sap flows. (It takes a full week to wash down all the equipment once the season is over. And Everett spends the remainder of the year cutting the many cords of wood needed to feed the fire under the evaporator.)

Nevertheless, the two never tire of the process. Visitors from as far away as Great Britain and Canada come to visit the Palmers and watch them make maple syrup. They love the constant flow of company and the opportunity to explain the rituals of a tradition of which they are extremely proud. And Kathryn gets up at 5 A.M. each morning to make her famous raised doughnuts which they serve to visitors to the sugar house. With the help of her daughter, she serves over 100 dozen doughnuts during sugar season.

Despite the demanding hours and strenuous work, Everett and Kathryn would never have it any other way. As long as they are able, they will continue making syrup.

HOW TO PURCHASE: Palmer's Maple Syrup is sold in containers ranging from ½ pint to a gallon. Syrup comes in light, medium, and dark amber. Prices are $4.40 per ½ pint, $7.60 for a pint, $12 per quart, and $40 per gallon. Prices are apt to change depending on the season so it's best to check with the Palmers before ordering. Shipping (by U.P.S.) is extra and varies with destination. Send check or money order payable to Palmer's Maple Syrup. They cannot accept credit cards.

TO VISIT: The Palmers love visitors. The best time to visit is March and April when they are sugaring. Take Route 100 and turn right onto East Warren Road in the direction of Waitsfield Village. In the middle of the village, you will go through a covered bridge. Continue 1 mile farther (in the direction of East Warren), and you'll see signs for Palmer's on the right.

Kathryn Palmer's Vermont Baked Beans

This is one tradition that New England will never surrender! Serve with Yankee brown bread or slices of pumpernickel bread.

> 4 cups dried yellow eye or soldier beans
> ⅓ lb. salt pork
> 1 medium onion, chopped
> 2 teaspoons salt
> ¼ teaspoon ground ginger
> 1 tablespoon dry mustard
> 1 teaspoon black pepper
> 1 cup Palmer's dark amber maple syrup

1. Set the beans in a large heavy pot, cover with water, and soak overnight. Drain the water and add fresh water to cover. Bring to a boil and simmer, covered, for 30 minutes.
2. Pour off all but enough liquid to barely cover the beans. Add the remaining ingredients. Stir and bake in a 300°F. oven for 6 hours, adding more water if necessary.

Serves 12.

BAKER'S SUPPLIES & BAKED GOODS

C O N N E C T I C U T

Chocolate Mousse Cake

THE CHOCOLATE MOUSSE CAKE
DESSERTS BY DAVID GLASS

DESSERTS BY DAVID GLASS. 140-150 Huyshope Avenue, Hartford, Connecticut 06106. 203/525-0345.

"Funny my cooking is so much better than my cakes," says David Glass. "I cook such wonderful sauces," says the culinary wizard who trained in three-star restaurants, pastry and chocolate shops in France.

But everyone likes chocolate. And for those of us who have eaten Glass's cakes, it's difficult to believe that anything could be better. Florence Fabricant of the *New York Times* calls his cake the "ultimate dessert." *New York* magazine's Gael Greene says it's "dark and wicked as a truffle." "It's the cheapest taste of sin you'll ever experience," says Candy Sagon of the *Dallas Times Herald*.

Glass started making chocolate mousse cakes in his kitchen in 1982. A "bootleg" operation, the big trucks would pull up to the slightly run-down Hartford address every day and load up with stacks of cakes ready for delivery to customers.

A year later, he opened a bona fide business in a factory where he makes 600 to 1,000 cakes per day. Glass has nearly all the same clients he started with and, of course, many more. None have really noticed that the formula keeps changing. Glass is on the 120th variation. Mostly the amount of chocolate and sugar have changed. He once tried a Belgian chocolate, too. Now he's back to his blend of several domestic and imported chocolates.

Glass does his own brand of marketing and public relations. He's written blurbs for trade journals that include suggestions that he be nominated for a Nobel Prize for his incredible desserts. His non-conformist sales approach includes walking into the plush offices of Stanley Marcus at the Neiman-Marcus Department Store in Dallas dressed in T-shirt and shorts. He gave Marcus a taste of chocolate mousse cake and clinched the sale.

Rumor has it that this legendary chocolate mousse cake is from a recipe imparted to Glass by a French woman on her deathbed. The woman made a surprise recovery and tried to sue Glass to get the recipe back, so the rumor goes.

Glass makes several renditions of his chocolate mousse cake — an espresso, an orange, and a bourbon flavored cake are all part of the repertoire. He also makes Chocolate Mousse Balls coated with hazelnut praline and a Bourbon Pecan Cake. His latest addition is an Old World cheesecake that he calls My Grandmother's Cheesecake. Rich and light with a farmer's cheese base, it is made according to his grandmother's recipe. "I grew up on this cake," he says.

What's next in the Glass product line? "I want to make another cake as great as the chocolate mousse cake!" he says.

HOW TO PURCHASE: Desserts by David Glass can be mail ordered. Prices are $9 for a 6-inch and $15 for an 8-inch Chocolate Mousse Cake. A box of 16 Chocolate Mousse Balls is $14. A 2-lb. Bourbon Pecan Cake is $17. My Grandmother's Cheesecake (1 lb.) is $9. Add $4 for shipments to New England and as far south as Washington, D.C., and add $7 per package for shipping and handling to all other addresses. Shipments are via U.P.S. overland and U.P.S. Second Day Air, respectively. Orders must be prepaid with check or money order.

Raspberry Sauce

The only thing that might be better than a David Glass Chocolate Mousse Cake straight up is one served with this wonderfully fruity sauce.

> *1 pint fresh or frozen raspberries*
> *1 tablespoon confectioner's sugar, sifted*
> *1 tablespoon raspberry brandy*
> *6-inch Chocolate Mousse Cake by David Glass*

1. Purée the raspberries and strain through a sieve to remove the seeds. Add the sugar and brandy and chill until ready to serve.
2. Spoon onto plates and top with a generous slice of David Glass Chocolate Mousse Cake.

Makes 8 servings.

Lemon Rum Sunshine Cake

MATTHEWS 1812 HOUSE. Box 15, Whitcomb Hill Road, Cornwall Bridge, Connecticut 06754. 203/672-0149.

The restored 1812 farmhouse that gives her business its name is the rural setting for the production of Deanna Matthews's crowd-pleasing cakes, which have been playing to appreciative audiences since 1979. With a mailing list from all fifty states and several foreign countries, Matthews has tantalized thousands with her mouth-watering cakes.

If cake can be exciting, this one is. This incredibly creamy, light, and velvety cake exudes lemon and rum the moment the lid is removed from the tastefully decorated, gold-colored box. "Moist and deliciously spirited," says *New York Times* food critic Marian Burros of Matthews's Lemon Rum Sunshine Cake.

Matthews started her mail order food business after leaving a 17-year career in the New York retail trade and moving to Connecticut. She had always enjoyed cooking as a hobby and had a yen "to be in the food business." Mail order foods seemed to fit the bill. Using a recipe that had been her grandmother's, Matthews started making a fruitcake appropriately named Heirloom Fruit and Nut Cake. Moist and fruity and laced with brandy, it is made with only all-natural ingredients. All Matthews's products (she also makes a Heritage Brandied Apricot cake) use plump dried fruits, nuts, real butter, and farm-fresh eggs. Homemade jams and jellies, assorted nuts, hard candies, and hand-dipped chocolates are recent additions to the mail order catalog.

Exquisite taste and glitzy packaging make these terrific gift items. The Matthews family will also write the greeting card to be enclosed with each gift order.

HOW TO PURCHASE: Most of Matthews's business is done via the mail. A beautiful four-color catalog of products is available by writing or calling. A 1¾-lb. Lemon Rum Sunshine Cake is $17. The Heritage Brandied Apricot Cake and the Heirloom Fruit and Nut Cake are each $14.25 (1½ lb.) or $26.50 (3 lb.). Postage is $2.50 per address and shipping is chiefly by U.P.S. All cakes are decorated with satin ribbons and wrapped in attractive, reusable tins. Matthews accepts all major credit cards.

Lemon Rum Sunshine Cake with Fruit Jubilee

As if a Matthews's Lemon Cake isn't occasion enough, this sauce makes it truly a holiday dessert.

1 pint fresh blueberries, washed
1 pint fresh strawberries, hulled and sliced
1 pineapple, cored and cut into bite-size pieces

Sauce

2 cups fresh or frozen orange juice
½ cup sugar
½ teaspoon almond extract
½ teaspoon vanilla extract
*1 tablespoon cornstarch mixed with 2 tablespoons
   orange juice*
¼ cup almond liqueur
Matthews 1812 Lemon Rum Sunshine Cake

1. Prepare the fruit. In a small saucepan, combine the orange juice and sugar. Bring to a boil and simmer until the sugar has dissolved. Add the two extracts and the cornstarch mixture and return to a boil. Stir vigorously while allowing the mixture to thicken. Remove from the heat and add the almond liqueur. Chill 1 hour.
2. Add the fruit and mix to coat with the sauce. Chill until ready to serve.
3. Cut 16 thin slices from the cake. (Cover the remainder and refrigerate for another use.) Arrange 2 slices on each plate. Allow to come to room temperature if the cake has been in the refrigerator. Spoon a generous amount of the topping over the cake. Serve.

Serves 8.

MAINE

Bakewell Cream & Biscuit Mix

BAKEWELL CREAM & THE APPLE LEDGE COMPANY.
R.F.D. #2, Box 6640, East Holden, Maine 04429.
207/942-5532.

If you've ever traveled to Maine during blueberry or strawberry shortcake season, then you probably know that Mainers can't live without their biscuits. An old-time Yankee mainstay, these chewy pillows of dough appear, heaped with fresh fruit and berries, in every little Down East diner during the summer months.

During World War II, however, a shortage of cream of tartar put that New England staple in jeopardy. (The aluminum in it was needed for wartime supplies.)

In 1940, chemist Byron H. Smith of Bangor saved the day by developing a substitute leavening agent that he called Bakewell Cream. It got Mainers through the war, and soon folks discovered there were some serious advantages to baking with Bakewell Cream. It produced lighter, fluffier biscuits and lasted longer on the shelf.

A totally unique product that's never been duplicated, Bakewell Cream became a highly prized commodity and for many years it sold well. Then Byron Smith died, leaving a business that was in decline, owing to its having never been advertised or actively marketed.

Smith's granddaughter Linda Smith Buckley, along with her mother and sister, took over management in 1979, and they faced major decisions about Bakewell Cream's future. In an effort to revitalize the foundering business, Buckley introduced a biscuit mix, called the Original Bakewell Cream Biscuit Mix, in 1985. Identical to the biscuit recipe that's on each can of Bakewell Cream, the mix was a response to customer requests for a more convenient way to make the same delicious Bakewell biscuits.

Buckley's marketing efforts and savvy food brokers put Bakewell Cream and the Bakewell Cream Biscuit Mix back on Maine grocery shelves.

Recently, the Smith family sold the business to Lolly and Paul Sevigny. Local folks, the Sevignys hope to expand distribution even farther, into all of New England and regions beyond. They continue to send packages of the cream and biscuit mix through the mail. Lolly chuckles each time she receives a letter stating, "I can't live without my Bakewell Cream."

One thing hasn't changed, however. The recipe for the original, mouth-watering biscuits is the same as it was when Byron Smith started Bakewell Cream so many years ago. And due to his ingenious offspring, and now the Sevigny family, this fascinating chapter in Maine food lore will be preserved for yet another generation.

HOW TO PURCHASE: The 16-oz. box of Original Bakewe Cream Biscuit Mix is $1.75, and the 8-oz. can of Bakewell Crea costs $2. There is a $1.75 fee for shipping and handling. Case price for biscuit mix are available and perhaps the best bet for biscu lovers. Price is $18.75 plus $6.50 postage.

Mom's Strawberry Shortcake

Many Mainers argue that the "proper" way to make a strawberr shortcake is to mix unsweetened cream with sliced berries and pou this over warm biscuits that have been cut and buttered. We alway made it a little differently. Whatever your preference, the biscui should be light and fluffy. For that, Bakewell Cream Biscuit Mix perfect.

The filling

*1 quart fresh strawberries, hulled, washed, and
  sliced
¼ cup sugar (or less, depending on the sweetness
  of the berries)*

The biscuits

*1 package Bakewell Cream Biscuit Mix
2 teaspoons sugar
1½ cups cold milk
5 tablespoons butter*

*1 cup heavy cream, whipped until it forms
soft peaks*

1. Combine the strawberries and the sugar and allow to sit in th refrigerator 1 hour.

2. Preheat the oven to 450°F. Add the sugar to the biscuit mix; the quickly mix in the cold milk all at once. Knead 4 or 5 times unt smooth and all dry ingredients feel moist. Pat or roll out to abou ¾-inch thickness and cut biscuits. Set each on cookie sheet an dot with 3 tablespoons of the butter. Bake 10 to 12 minutes or unt golden. Remove and allow to cool for 10 minutes. Cut in half throug the center of each biscuit and place a small pat of the remainin 2 tablespoons of butter in the center of each split biscuit.

3. Spoon strawberries into the center of each biscuit, replace top and spoon extra berries over each. Top with a generous dollop c whipped cream and serve.

Makes 12 shortcakes.

French Acadian Ployes de Boqouite

BOUCHARD FAMILY FARM. R.F.D. #1, Box 690, Fort Kent, Maine 04743. 207/834-3237.

At a time when many small family farms are taking their lumps, Rita and Alban Bouchard and family are making their proverbial "hay" with an ethnic commodity that's been a hit everywhere it's been tried. Their product, Ployes de Boqouite, is an original mix for a buckwheat pancake that's been a favorite, centuries-old Acadian substitute for bread. Low in calories and high in nutrition, these can be paired with dishes as diverse as spiced ground pork or vanilla ice cream.

Ployes (rhymes with boy) had been a staple with itinerant Acadians who, expelled from Nova Scotia, settled in the St. John Valley in northern Maine. Rough terrain and long hard winters made it impossible to grow wheat, but buckwheat did well in this valley. Thus, there were always ployes de boqouite, even when a loaf of bread was beyond the budget.

Unique to this region of the country, ployes had enjoyed only local popularity until a Maine author, Virginia Rich, wrote an intriguing mystery, *The Baked Bean Supper Murder*, which spurred national interest in these slightly nutty tasting crepes. Orders for valley-grown buckwheat began to pour into a local grocery store, and Rita and her daughter Jane Bosse decided to capitalize on the renewed interest for this Acadian specialty. Fortuitously, Alban had planted 100 acres of buckwheat to diversify his 500-acre potato farm. So the mother-daughter team began creating a ployes mix that would allow even the busiest cook to whip up a batch of the buckwheat pancakes in no time. (The original recipe used by their ancestors called for making a time-consuming sourdough starter.)

The two started making their ployes de boqouite mix in 1983 during off-duty hours from their regular jobs as registered nurses with a $100 investment for supplies. Production is currently about 10,000 pounds a year, and the Bouchard family team has had to move from their country kitchen into Alban Bouchard's two-car garage. Perhaps the burgeoning cottage industry will not make the family rich, but the Bouchards wouldn't mind if it did. They've tried many things in the past to make the farm profitable, from raising chickens and pigs to growing potatoes. "I'd really like to see the ployes become a full-time family business," says Bosse.

HOW TO PURCHASE: A 3-lb. bag of Ployes de Boqouite is $5.95 when shipped within a 600-mile range; $6.50 from 600 to 1,400 miles distance; and $7.25 if sent beyond 1,400 miles. Two bags sent to the same regions cost $8.75, $9.60, or $11.60 respectively. To order, send check or money order payable to Bouchard Family Farms.

Buckwheat Crepes with Cheddar and Apple

The Bouchard Family's Ployes de Boqouite mix makes the lightest nutty-tasting crepes ever to grace the palate. Combined with cheddar cheese and apples, this recipe is all–New England and a rare treat.

1 egg
1½ cups cold milk
1 cup Ployes de Boqouite mix
2 tablespoons melted butter
1 cup coarsely chopped apples (McIntosh are best)
2 tablespoons unsalted butter
1 cup grated medium or sharp cheddar cheese

1. In a medium mixing bowl, whisk the egg and the milk. Add the Ployes mix and whisk until smooth. Add the melted butter and whisk to combine. Allow batter to rest for 5 minutes.
2. Spray an 8-inch crepe pan with vegetable spray and set over medium heat. When hot, pour ⅓ cup of batter in the pan and smooth around with a spoon until ⅛ inch thick. Cook 2 minutes, flip, and cook another minute. Remove from pan and repeat until all the batter has been used. Batter will yield 8 to 10 large lacey crepes.
3. Sauté chopped apples in 2 tablespoons of butter for 2–3 minutes or until well coated and slightly soft.
4. Preheat oven to 325°F. Divide the apples among the crepes and sprinkle cheese over the apples. Roll the crepes and set in a lightly buttered pan. Bake 10 minutes or until cheese has melted.

Serves 4.

Sinfully Good Fudge Pie

EASTER ORCHARD FARM BAKERY. Box 1321, Wells, Maine 04090. 207/646-7177.

Mort Mather is a colorful character who would just as soon hoe his garden as anything else. That's not to say that he does that. Mostly he's running a major fund-raising effort that successfully turned the tide on a 250-acre seaside property destined to become an oil refinery. For that he received the 1987 Environmental Award from *Down East* magazine.

When he's not busy raising money for that endowment fund, he's also organizing the annual Harry S Truman Manure Pitch-Off held each year at the Common Ground Fair.

But, most of all, Mort and his wife Barbara run a small home bakery where they make a deep-dish, 10-inch fudge pie that's so sinful, it makes the chewiest, chocolatiest brownie pale by comparison.

Mort Mather started out as a theatrical stage manager and found his way to Maine in the late 1960s as stage manager of the Ogunquit Playhouse. Here he met Barbara, and the two bought a 100-acre farm in "back Wells" in 1969, spending $16,000 for their parcel.

Barbara had a recipe for an outrageously rich fudge pie. At the request of friends who ran a restaurant, the couple started making their fudge pies for them in 1973. The Ogunquit eatery would serve the pies with whipped cream in the indented center and a topping of green crème de menthe to complement the green and white motif of the restaurant.

For many years, the fudge pie business catered chiefly to this and many other restaurants. Occasionally someone would request a pie by mail, and the Mathers would send it in the same Pyrex dish they used to deliver their desserts to eateries. Later, Mort would go around trying to retrieve the plates.

In 1985, the two had a box designed to hold their pie, and it just happened to be suitable for mailing. Now, in addition to environmental preservation activities and manure pitch-offs, the Mathers mail fudge pies—2½ pounds of rich brownie with a soft fudge center—to any point in the continental United States. Made from top quality ingredients, including bittersweet chocolate, eggs, and butter, the fudge pies are baked in two large old pizza ovens in the Mathers' own kitchen.

And about the manure pitch-off. Mort devised a contest in which participants are judged for their ability to spread a truckload of manure evenly. It's one of the most popular events at the Windsor, Maine, fair each year and requires simply a durable sense of humor and large amounts of manure. Only government officials are barred from entering. "They're already much too good at spreading it," says Mort.

HOW TO PURCHASE: Mort and Barbara Mather will ship 2½-lb. 10-inch fudge pie anywhere in the United States for $1 including postage. Orders must be prepaid, and checks should b made out to the Mathers or Easter Orchard Farm Bakery.

Fudge Pie à la Fudge

This dessert takes the place of a multitude of sins!

10-inch Mathers' fudge pie
½ pint French vanilla ice cream, softened slightly

Chocolate Sauce (1 cup)

½ cup heavy cream
¼ cup sugar
5 oz. semisweet chocolate
3 tablespoons unsalted butter
½ teaspoon vanilla

½ cup heavy cream, whipped
Chocolate shavings, to garnish

1. Spread ice cream in the center of fudge pie. Chill in freezer whil preparing chocolate sauce. (Don't chill for more than 30 minute or pie will be too cold to taste its best.)
2. Heat cream and sugar in a heavy medium saucepan over mediu heat. Stir occasionally until sugar has dissolved. Add the chocola and the butter and stir until the chocolate is completely melted an sauce is slightly thickened. Remove from the heat and add the vanill Let cool slightly.
3. Just before serving, remove the pie from the freezer. Drizzle ha the chocolate sauce over the ice cream. Top with whipped crea and chocolate shavings. Serve with extra chocolate sauce.

Serves 1–2 real chocolate lovers or 8–10.

English Fruitcake, Cheesecakes & Christmas Pudding

ELFIN HILL. Business Route 1, P.O. Box 1317, Damariscotta, Maine 04543. 207/563-1886.

If there's any doubt that dreams are the stuff that make successful businesses, talk to Emma Stephenson and Don Smith. To visit them at their charming Elfin Hill Bed and Breakfast in tiny Newcastle, Maine, we'd never have suspected that an adjacent barn-turned-kitchen was the center of operation for a booming mail order business that produces more than a ton of English fruitcake and nearly as much chocolate cheesecake each year.

It's even harder to believe that the two started the business not very long ago—1983, to be exact. While serving us tea and bite-size pieces of their prize-winning fruitcake, Stephenson and Smith told us how they came to Maine via Wilton, Connecticut, where the two met while working for Nabisco Company. The company was threatening to move south, so Smith and Stephenson decided to move north.

They arrived in Maine equipped with a dream of starting a bed and breakfast; a life-sized elf from the now defunct Danbury Fair which they took as the name for their business; and Stephenson's favorite recipe for fruitcake, which she brought from her native Kent, England. The two found a charming house overlooking the Damariscotta River and set about to construct their dream. It happened to include a mail order business, and fruitcake was just what they needed. (There is not as much competition for English-style fruitcake in this country.)

Even people who hate fruitcake enjoy Stephenson's. While traditional fruitcake packed with citron, peel, and nuts is reminiscent of biting into a dirt road, hers uses no candied fruit, relying instead on nuts and spices to produce a dense cake that boasts the best traits of fruitcake without the bumps!

Success started when nearby L. L. Bean offered to carry Elfin Hill fruitcake in their Freeport store. From there, Stephenson and Smith expanded to include their Triple Chocolate Cheesecake, one of the most incredible eating experiences we've ever had. They added a carrot cake with cream cheese frosting, classic butter cookies, fruitcake mini-morsels (individually wrapped and packed in a decorative tin), and a mocha swirl cheesecake. The two are introducing a gingerbread and an English Christmas Pudding in their upcoming catalogs.

The mail order bakery business has been so good to Stephenson and Smith that they gave up their bed and breakfast operation, and in the summer of 1988, the couple moved to larger quarters in Newcastle's twin village of Damariscotta. Smith has converted yet another barn into a spacious kitchen—just in time for the next million or so fruitcakes and the upcoming busy season.

HOW TO PURCHASE: Elfin Hill's 2-lb. English-style Fruitcake is $15.95. Triple Chocolate Cheesecake (shipped only October to May 15) and Mocha Swirl Cheesecake are each $15.95; Classic Creamy Cheesecake is $13.95. Carrot Bundt Cake (1 lb. 12 oz.) is $12.95 and comes with its own pouch of cream cheese frosting. A Christmas Tuck Box is offered, with English specials including a 2-lb. fruitcake, a 2-lb. Christmas Pudding in its own bowl, a large jar (over a pound) of Elfin Hill marmalade, and a box of Christmas Crackers. Price is $38.95. All prices include shipping via U.P.S. Write or phone for a full catalog. Payment is by check, money order, MasterCard, or Visa.

Cumberland Rum Butter

This makes a delicious topping for Elfin Hill Christmas Pudding. It keeps well stored in the refrigerator, if given a chance!

>   4 tablespoons unsalted butter, softened to room
>   temperature
>   ½ cup dark brown sugar
>   3 tablespoons dark rum
>   ½ teaspoon vanilla extract

Beat the ingredients together until very smooth and fluffy. Refrigerate until ready to serve.

Yields ¾ cup (enough for a 2-lb. Elfin Hill Christmas Pudding).

Organically Grown Whole Grain Products

FIDDLER'S GREEN FARM. R.R. 1, Box 656, Belfast, Maine 04915. 207/338-3568.

Nancy Galland and Richard Stander are inclined to believe there's something providential about their being at Fiddler's Green Farm. The 115-acre organic farm in midcoast Maine was where Dave Kennedy had grown wheat for more than 10 years, just for the love of it. It was all part of his philosophy that the future of the small farm, once an integral part of American life, depends on ecologically sound farming techniques.

Kennedy died in a plane crash in 1985, and he left the farm to a trust charged with finding someone to carry on his vision. The farm would only be sold with the stipulation that organic methods would continue to be used in perpetuity. Galland and Stander heard the farm was for sale just about the time that chemical spraying was forcing them out of their organic vegetable operation in western Massachusetts.

The two were among fifteen qualified applicants who interviewed for the stewardship. "We never thought we'd get the appointment," says Galland, thinking their ages (43 and 52) would count against them. But the couple came out on top and took over in the spring of 1986. They began working toward turning Kennedy's dream into a truly self-sustaining, economically viable family farm. They continued wheat production but found ways to improve the yield of grains with better drainage and by rotating crops. And they continued to grind the farm's crop of soft winter wheat and Aroostook rye in the grist mill on the property.

The intrepid couple determined the best way to market their grain was by turning their crops into other, more salable products. So the two expanded the product line that had started back in Kennedy's day with Cap'n Dave's Pancake and Muffin Mix (still a favorite in coastal Maine). Stander and Galland added Irish Soda Bread Mix, the kind that doesn't crumble and makes divine toast; Penobscot Porridge, a tasty stick-to-the-ribs blend of wheat and rye berries, brown rice, and whole corn; and a versatile Buttermilk Spice Cake Mix. A new logo, new packaging, and some advertising, and the two were well on their way.

Stander and Galland also redecorated part of the big farmhouse and turned it into a thriving bed and breakfast. Here guests are served continental breakfasts of Cap'n Dave's piping hot blueberry muffins. And the two let guests know what they are eating and that it's available on the farm. A thriving mail order business, too, has helped boost sales of their wholesome products.

HOW TO PURCHASE: Fiddler's Green whole grain mixes are sold by the package. Penobscot Porridge (1-lb. bag) is $2.38; Irish Soda Bread Mix (1¾ lbs.) is $2.90; Cap'n Dave's Pancake and Muffin Mix (1½ lbs.) is $2.64; Buttermilk Spice Cake Mix (1½ lbs.) is $2.67. Gift packets of several Fiddler's Green items are available. Shipping is extra and is via U.P.S. (Be sure to include a street address. U.P.S. will not deliver to P.O. boxes.) Payment is by check, money order, Visa, or MasterCard.

Shaker Apple-Gingerbread Cake

A dense cake with lots of flavor and textures, this one's reminiscent of the kinds of cakes made by old-fashioned New England bakers.

> *2 medium apples, peeled, cored, and cut into*
> *¼-inch slices*
> *1 egg*
> *⅓ cup of milk*
> *⅓ cup vegetable oil*
> *⅓ cup molasses*
> *¼ cup honey*
> *2 cups Buttermilk Spice Cake Mix*
> *½ cup raisins*

1. Preheat oven to 350°F. Grease an 8-inch pan. Spread the apple slices evenly over the bottom of the pan.
2. Combine the egg, milk, oil, molasses, and honey and beat well. Add the cake mix and stir until moistened. Stir in the raisins and pour over the apple slices. Bake 35 minutes or until cake tester comes out clean. Let cool 10 minutes in pan then transfer to a serving plate. Brush warm cake with Lemon-Honey Sauce below.
Serves 8.

Lemon-Honey Sauce

> *4 tablespoons butter, melted*
> *4 tablespoons honey*
> *2 tablespoons freshly squeezed lemon juice*

Stir ingredients together until mixed and brush over warm cake. Serve the rest of the sauce with the cake.

Stone-ground Grains & Whole Grain Mixes

The Tribute Of The Current To The Source

MORGAN'S MILLS. R.D. #2, Box 115, Union, Maine 04862. 207/785-4900.

By the old mill stream in the sleepy hamlet of East Union, history is repeating itself. Credit goes to a Rhode Islander named Richard Morgan and his Ohio-born wife Helen. The two have restored a nearly 200-year-old grist mill that was built by one of the area's first settlers, John Lermond, in 1803.

Morgan, formerly a marine-engine mechanic and machinery repairman, had always dreamed of restoring a water-powered mill as a family business. In 1977, he began looking for a site that would fulfill his vision and, in 1978, happened upon the mill in East Union. Badly in need of repair and idle for more than 10 years, the mill required nearly 2 more years of hard work to restore it to working condition. Morgan added a hydro-powered electric generator that produces more than enough power to run the mill and excess to sell at a nice profit to Central Maine Power Company. The water source is the same Alford Lake and Lermond Pond that Lermond harnessed nearly 2 centuries ago to power his enterprise.

Morgan salvaged traditional granite stones from a Vermont mill to stone-grind all his grains. The mill made its debut in 1981 when the Morgans introduced Mainers to johnny cakes at a local country fair. Today Morgan's Mill is supplying bakers throughout New England with organically grown flour and meal. They grind many different grains, among them hard red spring wheat, soft winter wheat, hard winter wheat, rye, oats, barley, buckwheat, johnny cake flour, and three types of rice flour among them. Most popular, however, are their wonderful muffin mixes and Griffles (pancake and waffle) mixes. One of our favorites is the sweet and dense tawny-colored Maple Corn Muffin Mix (Helen's own recipe) that we cooked as a pie-shaped bread and served in wedges.

Business started slowly, and Helen maintained her outside job as a medical secretary and midwife, and Richard continued with his machinery repairs. Today, however, Morgan's Mills is processing about 63 tons of products a year, and neither Helen nor Richard has the time for outside work. With customers from Bangor to Boston and mail order requests coming from all over, the mill has become a full-time job for both. And the three Morgan children pitch in by pasting labels on packages.

HOW TO PURCHASE: Products are shipped in 1½-lb. or 5-lb. packages. Blueberry Griffles are $3.25 or $8.50. Buckwheat Griffles are $2.75 or $6.95. Maple Corn Muffin Mix is $2.75 or $6.95. Orange Bran Muffin Mix is $2.50 or $4.75. Stone-ground flour and meal are sold in the same weights, and prices range from $1.60 to $3.55 for smaller bags, and $3.25 to $10.35 for large sacks. Write or call for the latest list of prices. Gift packs are also sold. Prices include shipping, which is via U.P.S. Payment is by check or money order.

Whole Wheat Pizza with Caramelized Onion & Gorgonzola Cheese

A "white" pizza seems to bring out the full flavor of this marvelous crust. This caramelized onion and Gorgonzola cheese topping is our favorite.

> *¾ cup lukewarm water (105°F.–115°F.)*
> *2 packages active dry yeast (¼ oz. each)*
> *¼ cup Morgan's Mills whole wheat bread flour*
> *½ cup unbleached white bread flour*
> *¾ to 1 cup all-purpose flour*
> *½ cup Morgan's Mills whole wheat bread flour*
> *1 teaspoon salt*
> *3 tablespoons olive oil*

1. Combine the water, yeast, and the ¼ cup of whole wheat flour. Stir to dissolve. Let stand in a warm place for 15 minutes or until yeast begins to bubble and increase in size.
2. Combine remaining ingredients in a large bowl, using the smaller amount of all-purpose flour to start. Add activated yeast and mix. If dough is too sticky, add remaining flour as needed. Turn onto a floured surface and knead 10 minutes or until smooth, adding flour if dough becomes sticky. Set in a large bowl. Cover and allow to rise until doubled in size (about 1 hour).
3. Preheat oven to 450°F. Roll dough into a 14-inch circle and set on a pizza pan that has been dusted with cornmeal or on a pizza stone. Top with Caramelized Onion & Gorgonzola Cheese Topping (below). Bake 15 minutes in lowest part of the oven.

Makes one 14-inch pizza.

Caramelized Onion & Gorgonzola Cheese Topping

> *3 medium onions, thinly sliced*
> *2 tablespoons olive oil*
> *2–3 cloves garlic, minced*
> *14-inch whole wheat pizza crust*
> *¼ cup olive oil mixed with 3 cloves of crushed garlic*
> *4 oz. Gorgonzola cheese, crumbled*
> *3 tablespoons pine nuts*
> *3 tablespoons chopped fresh parsley*

1. Sauté the onions in the 2 tablespoons of olive oil over medium heat until they are quite brown (about 10–15 minutes). Add the garlic and sauté 2 minutes. Cool.
2. Brush the pizza dough with the olive oil and garlic mixture. Spread onions over the top, then sprinkle with the cheese, pine nuts, and parsley.

Yields topping for one 14-inch pizza.

Natural Sourdough Bread

BALDWIN HILL BAKERY. Baldwin Hill Road, Phillipston, Massachusetts 01331. 617/249-4691.

The words "bleached," "enriched," and "refined" are never spoken at the Baldwin Hill Bakery, a European-style bakery recreated on a 20-acre farm in the countryside of eastern Massachusetts. While many traditional bakeries have been replaced by large bread factories that turn out products tasting like balsa wood, Hy Lerner and his natural foods bread-making business are baking dense loaves of chewy sourdough bread that are uncommonly delicious.

From the ground up, Lerner and his staff of twenty control every aspect of the bread-making process. Hard wheat and spring wheat berries are purchased from an organic grower in Montana and stone ground as needed at a mill 2 miles from the bakery. Wheat berries are crushed and fermented to form the sourdough starter. No yeast is used, Lerner explains, as it will only break down the starchy part of the bread. Sourdough starter acts on all elements of the wheat and can leaven 30 times its weight. This makes the bread fully digestible — and irresistible, we might add. Unlike some sourdough breads which leave a strong, almost acidic taste, Baldwin Hill products are mild and satisfying.

Lerner started Baldwin Hill Bakery in 1974 after studying bread making with Omer Gevaert at the LIMA Bakery in Belgium. "I felt his bread should be introduced to this country," Lerner says. He returned to the States to duplicate the operation in Massachusetts, building a wood-fired brick oven that bakes up to 200 loaves of hard-crusted bread at once. The hardwood fuel also gives the bread a wonderful aroma.

Six varieties of bread are made based on the same recipe — whole wheat, no-salt whole wheat, sesame wheat (filled with sesame seeds), rye, sourdough French, and raisin bread. The last is chock full of raisins (about ¾ of a pound for each 1½-pound loaf) and is a hearty breakfast in itself.

Baldwin Hill Breads keep well for up to a week in unsealed plastic bags and may be frozen or refrigerated. The sourdough starter acts as a natural preservative that retards spoilage longer than most non-preservative breads, and a loaf is easily refreshed by steaming it for a few minutes.

HOW TO PURCHASE: All Baldwin Hill breads are available by mail. The whole wheat, no-salt whole wheat, rye, and sesame are made in 1¾-lb. loaves for $1.50 each, and whole wheat also comes in 1-lb. loaves for $1 each. The raisin bread is sold in 1½ lb. loaves for $1.90; and French sourdough bread (a 1¼-lb. loaf) is $1.55. There is a 12-loaf minimum order, but these freeze well and are wonderful to have on hand. Shipping is extra and based on weight and zip code. Write or call for the latest prices and a chart of shipping charges. Baldwin Hill Bakery accepts checks and money orders but no credit cards.

Sourdough Cheese Strata

This one adds a new dimension to ho-hum brunch or breakfast menus.

> *12 slices Baldwin Hill Bakery rye sourdough bread*
> *1 cup diced ham*
> *¼ cup chopped green onion*
> *2 cups grated mild cheddar or Swiss cheese*
> *6 eggs, lightly beaten*
> *1 cup milk*
> *1 tablespoon spicy mustard*
> *Salt and pepper to taste*

1. Preheat oven to 350°F. Butter a cookie sheet and arrange the slices of bread in one layer on the pan. Sprinkle ham, onion, and cheese over bread slices.
2. Whisk together the eggs, milk, mustard, and salt and pepper. Pour evenly over the bread slices. Bake 20–25 minutes or until bread is slightly puffed and edges are golden. Serve.

Serves 4–6.

Rugelach

CHRISTINE'S GOURMET BAKERY. 8 West Main Street, Wellfleet, Massachusetts 02667. 508/349-3100.

Bob Costa has been cooking most of his life. Both sisters hated the kitchen, so he was appointed to help his mother with the food preparation. "She was an unbelievable cook," recalls Costa, who says he learned everything about cuisine from her.

It was during this early part of his life that Costa and his family frequented a neighborhood fixture called Mother's Bakery in Riverdale, New York. They made the very best rugelach—tiny Eastern European roll-ups filled with raisins, nuts, and apricot or raspberry jam—and it was a recipe he always wanted to duplicate.

Years later, when Costa moved from Manhattan to Cape Cod, and he and his wife Christine decided to open a bakery, he still remembered the taste of that rugelach. He dug up every recipe he could find for this rich, buttery pastry and came up with a hybrid that's "as good or better," says Costa.

A horticulturist and landscape artist by training, Costa had run a restaurant in lower Manhattan for years—a sort of blue-collar lunch and dinner bistro—before moving to Wellfleet in 1980. In Wellfleet, he continued with his real profession until the town's only bakery closed. The two couldn't imagine a town without a bakery so they gave it a try. That was back in 1984. Today they make an extensive assortment of pastries with only pure butter, cream cheese, sour cream, and flavorings. It's all "just like grandma used to make," says Costa.

Of all their products, however, the rugelach is the most popular, and it's requested by people from all over the country. Ironically, 30 to 40 percent of Christine's mail order requests for rugelach come from New York addresses, a fact that tells Costa he's doing something right.

In addition to rugelach, Christine's bakery takes mail order requests for their fudge brownies, which are nearly as rich and second in popularity. The lemon tea cake, French loaf cake, and sour cream coffee cake are also on top of the list, and Costa hopes he'll be able to mail order some or all of those items soon.

HOW TO PURCHASE: Christine's Bakery will ship a 1-lb. box of rugelach (17–20 pieces) for $12.50. One pound of Fabulous Fudge Brownies (yields seven 2x2-inch squares) is $10. Shipping is extra and varies with destination. Outside of New England, they ship U.P.S. Second Day Air. Orders must be prepaid, and Christine's accepts Visa and MasterCard.

Gourmet English Muffins

JOYCE'S GOURMET ENGLISH MUFFIN COMPANY. 4 Lake Street, Arlington, Massachusetts 02174. 617/641-1900.

Thomas' move over. Joyce Kazanjian is making English muffins—nearly 2 inches high and about 4 inches round—that are likely to revolutionize the industry. Every mouthful is packed with a taste that's as gargantuan as the muffins themselves.

Kazanjian began making her oversized muffins in the kitchen of her home for family and friends. She made about 10 dozen of the finely textured muffins at a time. She even designed food baskets around her products, featuring teas, coffees, and jams to complement them. Friends kept telling her she should market them.

In early 1987 she tapped into a local bakery shop where she could turn out 40 dozen a day. Then in August, Willard Scott, on NBC's "Today Show" rated them a "gangbusters 11" on a scale of 1 to 10. Next a mention in the *New York Times* advised, "Discard all other English muffins and switch to these crispy-crusted moist gems." Apparently many followed this advice for Kazanjian was swamped with requests.

Just 7 months after Kazanjian began her enterprise, Joyce's Gourmet English Muffin Company moved into its own shop. By the end of the first year in business, Joyce's was selling more than 30,000 muffins a month. They were soon carried in many "gourmet" delis throughout the Northeast. Now a family business, Kazanjian employs fourteen, including daughter Lil Vickers and her three sons.

Kazanjian's creations are baked rather than grilled as are most English muffins. In addition to plain muffins, she makes a cinnamon raisin and a honey wheat raisin, both full of raisins. Her cheese muffins each boast 1 to 1¼ ounces of cheese (a blend of five different cheeses). Her latest, onion muffins with a subtle onion taste, are a savory addition to the line.

Currently the muffin maker is experimenting with an apple spice muffin with chunks of apple. "It's unlimited, what you can do with muffins," says Kazanjian, who still gloats over the fact that a basket of her muffins brought in more money than Bobby Orr's hockey stick at a recent charity auction.

HOW TO PURCHASE: A dozen muffins, one flavor, are $12.95; assorted are $11.40. Add $1.95 for handling. Add $2.41 for shipping, which is via U.P.S. (There is a small extra charge for U.P.S. Second Day Air.) MasterCard and Visa are accepted, as are check and money order.

Gourmet Muffins Benedict

The possibilities for Joyce's Gourmet Muffins are endless. Here an updated version of an old standby.

> *½ lb. young asparagus spears, washed*
> *4 Joyce's Cheese English muffins, split*
> *½ lb. prosciutto ham, in thin julienne strips*
> *8 large eggs*
> *1 recipe of Chive Hollandaise Sauce*
> *Extra chopped chives for garnish*

1. Bring a pot of water to a boil. Trim the asparagus and cut eac spear in half lengthwise. Boil 3–5 minutes or until lightly cooke but still crunchy. Remove and rinse under cold water. Drain ar reserve.

2. Make the hollandaise sauce according to the directions belov Spread the muffins on a baking sheet and warm in a 400°F. ove for 5 minutes. Remove muffins and set oven to broil. Top each muff with ⅛ of the prosciutto ham. Cut each spear of asparagus into thir and lay 6–8 pieces on top of the ham.

3. Poach the eggs for 4 minutes. Remove with a slotted spoon. T each muffin with an egg. Then cover each with 2–3 spoonfuls hollandaise sauce. Set under the broiler 1–2 minutes or until edg of sauce are brown. Garnish with additional chopped chives ar serve.

Serves 8.

Chive Hollandaise Sauce

> *4 egg yolks*
> *1 tablespoon cold water*
> *½ lb. unsalted butter, cut in pieces*
> *Juice of 1 lemon*
> *Salt and pepper to taste*
> *2 tablespoons fresh chives, chopped*

In the top of a double boiler set over medium heat and with wat simmering, whisk the egg yolks and cold water together. Whisk un mixture is smooth, pale yellow, and warm. Add the butter, a fe pieces at a time, whisking until the butter has been absorbed. Co tinue until all the butter has been added. Add lemon juice, salt ar pepper, and chives. Reserve.

Yields about 1½ cups of sauce.

Emily Dickinson Raisin Brandycake

Judy Fersch

Teacakes Etcetera, Inc. • P.O. BOX 134
CONCORD, MASS. 01742 • (617) 369-7644

TEACAKES ETCETERA, INC. P.O. Box 134, Concord, Massachusetts 01742. 508/369-7644.

Taking a bite of Judy Fersch's Emily Dickinson Raisin Brandycake is like sampling a bit of history. The dedicated cook from Concord faithfully reproduces the nineteenth-century author's recipe in a business that's dedicated to producing fine baked products, some of which are made according to historically based recipes.

Fersch hesitates to call this spice cake—chock full of raisins and generously soaked in brandy—a fruitcake because she says "people give fruitcakes, but they don't eat them." Marian Burros, *New York Times* food critic, says, "This one you will eat." The *Concord Journal* goes so far as to call it a "fruitcake fit for the Queen of England at high tea." Fruitcake lover or not, Fersch's Raisin Brandycake is almost guaranteed to make a fruitcake fancier out of you.

With the help of her friend Joel Porte, then chairman of the English Department at Harvard University, Fersch found Dickinson's original recipe for New England Black Cake. Fersch followed the recipe closely with some modifications for the sake of modernization. (Sketchy details and skimpy instructions often stand in the way of turning historical recipes into dishes that appeal to modern tastes. However, Fersch, an accomplished baker who enjoys that sort of challenge, was able to do just that.) Her recipe remained authentic enough to allow her cakes to be included in recent Emily Dickinson centennial celebrations in Washington, D.C., and at Dickinson's homestead in Amherst, Massachusetts.

Teacakes Etcetera was started by Fersch in 1984. Today her company, which includes a wholesale, retail, and mail order business, offers several other cakes from Fersch's own repertoire. A very dense, moist cake with a chocolate glaze is appropriately named Chocolate Chocolate Cake. The Almond Lemon Cake has also received accolades for being very tangy, moist, and filled with ground almonds and a distinctive citrus flavor. Cinnamon Apple Cake, filled with fresh apples and pecans, and Dark Gingerbread Cake that's moist and spicy round out the list.

HOW TO PURCHASE: All Teacakes Etcetera cakes are available by mail. They are nicely packaged with hand-tied ribbons. The Raisin Brandycake comes in a 24-oz. loaf for $16 and a 12-oz. loaf for $10. The Almond Lemon Cake, Chocolate Chocolate Cake, Cinnamon Apple Cake, and Dark Gingerbread all come in an 8-inch bundt shape for $13 each. Prices include shipping, which is via U.P.S. Orders must be prepaid by check or money order. Cakes are shipped only between October and May.

Honey Nut Granola

RR#1 Box 792 Austin Farm Rd
Exeter, RI 02822

AUSTIN FARM. R.R. #1, Box 792, Austin Farm Road, Exeter, Rhode Island 02822. 401/392-0212.

Lorilynn and Brian Bishop's granola was always the star attraction when the two trundled their pony cart through the streets of Providence peddling home-grown organic vegetables, goat's milk, cheese, and yogurt. It was with good intentions that these Michigan natives purchased the turn-of-the-century Austin Homestead Farm in 1982. All their vegetables would be organically grown and hand harvested. They would raise their own chickens and tend a flock of goats.

But the two hadn't planned on the back-breaking work their ambitions would bring. So, in 1985, the young couple decided to give up farming and devote their time to making the delectably crunchy, chewy fruit and nut granola that has become their trademark. There was no question that success was on the horizon. A blend of sixteen ingredients, including almonds, apple bits, cinnamon, raisins, rolled oats, safflower oil, sesame seeds, sunflower seeds, walnuts, and wheat germ that's sweetened with plenty of clover honey, makes this granola expensive and sweet. "But it always sells out immediately," according to the owner of the Harvest Health Food Store in Newport, who told us about Austin Farm.

Austin Farm also makes spice and herb blends and an all-natural peanut butter. A favorite is their Versatile Blend, a mixture that's made with basil, cayenne pepper, lemon peel, sesame seed, and thyme and has no salt or sugar. People just leave it on the table and use it in place of salt and pepper, says Lorilynn.

The 110-acre farm, once a major agricultural center of Rhode Island, is now a National Historic Registered farm. To help defray expenses, the two have made the farm into an equestrian center where they conduct lessons and board horses.

HOW TO PURCHASE: The granola is $4.00 for a 1-lb. bag, $5.00 for a 1-lb. jar. The Versatile Blend is $5.00 for a small jar, $6.00 for a large jar. The all-natural peanut butter is $3.75 for a 1-lb. jar. Shipping and handling are extra charges. Shipping is via U.P.S. Personal checks are accepted. Austin Farm does not take credit cards.

Austin Farm Granola Apple Crunch

Something on the order of an apple Betty, the granola adds extra crunch.

Apple Mixture

4 cups peeled, cored, and thinly sliced Granny Smith apples
⅓ cup sugar
1 tablespoon all-purpose flour
½ teaspoon cinnamon
Pinch of nutmeg
Pinch of salt

Topping

½ cup loosely packed light brown sugar
⅔ cup Austin Farm honey nut granola
½ cup all-purpose flour
¼ teaspoon cinnamon
¼ teaspoon nutmeg
Pinch baking soda
Pinch baking powder
6 tablespoons melted butter

Heavy cream (whipped) or vanilla ice cream (optional)

Combine apple mixture ingredients and layer in an ungreased 8x8-inch pan. Combine dry topping ingredients. Add melted butter and mix well. Sprinkle over apples. Bake in preheated 375°F. oven for 30 minutes. Serve warm, topped with half-whipped cream or vanilla ice cream, if desired.

Serves 6–8.

Johnny Cake Mix

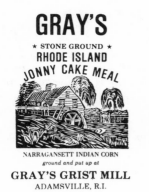

GRAY'S
★ STONE GROUND ★
RHODE ISLAND
JONNY CAKE MEAL

NARRAGANSETT INDIAN CORN
ground and put up at
GRAY'S GRIST MILL
ADAMSVILLE, R.I.

GRAY'S GRIST MILL. P.O. Box 422, Adamsville, Rhode Island 02801. 508/636-6075 (Gray's is on the Rhode Island/ Massachusetts line).

For Rhode Islanders, politics and religion have never generated the heated discussions that arise at the mention of johnny cakes. A legacy from pioneer days, these stone-ground corn cakes are as indigenous to the state as the right to vote. And the ways of preparing them might well be as numerous as the candidates in some elections.

Around the Kingston area, home of Kenyon Corn Meal Company (also listed in this book) the locals know for certain that the only way to make a johnny cake is by adding boiling water to the cornmeal and cooking up thick cakes that are crispy around the edges, but soft in the middle.

Tim McTague, part owner and manager of Gray's Grist Mill, would sooner be caught dead than make his johnny cakes with scalding water. McTague maintains that adding anything hot takes the ''zip'' out of the meal. Instead, he thins his johnny cake mix with cold water until the batter is soupy, just as his mentor and former owner of the mill John Hart has done every day for 70-odd years.

McTague was a carpenter working in Adamsville, a tiny town that sits on the bank of the Westport River on the Rhode Island/Massachusetts border, when he heard about an apprenticeship at the grist mill. The moment he met Hart, he was filled with admiration. The prospect of acquiring a real craft with years of tradition behind it suited the young man.

Gray's has been the site of an operating grist mill for more than 300 years. Early on, it was powered by water from the west branch of the Westport River. Today, the four giant granite stones that grind the corn, rye, and wheat are powered by a 1946 Dodge truck that sits outside.

The present mill was started in 1878 by James L. Gray. Hart came along in the early part of the 1900s and married Marion Gray, the granddaughter of the original owner. During World War II, gas rationing caused most of the grist mills in the area to fold. But Hart, who likes his johnny cake, kept the business going.

Gray's still grinds true Rhode Island johnny cake meal that's harvested from Narragansett Indian Flint Corn grown in the fields of nearby Little Compton, the southeasternmost tip of Rhode Island. The grist mill also makes a New England Brown Bread and Muffin Mix that's been used for more than a century to make the steamed brown breads that Yankees ate with their Saturday night baked bean dinners. And McTague has added a whole grain pancake mix that even John Hart thinks is pretty good!

HOW TO PURCHASE: Two-pound bags of Johnny Cake Meal, Brown Bread and Muffin Mixture, and Pancake and Waffle Mix are $5.25 per bag. These all come in 5-lb. bags for $10.95 each. Two- and five-pound bags of whole wheat flour and rye flour are sold for $4.25 and $10.25 respectively. Shipping (via U.P.S.) is included. Send check or money order payable to Gray's Grist Mill. Credit cards are not accepted.

TO VISIT: These products are also sold on the premises, and McTague welcomes visitors, particularly between 10 A.M. and 2 P.M., Saturday and Sunday. To get to Gray's, take Route 195 east from Providence until it intersects with Route 24. Follow Route 24 south to Route 81 south and follow 81 until it ends in Adamsville. At the end of Route 81, bear left and follow this road ¼ mile. The grist mill is across from the pond.

Polenta with Escargot in Tomato Cream Sauce

A discussion about the many uses for Gray's cornmeal inspired this recipe which chef Steve Kantrowitz features on the evening menu at Hartford, Connecticut's Max on Main. We loved it, and he graciously agreed to let us include it here.

Polenta

2 cups water
1 teaspoon salt
1 cup Gray's Stone Ground Johnny Cake Meal
1 egg white, stiffly beaten
2 tablespoons unsalted butter for frying the polenta

1. Butter a loaf pan. Bring water and salt to a boil in a medium saucepan. Sprinkle the cornmeal over the boiling water, whisking constantly until mixture is smooth. Simmer 3 minutes, stirring with a wooden spoon. Mixture will become very thick. Remove from heat and fold in the egg white. Spoon into loaf pan and smooth mixture out evenly. Cool for at least 2 hours or overnight in the refrigerator.
2. Slice into 4 pieces. In a large skillet, melt the butter over medium heat. Add the polenta slices and fry on both sides until browned. Remove from pan and slice in half diagonally. Place 2 triangles on each of 4 plates and spoon one-fourth of the escargot and sauce (below) over each.

Escargot with Tomato and Cream Sauce

12 canned giant escargot, rinsed and drained
½ cup white wine
½ cup water
1 sprig fresh thyme
6 leaves fresh oregano
1 bay leaf
1½ tablespoons extra virgin olive oil
2 teaspoons finely chopped garlic
1 large ripe tomato, seeded and chopped
6 leaves fresh basil, in thin strips
1 tablespoon capers, drained
¼ cup white wine
¾ cup heavy cream
Salt and pepper to taste
1 tablespoon unsalted butter

1. In a saucepan, combine the escargot, ½ cup white wine, water, thyme, oregano, and bay leaf and bring to a simmer. Simmer 4 to 5 minutes. Remove from heat and drain. Reserve.
2. Coat a sauté pan with the olive oil and set over medium heat. Add the garlic, tomato, basil, and capers and sauté for 1 minute. Deglaze with the ¼ cup white wine and reduce by half. Add the cream and reduce by half. Add the escargot and salt and pepper. Stir and remove from the heat. Swirl in the butter and spoon over the polenta triangles. Serve warm.

Serves 4.

Johnny Cake Mix/Stone-ground Meals and Flour

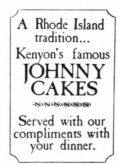

A Rhode Island tradition... Kenyon's famous **JOHNNY CAKES** Served with our compliments with your dinner.

KENYON CORN MEAL COMPANY. Usquepaugh, West Kingston, Rhode Island 02892. 401/783-4054.

For more than 90 years Kenyon Corn Meal Company has helped perpetuate the legacy of the johnny cake, but only if it's made their way.

The folks at Kenyon's travel all over New England demonstrating the "right way" to make these round griddle cakes. Kenyon's owner Paul Drumm insists it's necessary to scald the cornmeal with boiling water before cooking it. He and the folks around Usquepaugh and the South County make their johnny cake thick and soft in the middle, crispy around the edges and the outside.

But the one place that a Kenyon proponent cannot show his or her face is around the Newport area. That's the home of Gray's Grist Mill (also listed in this book).

The food lore about the johnny cake goes back to when the Pilgrims adopted the corn cakes during their first winter in this country. It seems all the wheat they had brought from England had spoiled. A plentiful native corn crop and a friendly Pawtuxet Indian named Squanto saved the early settlers from starvation that year, according to local history.

Several sources say the name, johnny cake, is believed to be an adaptation of journey cake. Colonial travelers made up the cakes to carry on a trip because they would keep a long time. This way they always had something in their pocket to eat while they journeyed.

Today the johnny cake has moved from the mainstay of pantry staples to a food that has earned a place of honor in the annals of regional lore.

Despite the good-natured rivalry that continues to divide Rhode Island on this subject, all the experts agree that the corn must be milled a special way to produce johnny cake meal. It must be ground until flat, not round, and it must be very fresh when it's used for johnny cake batter.

Set at the edge of the peaceful Queen's River Mill Pond and waterfall, Kenyon's is one of Rhode Island's two foremost producers of the stone-ground corn meal that's needed to make these cakes. (Stone grinding means the meal is rubbed between two great granite stones following much the same principle as the granite mortar and pestle method used long ago by the Indians.) Since 1711, a grist mill has stood at the water's edge grinding corn into johnny cake meal and Kenyon's is the most recent of those mills.

In addition to cornmeal, Kenyon's makes an impressive list of stone-ground grains and packages them in mixes such as a traditional New England Brown Bread mix, and a clam fritter mix for which they are nearly as well known.

HOW TO PURCHASE: Kenyon's products are available by mail. A 1-lb. box of Johnny Cake Corn Meal (shipping weight, 2 lbs.) is $1.92; a 3-lb. box (shipping weight, 4 lbs.) is $4.50. Kenyon's Brown Bread Mix is $2.21 for a 1-lb. box (shipping weight, 2 lbs.); Clam Cake and Fritter Mix is $1.83 for a 1-lb. box (shipping weight, 2 lbs.). There is a 50¢ handling charge for each order. All products are shipped U.P.S., and shipping costs range from $1.35 to $1.9 for a 1-lb. order, depending on the zone, to $2.99 to $10.60 for a 20-lb. order. Write or call for Kenyon's latest price and product list. Visa, MasterCard, personal checks, and money orders are all accepted.

The World's Best Cornbread

This, too, was inspired by our friend Steve Kantrowitz. He makes this bread to use in his Corn Pudding recipe, included on page 100. It just happens the bread, itself, moist and not too crumbly, is the best corn bread we've ever eaten. Save half of this for a corn pudding and devour the rest.

> *2⅔ cups all-purpose flour*
> *1⅓ cups Kenyon's Johnny Cake Mix*
> *1⅓ cups sugar*
> *1 tablespoon salt*
> *10 teaspoons baking powder*
> *2⅔ cups milk*
> *2 eggs, beaten*
> *5 tablespoons melted butter*

1. Preheat oven to 350°F. Butter a 9x13-inch pan. In a large mixing bowl, combine the flour, Johnny Cake Mix, sugar, salt, and baking powder. Beat the milk with the eggs and butter and add to the dry ingredients. Mix until moistened, but do not overmix.

2. Pour batter into prepared pan and bake 30–35 minutes or until bread pulls away from the sides of the pan and a cake tester inserted in the middle of the bread comes away clean. Transfer to a rack and cool completely before storing, or eat while still warm.

Serves 12.

VERMONT

Stone-ground Organic Flour & Meal

Brewster River Mill
Organically Grown
Stone-ground Flour & Meal

BREWSTER RIVER MILL. Mill Street, Jeffersonville,
Vermont 05464. 802/644-2987.

There are old mills. There are restored mills. Then there is the
one-of-a-kind Brewster River Mill, an historic landmark that's tied
to centuries of milling and, had it not been for the Albrights, might
have been lost forever due to years of neglect.

David Albright, who was a welder, owned a wood-splitter manufacturing business, and his wife Sandy was his bookkeeper. But the
two wanted to find a livelihood that was less harmful to the environment. They also shared a commitment toward preserving local traditions. After all, Sandy's family had lived in Jeffersonville for 150 years,
and David, although a newcomer, had been there for 30. In 1977,
the two decided to restore the old Brewster mill and go into the
business of running a grist mill. "It was our therapy," says Sandy.

The couple spent the next 6 years faithfully rebuilding the ancient
mill, which has overlooked the Brewster River since the late 1700s.
The aging structure fell down in the 1940s, but the Albrights rebuilt
the entire mill on the original foundation, using traditional materials
and techniques gleaned from old milling publications.

Although they could not restore the dam over the stream, David
painstakingly engineered a waterwheel powered by water pumped
from the stream. For backup, the mill is also powered and heated
by a 1922 Frick horse-drawn steam engine affectionately named
Herman, and an unnamed boiler that's fired by wood. The system
is connected to French Burr grinding stones that put the mill back
in operation in 1983.

The Albrights use only organic grains in their grist mill operation
and grind everything in small batches. They regularly make whole
grain wheat, corn, oat, rye, and buckwheat flour. They will also custom grind any blend, and they make their own four-grain pancake
mix. The cold grinding process used at the mill keeps the oils within
the grains from heating so they cannot become rancid. The result
is a nutty freshness in their product that makes breads tasty beyond
belief.

Next to the grinding room is a shop where the Albrights sell their
flour and a host of other locally made products. "The bulk of the
maple syrup comes from my father's sugar-place," says Sandy. And
all the other products "meet our own stringent guidelines. Everything is locally made and contains 'real' ingredients that we all can
pronounce and recognize," the Albrights promise.

HOW TO PURCHASE: A 5-lb. bag of whole wheat or hi-gluten
white flour is $2.75. Two-pound bags of other stone-ground grains
are oat flour, $2.40; rye flour, $1.35; rolled oats, $1.50; cornmeal,
$1.50; hi-lysine cornmeal, $2.95; cracked wheat, $1.25; buckwheat
flour, $2.75. A 2-lb. bag of four-grain Pancake Mix is $2.95. Shipping
is extra and is based on destination. The Albrights accept MasterCard
and Visa. Write or call for Brewster River Mill's latest price list and
a chart of shipping charges.

Brewster River Mill Anadama Bread

This multi-purpose, all–New England loaf is the kind to have on
hand for just about any occasion. But watch out if someone gets
a whiff of the slightly sweet aroma as it comes out of the oven. There
won't be any left for supper!

> *2 cups boiling water*
> *½ cup cornmeal*
> *1 package active dry yeast*
> *½ cup warm water (about 105°F.)*
> *½ cup molasses*
> *2 teaspoons salt*
> *1 tablespoon solid vegetable shortening*
> *2 cups Brewster Mill River whole wheat flour*
> *2½ to 3 cups Brewster Mill River unbleached*
> *   white flour*

1. Combine the boiling water and cornmeal, mix, and let stand 1
hour.
2. Dissolve the yeast in the warm water. Add 1 tablespoon white
flour, mix, and let stand until mixture is bubbly.
3. In a large mixing bowl, combine the cornmeal, the yeast mixture,
molasses, salt, shortening, whole wheat flour and 2½ cups of white
flour. Mix well. Turn onto a lightly floured surface and knead 10
minutes or until smooth. Return to mixing bowl, cover with a towel,
and let rise in a warm spot until doubled in size (about 1 hour).
4. Preheat oven to 350°F. Spray 2 loaf pans with vegetable spray
and dust with cornmeal. Punch dough down and cut in half. Form
into loaves, placing one in each loaf pan. Cover pans with a towel
and let rise until dough reaches the top of the pans. Bake in the
middle of the oven 45 to 50 minutes or until loaves sound hollow
when tapped. Turn onto a wire rack and cool.

Yields 2 loaves.

Whole Grain Granola and Baked Goods

✓

LOAFERS' GLORY. R.F.D. #3, Box 895, Westminster West, Vermont 05346. 802/869-2120 & 802/869-2711 on Fridays.

Gaelen Ewald began baking whole grain foods when she was pregnant with her daughter Alyson more than 20 years ago. When her son Alec came along, she started to fashion her own granola after the store-bought Familia that he loved. She varied the ingredients to their own tastes, serving the uncooked granola to her young son and baking the rest for family use.

Soon Ewald became committed to making whole grain products — breads, granola, and her own special brand of pastries — for people who care as she does about the quality of food they eat. In 1978 her husband Richard built a modest structure in the small Putney suburb of Westminister West, and Ewald opened her wholesale and mail order bakery. She named it Loafers' Glory after the small town in North Carolina where she first started marketing her breads in the late 1970s. During that time the family had been traveling around the country in a bread truck that Richard had outfitted as a mobile home. The family of four first landed in Bakersville, then in Loafers' Glory, auspicious-sounding choices now that Ewald can look back on those times.

The small Vermont bakery uses only organically grown, stone-ground whole wheat flour. And most of the other ingredients are locally produced. Gaelen's Maple Shortbread, for instance, use Westminister maple syrup. (For Christmas, this 9-inch round, butter-rich shortbread is also sold with a thick coating of Callebaut chocolate.) Ewald's chewy and cheesy Cheddar Pepper Biscuits are filled to brimming with cheddar from neaby Grafton Village Cheese Company and a hint of pepper. The same cheese appears in the Vermont Cheddar Bread (without the pepper).

Only Gaelen's French Bread is predominantly unbleached white flour with some whole wheat and rye flour added. The breads at this unique bakery are a toothsome lot. Anadama, Black Russian Rye, and a new product, Mediterranean Olive Bread (with it's own hint of spiciness), boast crusty exteriors and dense interiors. And Loafers' Glory makes Vermont Maple Cream Buns that are a true northern delicacy. Swirled with maple syrup, cinnamon, and raisins and topped with a maple cream glaze and toasted walnuts, these are the perfect out-of-hand breakfast for hurried skiers.

Not to be overlooked are Ewald's granola products, which are still intertwined with Alec Ewald's childhood. As You Like It unsweetened granola, and Maple Almond Granola might have remained a secret to us had it not been for a friend and former Vermonter, Susan Stillman, who mail orders both in 5-pound boxes and can't live without her nighttime snack. These multigrain cereals are chocked full of nuts and sunflower seeds. As You Like It trades sweeteners for a triple helping of almonds, cashews, and walnuts.

HOW TO PURCHASE: All Loafers' Glory products are availabl by mail. Order ahead for Loafers' Glory granola items as Ewal makes it to order. As You Like It Granola and Maple Almond Granol are sold in 5-lb. units for $11.25. Breads range from $2.05 a loa for Mediterranean Olive Bread to $1.90 for Anadama and $1.65 pe loaf of French Bread. Cheddar Pepper Biscuits are $1.75 for an 8-oz package containing 6 biscuits. A package of 6 Maple Cream Bun is $4.10 (available only in the winter), and a 9-inch round Mapl Shortbread is $5.10. Shipping charges are extra and vary wit destination.

Maple Almond Granola Cookies

Although the granola from Loafers' Glory needs nothing to im prove its taste, this recipe transforms the crunchy, crumbly cerea into a portable feast!

> ½ cup unsalted butter, softened
> ⅔ cup firmly packed light brown sugar
> 1 egg
> 1 cup all-purpose flour
> ½ teaspoon baking powder
> ¼ teaspoon salt
> ¼ teaspoon nutmeg
> ¼ teaspoon cinnamon
> 2 cups Loafers' Glory Maple Almond Granola
>   (about ½ lb.)

1. Preheat oven to 350 °F. In a large mixing bowl, cream the butte with the sugar until light and fluffy. Add the egg and beat well. Com bine the flour, baking powder, salt, nutmeg, and cinnamon and add to the butter mixture. Beat to combine. Stir in the granola just unti blended.

2. Drop batter by rounded teaspoonfuls onto an ungreased cookie sheet, leaving about 1 inch between cookies. Bake 12 minutes o until lightly browned. Loosen with a spatula immediately and re move from pan when slightly cooled.

Makes 3 dozen cookies.

Vermont Velvet® Cheesecakes

NEW ENGLAND DAIRY FOODS. 398-400 Pine Street, Burlington, Vermont 05401. 1/800-447-1205 or 802/864-7271.

Patricia Novotny and Victoria Purdy were two of New England Dairy Foods' best customers when they heard the business was for sale. The two had been involved in specialty foods for years: Novotny as a cooking teacher and recipe developer who also did some catering when her husband was in graduate school; and Purdy as the owner of Sledrunner Farm raising beef cattle, sheep, and rabbits and tending a giant herb garden.

The two were looking for a way to combine their respective interests. "When we heard a business we both loved was offered for sale, we bought it!" says Novotny who is now the president of New England's largest manufacturer of cheesecakes and quiche puffs. The two purchased the 10-year-old concern in 1987.

New England Dairy Foods cheesecakes have continued to be the same rich, dense, and silky smooth products that were always made by this company under the registered name Vermont Velvet.® *Gourmet* Magazine called the cakes " . . . a velvet-soft monument to American cream cheese."

Today the company produces some 3,000 cheesecakes a week in flavors such as a decadent, not subtle, dark chocolate fudge (which uses real fudge), Kahlua, almond Amaretto, Black Forest, and chocolate chip. They also make some 30,000 Quiche Puffs, an invention of the former owner, Susan Callahan. These are light pastries filled with rich cream cheese and tastes such as mushroom or spinach.

Although Novotny and Purdy turn out thousands of items weekly, they are hardly the "stamped out" variety. Careful attention is paid to quality and flavor, and cheesecakes are still handmade by bakers. Fillers and additives are out of the question. The list of ingredients reads like a farmer's inventory with fresh eggs, cream, and cream cheese at the top of the list.

Sold chiefly to food service companies and via their retail outlet, the Cheese Outlet next door to the factory, the cheesecakes are also sold to individuals via mail and come well packed in dry ice. Quiche Puffs are not yet available by mail.

New England Dairy is one of the early pioneers in selling precut cheesecakes. Their large, 4½-pound cake comes in sixteen slices, each separated with paper for individual servings.

HOW TO PURCHASE: A Vermont Velvet® pre-sliced cheesecake (4 lbs. 8 oz.) sells for $34.95. Flavors are chocolate fudge, vanilla, Kahlua, chocolate chip, and fudge marble. A 28-oz. cheesecake (not sliced) is sold for $19.95. Prices include shipping (via U.P.S. Second Day Air). To order, send check or money order payable to The Cheese Outlet. Major credit cards are accepted.

Strawberry Glacé Cheesecake

This beautiful topping makes any cheesecake look as though you've been working on it for hours. But it takes just a very few minutes to prepare with a New England Dairy Vermont Velvet® cake on the bottom!

> *1 quart of fresh strawberries or a 16-oz. bag whole frozen berries*
> *½ cup water*
> *½ cup sugar*
> *1½ tablespoons cornstarch, thinned with 1–2 tablespoons water*
> *2 teaspoons lemon juice*
> *28-oz. New England Dairy vanilla cheesecake (about 8-inch diameter)*

1. Chop half the strawberries and combine with water and sugar in a small saucepan. Bring to a simmer and cook 15 minutes. Transfer to a blender and purée. Return to saucepan and heat. Stir in the cornstarch mixture and bring to a boil. Stir until thickened. Remove from heat and add the lemon juice. Chill.
2. Slice the remaining berries and arrange, overlapping slightly, around the cake. Brush the chilled strawberry sauce over the berries, filling in any spots where the cake shows through. Chill until ready to serve.

Serves 8.

Maple Sprinkles

VERMONT COUNTRY MAPLE, INC. P.O. Box 53, Jericho Center, Vermont 05465. 802/864-7519.

Money doesn't grow on trees, but Lyman Jenkins has found that there's cash *in* trees—if they're maple, that is. The creative-thinking young man had been a research chemist for the Forest Service when he happened on a new process for drying maple syrup. No one else seemed to be interested in marketing the technique that produces tiny maple crystals, so Jenkins decided to do it himself. He had absolutely no business experience, only a gut feeling that what he was doing was right.

Following his instincts, Jenkins founded Vermont Country Maple in 1980 and patented his three-step process for drying maple syrup, thus bringing maple syrup from tree to table all over the world. He starts by using a vacuum evaporator to remove the water from the syrup. Once done, he stirs it rapidly until crystals form. Forced warm air drying is the final step before the sprinkles are packed in 2½-ounce shakers and larger bakers' canisters.

He bought the sole license for manufacturing sprinkles from Amstar, the largest sugar manufacturer in the world. While looking for investors, he was carting gallons of local maple syrup to their Brooklyn plant for processing into granules. A lucky break came when American Maple Products in Newport, Vermont, bought shares in Jenkins's company. That allowed him to use their equipment rather than make the regular trek to New York.

Jenkins is quick to point out that start-up costs were much greater than expected. "Everything takes longer and costs more than you think it's going to," he says of founding a business. In 1987, Jenkins saw his first glimpse of profit, by selling some 250,000 pounds of maple sprinkles in gourmet shops, health food stores, bakeries, and mail order catalogs throughout the United States and as far away as Europe and Asia.

However, most of his marketing energy has been aimed at convincing a doubting public that maple doesn't necessarily mean syrup. It seems to be working. Today, Jenkins has cornered a tidy little market as the only manufacturer of a dry, all-natural sweetener in the world.

HOW TO PURCHASE: A package of 3 shakers (2½ oz. each) is $8.50. A 14-oz. canister is the same price. Jenkins also sells a case of 24 shakers for $60 and a 5-lb. bag of sprinkles for $40. A box of two hundred and fifty 4-gram packets, for $20, is ideal for traveling and camping. Shipping is included in these prices. Mail check or money order to Vermont Country Maple, Inc.

Vermont Maple Flan

Maple adds a subtle flavor to this already delicate dessert. Thanks to Maple Sprinkles, it's easy to prepare. The sprinkles need only a touch of moisture to produce a consistency like that of caramelized sugar.

> *3 cups milk*
> *6 eggs*
> *¼ cup granulated sugar*
> *½ cup maple syrup*
> *1 teaspoon pure vanilla extract*
> *⅓ cup Vermont Maple Sprinkles*

1. Preheat oven to 350°F. Heat the milk until scalded. Remove from heat. In a large mixing bowl, beat the eggs well. Add the sugar while beating and mix to combine. Add the hot milk in a slow, steady stream, beating continuously. Beat in the maple syrup and the vanilla extract.

2. Spread the Maple Sprinkles over the bottom of a shallow 6-cup baking dish. (A deep-dish pie plate is perfect.) Sprinkle 1 to 2 teaspoons of water over the sprinkles and mix so that the sprinkles are moist. Set in the oven for 5 minutes to melt the sprinkles and evaporate the water. Remove from the oven and gently pour the flan mixture over this. Set in a larger pan filled with enough hot water to come halfway up the sides of the smaller pan. Bake 45 minutes or until a knife inserted into the center of the flan comes away clean.

3. Carefully remove the flan from the water bath and refrigerate for at least 2 hours before serving.

Serves 8.

CONDIMENTS

CONNECTICUT

Cider Jelly & Cider Vinegar with Herbs

BLACK LAMB HERB FARM. 90 Sawyer Hill Road, New Milford, Connecticut 06776. 203/354-5634.

Laura Perkins tells you modestly that she left a high-powered job as a producer of "Mr. Rogers' Neighborhood" and the hubbub of city life to move to quiet Litchfield County and "do nothing" but raise her two children. "Nothing" to Perkins means collecting the eggs from 400 chickens, some on her farm and many more down the road on a neighboring farm. It means tending her ¼-acre herb garden and 4 acres of herbs at the nearby Connecticut Junior Republic property. It includes caring for two lambs. "Nibbles" is the black one for which her business is named.

This lady dashes everywhere, juggling the care of chickens, herb gardens, and lambs with dropping off and picking up children. Along the way are sudden stops along rural roadsides to pick and sample wild plants. Perkins is "in the process of learning what is edible in the wild." "I go out there and taste everything," she explains.

Perkins's serious business, however, is selling dried herbs, herb vinegars, and herbed cider jellies. She created the Black Lamb Herb Farm in 1986, motivated by a love of herbs, the desire to work at home, and an abundance of "leftover" cider from a local orchard. She starts with a mild, mellow-tasting cider vinegar — "the best in Connecticut," says Perkins. She adds her own blends of aromatic herbs, cut fresh the day they are used. They are steeped in vinegar for several months before bottling takes place. Then full stalks of herbs with flowers are added to the vinegar before it's capped for sale.

Perkins also makes a cider jelly starting with a light jelly, not the kind that's boiled down. Slightly sweet and with a smooth fruity taste, it doesn't overpower the delicate herb flavors. Herbs are either cooked with the cider or added later depending on their durability. Vinegars are sold with almost any combination of one or more herbs imaginable. Cider jellies are done primarily with rosemary, fennel, mint, and sage.

There's no doubt this is a cottage industry. Products arrive wrapped in newspaper and stuffed into used cartons. Aside from attractive silver and black striped wrappings, containers are ordinary canning jars and bottles. And Perkins asks that you return the empties!

HOW TO PURCHASE: Perkins's products are sold informally at her farm and are available at several specialty food stores in Connecticut. Herb cider vinegars and cider jellies can be mail ordered. Herb vinegar and herb cider jellies are $3. Add $1.50 for postage per order. Shipping is via U.P.S. Make checks payable to Black Lamb Herb Farm.

HINTS FOR SERVING: Use herb vinegars for salad and cole slaw dressings and in homemade mayonnaise. Jellies are superb as glazes for meats. Also try them in place of sugar or honey in quick bread recipes. Pair the herbal tastes with recipes as you would the fresh and dried ones. The cider jelly with fresh sage is wonderful with pork, as in the following recipe.

Cider Jelly Glazed Pork Tenderloin

This absolutely magnificent-tasting dish can also be done with a boneless pork loin roast.

2 pork tenderloins (about 1.4 lbs.)

Dry marinade

1 teaspoon ground thyme
1 teaspoon ground sage
1 teaspoon ground black pepper

2 tablespoons butter
2 tablespoons Black Lamb Herb Farm
Cider Jelly with Sage

1. Rub the tenderloins with the herb marinade. Allow to sit in the refrigerator for 2–4 hours. Preheat the oven to 400°F. Melt the butter in a sauté pan over medium-high heat. When butter foams, add the tenderloins and brown on all sides.

2. Transfer meat to an oven-proof platter. Melt the cider jelly over low heat and brush on all sides of the tenderloin. Bake the meat, uncovered, for 20 minutes or until inside is slightly pink. (While the meat is cooking, prepare the sauce below.) Remove from oven. Allow to stand 5 minutes, then slice. Add the juices to the sauce below.

Sauce

2 tablespoons butter
1 small onion, finely chopped
⅓ cup dry vermouth
½ cup veal or chicken stock
¼ cup Black Lamb Herb Farm Cider
Jelly with Sage

Using the same sauté pan, melt the butter over low heat. Add the onion and sauté 1 minute. Add the vermouth and simmer until most of the liquid has evaporated. Add the stock and the cider jelly. Whisk until combined. Allow to simmer until sauce is reduced to a thick glaze. Add the pan juices from the cut meat. Mix and spoon over the tenderloin slices.

Serves 4–6.

MAINE

Chutneys/Relishes/Sweet Sauces

DOWNEAST DELICACIES. Cape Porpoise Chutney, Ltd., P.O. Box 1281, Kennebunkport, Maine 04046. 207/967-5327.

Down East enthusiasts agree that Cape Porpoise Peach Chutney is "the best chutney you evah et." A truly Calcutta-style condiment with chunks of peaches, plump raisins, ginger, and spices, the chutney made by Jane Lamont at her small cottage enterprise is pretty "dahn gud."

Lamont began jarring her chutney recipe and one for a New England cranberry apple relish at the request of friends and their friends after they had received jars of the two condiments as Christmas gifts. Soon Lamont realized she enjoyed the creativity of being a relish maker more than her profession as an insurance executive in the corporate world. In 1987, she turned in her briefcase for a spot behind the canning pot and Downeast Delicacies was born.

Today her business turns out six flavorful condiments: Gingered Pear Chutney, three sweet sauces—Magical Maine Wild Blueberry, Pear & Lemon Ambrosia, and Honeyed Strawberry—as well as the two original products. Each recipe is all natural and cooked in very small batches. The chutneys simmer for several hours before actually being packaged. Then they are aged at least 2 months before they are sold.

Determined to offer a consistently excellent gourmet product that can only be achieved with the slow cooking process and mellowing time, Lamont refuses to take shortcuts to rush through the preparation. "There are too many items in the marketplace that have taken this route, and the end result is self-evident," she says. Lamont's commitment to quality has never put her behind in meeting orders, however. "We just add people and kettles," she says. "Besides, there's lots of free time during the winter," explains the executive-turned-relish-maker. "Plenty of time to let the chutney mellow."

All Downeast Delicacies are made on the four-burner commercial range in the kitchen of Lamont's 1855 restored farmhouse, which is set at the water's edge in the picturesque fishing village of Kennebunkport. She uses native fruits as much as possible, especially in the Cranberry Relish which, in itself, is a New England cornucopia.

Lamont is continually working on new ideas for her product line and has cultivated a following of local tasters who are "so critical and fussy that when I get something positive out of them, I feel like I've conquered the Matterhorn!"

All of Lamont's products have passed muster with her critics. "One taster ate the whole jar before she had finished her taste test routine," says Lamont, who found herself furnishing additional samples before the testing was over.

HOW TO PURCHASE: A jar of Peach or Gingered Pear Chutney or Cranberry Apple Relish (about 12 oz.) sells for $6.50. The three sweet sauces—Wild Blueberry, Pear & Lemon Ambrosia, and Honeyed Strawberry—in the same sizes, sell for $6.65 each. Packaging and shipping are included. Orders must be prepaid, and checks should be made to Downeast Delicacies.

Tuna Pockets with Peach Chutney

The combination of Cape Porpoise Peach Chutney with a can of tuna is amazing, and that's coming from a non-tuna-fish lover.

> 6½-oz. can solid white tuna
> ¼ cup Cape Porpoise Peach Chutney
> ¼ cup good quality mayonnaise
> Two 6-inch whole wheat pita breads, cut in half
>   and warmed
> 4 lettuce leaves, washed and patted dry
> ½ red onion, thinly sliced
> 8 cherry tomatoes, halved

Mix the tuna with the chutney and the mayonnaise until well blended. Line the 4 pita pocket halves with the lettuce and spoon ¼ of the tuna mixture into each. Arrange red onion slices and tomato halves in each pocket. Serve at once.

Yields 4 sandwiches.

Mother's Mountain Sweet/Zesty Mustard

MOTHER'S MOUNTAIN MUSTARD. Tan-Man, 110 Woodville Road, P.O. Box 6044, Falmouth, Maine 04105. 207/781-4658.

Mother would be proud of Carol Tanner and partner Dennis Proctor. The two have created products from Tanner's mother's secret Depression-era mustard recipe that have become a hit throughout New England and beyond. One slightly sweet (to please young palates) and one a bit spicy (thanks to Carol's father's Creole background), these mustards are ideal for dipping with salami, sausage, and cheese and great for glazing hams and marinating fish, chicken, or lamb.

Although the original recipe was in Tanner's family for more than 50 years, Mother's Mustard evolved only in 1982 when the misplaced recipe happened to fall out of a cookbook that Tanner was reading. The first year, she made mustard by day and worked by night as a customer service operator for L. L. Bean. Here Tanner met coworker Dennis Proctor. About the same age as Tanner's oldest son, Proctor had just completed college in Boston and was wondering what to do with his life.

At the same time, someone brought Tanner a jar of specialty mustard. She knew hers was much better. With Proctor's enthusiasm and Carol's energy, a partnership soon followed. They began taking samples of their mustard to natural food and crafts fairs. After much tasting and testing, Mother's Mustard was launched in earnest.

Today Mother's Mustard produces about 12 tons of mustard a year, some out of their recently upgraded kitchen-in-the-barn and the rest from a nearby factory. Along with their zesty and sweet Mother's Mustards, the two also make a delightful Dijon mustard, and they have recently introduced Mother's Mountain 1880 New England Chili Sauce. A new ketchup and a Portland Beer Mustard will be coming out soon.

Their products boast "no salt, no sugar, no flour, no water, and no preservatives." Their business is primarily mail order although Mother's does supply several local grocery stores and gourmet shops. And customers include a host of celebrities, Brooke Shields and Boston Marathon–winner Joan Benoit Samuelson among them.

The industrious duo is always eager to talk about their mustard and their success story and has never been known to discourage a visitor to their "home" office or to turn anyone away without a jar of mustard.

HOW TO PURCHASE: Mother's Mountain Mustard comes in zesty, sweet, and country Dijon. A case of twelve 6-oz. jars of any of the mustards is $30. A Sample Mailer (two 6-oz. jars—your choice) is $9. A case of twelve 8-oz. jars of Chili Sauce is $30. One 8-oz. jar of Chili Sauce is $4.50. Prices include shipping, usually via U.P.S. Orders must be prepaid with check or money order payable to Mother's Mountain Mustard.

Carrots au Gratin with Mother's Mustard

This seems an unlikely combination, but the slightly sweet and hot taste of Mother's Mustard with a mellow cheese and fresh carrots produces one of the best vegetable dishes we have ever tried. It's also great with fresh broccoli.

> *2 lbs. carrots, peeled and cut into 1-inch pieces*
> *2 tablespoons butter*
> *Salt and pepper to taste*
> *3 tablespoons Mother's Zesty Mustard*
> *4 oz. Mozzarella cheese, grated*

1. Cook the carrots with enough water to partially cover. Simmer about 8 minutes or until carrots are fork tender. Drain and toss with butter, salt, pepper, and mustard.
2. Transfer to a baking dish and sprinkle cheese over the carrots. Set under broiler for about 5 minutes or until cheese has melted and edges start to brown. Serve immediately.

Serves 6.

Wild Maine Blueberry Ginger Conserve/Hot Tomato Jelly

NERVOUS NELLIE'S JAMS AND JELLIES. Sunshine Road, R.F.D. 474A, Deer Isle, Maine 04627. 1/800-346-4273 or 207/348-6182.

Nervous Nellie, in the form of one Michal McKeown and Peter Beerits, makes a creative and unusual line of jams and jellies that shouldn't make anyone anxious. Nellie turns out unique flavors such as Hot Tomato Jelly, Red Tomato Marmalade (a turn-of-the-century favorite), Sunshine Road Marmalade (with oranges, pink grapefruit, and lemons) that's perky enough to brighten up the soggiest of April mornings, and Wild Maine Blueberry Ginger Conserve that's sparked with crystallized ginger, oranges, and lemons. Even the more ordinary are intensely flavored: Red Raspberry Jam, Strawberry Marmalade (based on a birthday party punch from Nervous Nellie's childhood), Spicy Apple Cider Jelly, and Wild Maine Blueberry Jam.

The husband and wife team of McKeown and Beerits began by selling their preserves at craft fairs and specialty gourmet shops in the coastal Maine area. They broke into the wholesale market in 1986 and then started selling their product by mail to people who had sampled their items in other ways. The response was overwhelming. "Would you believe there are a lot of people who have never ever tasted red tomato marmalade? No wonder the country is in such a mess!" wrote one customer. Another said, "I don't think Nellie was nervous the day she made Deer Isle Maine Wild Blueberry Ginger Conserve because I had some on my English muffin this morning and it sent me into orbit!"

The products surely deserve no less enthusiastic response. However, we think it is Nellie's at once homespun and uplifting packaging that inspires this kind of following. Like some boxed breakfast cereals, Nellie's makes for delightful reading. "Our jams are louder and funnier than ever!" shouts Nellie from the pages of her mail order flyer. After setting the mood for folks to share Nellie's cider time, she says, "Next stop is the cider press, set up for those brief weeks when it's too cold for yellow jackets and too warm to snow."

"Nervous Nellie is off to the jelly kitchen where she works a magic of steaming kettles and bobbing spice bags — and the bounty of another autumn finds a home in quiet splendor on the pantry shelf." We couldn't have said it better.

HOW TO PURCHASE: Two-jar gift boxes (any flavors) are $16.95. Four 11-oz. jar gift boxes are $26.95. Shipping is included and is via U.P.S. Nellie will send gifts for you. Jars come complete with glitzy hats, shiny bows, and entertaining tags. Orders must be pre-paid. Nervous Nellie does not accept credit cards.

New England Cheddar Cheese Muffins with Hot Tomato Pockets

We took Nellie's cue about Hot Tomato Jelly and cheddar cheese and came up with this toothsome recipe. It's a terrific accompaniment to a Sunday supper of tummy-warming soup.

> 2 cups sifted flour
> ¼ cup sugar
> 3 teaspoons baking powder
> ½ teaspoon salt
> ⅛ teaspoon cayenne
> 1 cup milk
> ¼ cup vegetable oil or melted shortening
> 1 egg, slightly beaten
> 1 cup grated extra sharp New England
>   cheddar cheese
> ⅓ cup Nervous Nellie's Hot Tomato Jelly

1. Preheat oven to 425 °F. Spray a 12-cup muffin tin with vegetable spray. Combine flour, sugar, baking powder, salt, and cayenne in a medium mixing bowl. In another bowl, beat the milk, vegetable oil, and egg to combine. Add to dry ingredients and mix just until thoroughly moistened. Do not overmix. Fold in the cheese.
2. Fill muffin tins about ¼ full with batter. Spoon a generous teaspoon of jelly over batter and top with enough batter to fill each tin ¾ full. Bake 20 minutes or until golden and muffins have pulled away from the edges of the tin.

Makes 1 dozen muffins.

Mos-ness French Dressing

SCHLOTTERBECK & FOSS COMPANY. 117 Preble Street, P.O. Box 8609, Portland, Maine 04101. 207/772-4666.

To many families in Maine (including this author's), Mos-ness is the only bottled salad dressing that's earned its way to the dinner party. A one-of-a-kind product, this fine dressing has been on Maine pantry shelves since the 1950s.

Created by a gentleman named Leonard Mos-ness, it originally found favor with the Boston-based food house, S. S. Pierce, which started making the homespun product for Mos-ness in the twenties. In 1953, S. S. Pierce sold the recipe to Schlotterbeck & Foss, a large food company in Portland specializing in the wholesale production of pure flavorings, dressings, and toppings. And this family-run operation has been producing it ever since.

Although Mos-ness is not one of Foss's principal products, it is decidedly the most unique. A secret blend of onions, vegetables, spices, oil, and vinegar, the aging process is as critical to the flavor of this dressing as are the ingredients. The handling, too, seems to be an important factor in making this product—from a very special way of handling the onions and vegetables that produces the special Mos-ness flavor to the way it sits, like a fine red wine, improving each day that it's on the shelf after it's bottled.

This rich dressing is made in small batches and about 50,000 pounds are sold each year. Most is sold either on Maine grocery and gourmet store shelves or by mail. The latter accounts for a large part of the Mos-ness business.

People who have grown up in Maine and moved away tend not to be able to live without their Mos-ness. They write to Schlotterbeck & Foss requesting the dressing that they can't get outside the state. And the company gladly sends case-size gift boxes to its loyal following.

A legend in itself, the Schlotterbeck & Foss Company was founded back in 1866 and is the oldest family food manufacturing company in the state of Maine. Now third and fourth generations manage the company. Richard and his brother Clifton are the current owners, along with Richard's son Peter.

HOW TO PURCHASE: A case of twelve 8-oz. bottles of Mos-ness Dressing is $19.60 plus shipping, which is via U.P.S. and determined by destination. Schlotterbeck & Foss Company will send a mail order form that includes a chart of shipping charges. Orders must be prepaid, and checks or money orders should be payable to Schlotterbeck & Foss Company.

Beef and Green Bean Salad

Hearty and tangy, this recipe is perfect for a summer picnic.

1½ lbs. London broil

Marinade

½ cup dry red wine
¼ cup olive oil
¼ cup soy sauce
1 clove garlic, crushed
2 green onions, cut into 1-inch pieces

2 cups fresh cut green beans
2 large potatoes boiled, peeled, and cubed
1 cup quartered steamed or canned artichoke hearts
1 small red onion, chopped
2 teaspoons fresh thyme
¼ cup chopped fresh parsley leaves
⅓ cup Mos-ness Dressing
8 red leaf lettuce leaves, washed and patted dry
Tomato wedges for garnish

1. Marinate the beef in the marinade ingredients for 6 hours. Broil about 10 minutes or until beef is medium rare. Cut into julienne strips.
2. Cook the beans 3 minutes in lightly salted boiling water. Drain and rinse under cold water. Drain and pat dry.
3. In a large bowl, combine the beef, potatoes, beans, artichoke hearts, red onion, thyme, and parsley. Toss with the dressing.
4. Arrange the lettuce leaves on a serving platter and spoon the salad over them. Garnish with tomato wedges. Chill and serve.

Serves 6–8.

Blueberry Chutney & Conserve

SPRUCE MOUNTAIN BLUEBERRIES. Mt. Pleasant Street, P.O. Box 68, West Rockport, Maine 04865. 207/236-3538.

When Molly Sholes started her own blueberry company, she brought together two of her great passions—one for the East and one for Down East. Now her slightly renovated and very antiquated 1825 farmhouse kitchen fills with the aroma of ginger, cinnamon, cardamom, and the like as they simmer with wild Maine blueberries to produce Spruce Mountain chutneys and conserves.

Sholes spent 19 years in India and Pakistan as a United States Information Agency wife. Summer vacations would bring the family back to a farm they had purchased on the coast of Maine in 1971.

When Sholes returned to the United States permanently in 1983, she settled on the family farm in West Rockport. She came equipped with a vast knowledge of Eastern spices and recipes for some of the world's finest chutneys. And she had her hands on more wild Maine blueberries than she knew what to do with. Her farm, 136 acres nestled in the shadow of Spruce Mountain, had between 25 and 30 acres of lowbush blueberries growing wild on the property.

The grand yellow farmhouse was without electricity, and the blueberries were waiting to be harvested. She hired a crew to help rake the berries, and she installed electricity in the place. Then Sholes did over the kitchen for chutney production. She combined the stock of fragrant spices she'd brought back from the East with the abundant blueberry crop and turned them into exciting condiments.

Spruce Mountain Blueberry Chutney comes plain and with almonds and raisins. Adapted from a traditional north Indian chutney recipe, both have a sweet spicy-hot flavor that's filled with the tastes of exotic spices, but without the sharp bite of red-hot relishes. The conserve, too, has a sweet and sour flavor.

Sholes starts with her own blend of spices, roasts them, and grinds them in small batches to make her own garam masala. Some of the spices are still imported from India, but the gingerroot is fresh and purchased locally.

"What better way to express these two great loves," says Sholes of her one-person cottage industry.

HOW TO PURCHASE: All Spruce Mountain products are available by mail. Blueberry Chutney is $4.60 per 10-oz. jar. Blueberry Chutney with Almonds and Raisins costs $2.75 for a 10-oz. jar. Blueberry Conserve is $4 for a 10-oz. jar. Packing and shipping are included. Spruce Mountain features a pack of three 10-oz. jars (one of each flavor) for $14.50 including postage. Send check or money order. Sholes does not accept credit cards.

Spruce Mountain Blueberry Chutney Chicken

Last-minute company helped devise this simple recipe. It was just a case of whatever-was-on-hand until the Spruce Mountain Chutney was added.

> *1 lb. boneless chicken breasts*
> *Salt and pepper to taste*
> *4 tablespoons unsalted butter*
> *1 bunch green onions, top third discarded*
> *⅓ cup blueberry vinegar*
> *½ cup chicken stock*
> *⅓ cup Spruce Mountain Chutney (plain or with almonds and raisins)*
> *⅓ cup sour cream*

1. Place the chicken pieces between sheets of wax paper and pound with a kitchen mallet until fairly thin. Sprinkle with salt and pepper. In a large skillet set over medium heat, melt 2 tablespoons of the butter. Add the chicken breasts and brown on both sides (about 1 minute on each side).

2. Remove to an oven-proof platter, cover with aluminum foil, and keep warm in a 350°F. oven. (Breasts will continue cooking so do not allow to sit more than 10 minutes.)

3. In the skillet, add remaining butter and sauté green onions for 30 seconds. Add the vinegar and simmer until reduced to a syrupy liquid. Add the stock and simmer 5 minutes or until reduced by half. Add the chutney and the sour cream and whisk. Pour any liquid from the chicken into the skillet and warm. Pour over the chicken and serve.

Serves 4.

Maple Barbeque Sauce

'STACHE FOODS. P.O. Box 705, Damariscotta, Maine 04543. 207/529-5879.

Stewart Blackburn grew weary of his job as a chef and sought another profession that would be creative without leaving him tied to a restaurant and the long hours of cooking on a grand scale. He turned to catering, especially theme parties, barbecues, and clambakes. But most importantly, he started producing a barbecue sauce that's taken Maine by storm.

"Maine needed its own distinctive barbecue sauce," he says of his choice of products. So, in 1985, he started his own barbecue sauce company and named it 'Stache Foods for the rolling red handlebar mustache that he proudly sports. He makes his sauce by combining the finest Maine maple syrup, tomato paste, and apple cider vinegar. Then he simmers his gustatory concoction for hours until it's perfect. The result is a rich, full-bodied mixture with a moderate amount of spiciness that's a versatile marinade and basting or dipping sauce.

Blackburn is the major attraction when he takes his deep mahogany red sauce to food shows. Here, adorned with a rakish chef's hat, he serves up skewered tidbits of well-doused barbecued pork with Yankee gusto.

The son of a navy admiral who summered in Maine, Blackburn calls himself a Bremen, Maine, local. However, he spent a good deal of time traveling before settling back in New England. He studied mycology in New Zealand on a Watson Fellowship, then went to San Francisco where he trained to become a chef. Next followed stints in professional kitchens in St. Croix; Fairbanks, Alaska; and finally Martha's Vineyard before he returned to Maine in 1985. "It was the only place that felt like home," explains Blackburn, who launched his barbecue sauce venture the year he "came home."

Blackburn next opened a specialty foods store in Bremen in 1986 and called it Hocamock Hollow. The store closed the same year, but the building now serves as headquarters for 'Stache Foods catering and barbecue sauce.

HOW TO PURCHASE: Maple Barbeque Sauce comes in 8- and 16-oz. jars. The prices are $2.50 and $4.50. Shipping is via U.P.S., and there is an additional charge based on destination. Case prices are available.

Stewart's Maple Barbeque Ribs

Blackburn can be found making these yummy ribs for visitors at the Maine Festival and Common Ground Fair in Windsor each year.

3 lbs. country-style pork ribs (or 2 racks of pork ribs)
¼ cup soy sauce
2 teaspoons granulated garlic (or garlic powder)
1 cup Maple Barbeque Sauce

1. Brush the ribs with the soy sauce then sprinkle with garlic. Spread over a cookie sheet so that ribs do not overlap and bake in a 325 °F. oven for 2 hours. Turn after the first hour and brush with more soy sauce. Remove and cool. If using racks, cut into individual ribs.
2. Start a charcoal fire and let burn down for 20 to 30 minutes after coals have turned gray. Dip the ribs in Maple Barbeque Sauce and put on grill. Grill slowly until deep maroon (about 20 minutes). Baste with more sauce and turn occasionally while grilling. Serve immediately with plenty of napkins.

Serves 4 to 6.

Cranberry & Apple Catsups/Herb Jellies

BEAR MEADOW FARM. Route 2, Moore Road, Florida, Massachusetts 01247. 413/663-9241.

Hilary and George Garivaltis were working in Boston and looking for a way to return to the "country" when they saw an ad that Bear Meadow Farm was for sale. George was originally from nearby Pittsfield, Massachusetts, and Hilary was a New Hampshire native with a degree in agronomy and a background in interior landscapes and nurseries. The already established farm business was just the opportunity the two were looking for to make use of their combined talents and passions.

The farm had been established by the Shays, an elderly couple who had operated Bear Meadow Farm for 12 years. The agrarian business was in two parts. The first was the production of a roster of unique-sounding condiments. The second, and more attractive to Hilary, was an herb nursery in need of repair. The Garivaltises bought the farm in 1985 and decided to put their energies into the products first.

The Garivaltises offer all the selections developed by the Shays—from the unusual Apple Catsup and Cranberry Catsup to ever-flavorful jams and jellies. Products include an extensive line of apple-based herb jellies—Rose Geranium, Garden Mint, Rosemary, Sage, and Tarragon—and a grape-based herb jelly that's flecked with flakes of fresh thyme. Bear Meadow Farm also offers nine varieties of herb vinegar, Garlic-Wine and Mint among them, and mouth-watering Cranberry and Rhubarb Chutneys. Many products are so unusual and hard to find elsewhere that when customers take a liking to Bear Bite Mustard (made with lemon and green peppercorn), Monk's Mustard (cracked black mustard seed), or Mint Vinegar, they keep coming back for more.

The two young entrepreneurs continue to develop new products as well. All are made in small batches, and orders are filled as they are received. Jams, jellies, and preserves are made with a minimum of cooking as overcooking destroys the delicate flavors, explains Hilary. As a result, some of their products are a bit softer in consistency than the run-of-the-mill jams and jellies.

In 1986, the new business began to take off, but the two found a bit of leftover energy to build up the herb nursery business. Visitors to Bear Meadow Farm can now buy perennial plants and herbs of uncommon quality to take home with their Bear Bite Mustard.

HOW TO PURCHASE: Cranberry, Apple, and Rhubarb Chutneys are sold in 10-oz. jars for $4.15 each. Apple Catsup and Cranberry Catsup, in ½-pint jars, are $4.15. Bear Bite, Monk's, Honey-Herb, and Horseradish Mustard are $4.15 each. Herb vinegars range from $2.50 per bottle for flavors such as Basil, Dill, Mint, and Thyme to $3 for blends such as Garlic-Herb. Herb jellies are available in 10-oz. jars for $3.15 each. Shipping, extra, is via U.P.S. Payment is by check or money order. Write or call for the latest Bear Meadow Farm price list.

Turkey Club Sandwich with Cranberry Russian Dressing

This divine combination of tastes makes for an extraordinary sandwich that's a meal in itself. In testing this recipe, we used whatever happened to be on hand, in this case some of the best ingredients imaginable—Granville Extra-Sharp Cheddar, Joyce's Gourmet English Muffins (plain), and Smith Smokehouse Blackstrap bacon.

12 slices pumpernickel or whole wheat bread
⅓ lb. extra sharp cheddar cheese, thinly sliced
¾ lb. boneless turkey breast, thinly sliced
2 tomatoes, sliced
4 large leaves Romaine lettuce, washed, leafy part only
8 slices bacon, cooked and drained

Cranberry Russian Dressing

⅓ cup Bear Meadow Cranberry Catsup
⅓ cup mayonnaise

Toast bread. Spread cheese over 4 slices of warm toast. Top with the turkey (divided into 4 portions). Combine catsup and mayonnaise to make Cranberry Russian Dressing; spread some of it on 4 more slices of toast. Top each with a quarter of the tomato slices, lettuce, and 2 slices of bacon. Spread more dressing on the remaining toast and top each sandwich.

Makes 4 large sandwiches.

CHICAMA VINEYARDS
STONEY HILL ROAD
WEST TISBURY
MA 02575
617-693-0309

CHICAMA VINEYARDS. Stoney Hill Road, West Tisbury, Massachusetts 02575. 508/693-0309.

When Catherine and George Mathiesen took a sailing trip from New York to Martha's Vineyard in 1969, they fell in love with the area and bought a summer house there. The couple had lived for years near California wine country, and on weekends they would tour the wineries. They figured it was about time to start their own winery, and Martha's Vineyard looked like the right spot.

In 1971, with the help of their six children, the Mathiesens carved out the first commercial vineyard on the island. They didn't realize that the town of West Tisbury was dry until they'd already cleared their 50-acre wooded plot and produced their first wine, a zinfandel. After pleading their case at a town meeting, they finally got the go-ahead to sell and taste wine on their property.

Today, two sons and one daughter are still active in the business. Tim Mathiesen left the island to work in the theater and performing arts but later returned to become the winery manager at Chicama Vineyards.

As a natural addition to a business that now produces 8,000 cases of wine each year, the Mathiesen family decided to turn a little of their spirits into vinegar. Three types are made: natural wine vinegar, herb vinegar, and fruit wine vinegar. All are aged in oak barrels by the Orleans method—a little of the vinegar remains in the barrel each time to act as a kind of "starter" for the next batch of vinegar.

The end result is a visual delight. The flasks are filled with liquids of luminous hues ranging from the golden-yellow of the Ginger & Lemon-flavored Vinegar and vibrant flame-colored Spicy Orange to ruby-toned Cape Cod Cranberry. A piece of herb or fruit floats gracefully in each bottle.

Twenty-three varieties of vinegar are made, and the product line has been expanded to include two types of salad dressings, two mustards, and, most recently, two new spicy cooking oils.

HOW TO PURCHASE: **Chicama's vinegars are sold in the winery and are available by mail. There are 23 flavors, including Lemon Thyme, Jalapeno Pepper & Garlic, Cape Cod Cranberry, Spicy Orange, Opal Basil, Chive, and Cracked Peppercorn. All are $3.95 per 375-ml. bottle. Salad dressings (Classic Vinaigrette and Raspberry Honey-Poppyseed) are $4.49 per bottle. Raspberry Honey-Poppyseed and Spicy Orange Mustard are each $3.25. Moroccan Oil and Cajun Oil are $5 each. Shipping is by U.P.S. Add $1.95 for the first $10; $3.95 for a $10–$20 purchase. West of the Mississippi, shipping is more.**

This easy, yet elegant recipe is great for company, especially the last-minute kind. It calls for two versions of a favorite New England food, Chicama Vineyards Cranberry Vinegar and whole fresh cranberries.

> *2 whole chicken breasts, boned, skinned, and*
> *fillets pounded*
> *Salt and pepper to taste*
> *2 tablespoons orange zest, cut into julienne strips*
> *4 tablespoons unsalted butter*
> *2 shallots, minced*
> *⅓ cup Chicama Vineyards Cranberry Vinegar*
> *½ cup freshly squeezed orange juice*
> *1 tablespoon lingonberry jam*
> *¼ teaspoon ground cinnamon*
> *¼ cup sour cream*
> *½ cup whole fresh cranberries, washed and picked*
> *clean*

1. Sprinkle the chicken fillets with salt and pepper. Bring a small pan of water to a boil and poach the orange zest for 1 minute. Remove, rinse under cold water, and drain.

2. In a large skillet set over medium-high heat, melt 2 tablespoons of the butter. Sauté the chicken pieces until brown on both sides (about 3 minutes per side). Remove to a serving platter and keep warm. Lower the heat. Add the remaining butter and sauté the shallots about 1 minute. Add the cranberry vinegar and simmer until reduced to a thick syrup. (Watch carefully so that it doesn't evaporate completely.) Whisk in the orange juice, jam, and the cinnamon. Return the chicken to the skillet. Cover and cook 5 minutes.

3. Remove the cover. Move the chicken to one side. Whisk the sour cream into the liquid. Add the whole cranberries and the orange zest. Stir to combine. Turn chicken pieces in the sauce once or twice. Cover and cook 2 minutes or just until the cranberries begin to pop. Remove from heat and serve.

Serves 4.

Greek Salad Dressing

CHRISTIE FOODS. P.O. Box 314, 10 Charlam Drive, Braintree, Massachusetts 02184. 617/848-7200.

Dean Christie has been in the food business most of his life. He started out in the restaurant and hotel side of things. But a combination of factors including lack of any good Greek dressing on the market prompted him to go into business for himself.

In 1957, Christie founded Christie Food Products, aiming chiefly to sell to the restaurant and hotel chains he had just left. With his knack for coming up with recipes, he devised his own soup bases—chicken and beef stocks and gravies from which many food service companies create their soups, stews, sauces, and such.

Today Christie Foods manufactures 165 items including salad dressings, dessert mixes, and beverage powders—not exactly a cottage industry. Christie makes one item, however, which should be in everyone's cottage! A wonderful dressing with just the right amount of spice, Christie Greek Salad Dressing is a rich and tangy salad seasoner that needs only crumbled Feta cheese to taste absolutely authentic. It's also the only suspended dressing on the market, meaning it doesn't separate while it sits. Christie lays claim that he is the first ever to suspend a dressing without homogenizing it.

Since Christie Foods began, its Greek salad dressing has been a trademark to people in New England and beyond. People who have tasted the dressing always send back rave reviews. (Christie sells it to airlines such as TWA and in restaurants and New England salad bars.) It didn't take long before Christie Foods was flooded with complimentary letters and inquiries about where individuals could purchase the salad dressing. That prompted Dean Christie to begin selling the dressing to gourmet and specialty shops in 1976.

Going "retail" has met with such favorable response that Christie began selling his dressing to supermarkets, and it now appears on grocery shelves in twenty-two states. If that's not sufficient, however, for those who are still unable to buy Christie's Greek Dressing locally, Dean Christie sells this one product by mail.

If you've ever stopped in a New England restaurant and sampled a dressing you wished you could buy, it was probably one of Christie's.

Asked how he came up with the recipe for this delectable dressing, Dean Christie gave the answer he does for most of his products: "Out of my head."

HOW TO PURCHASE: Christie Foods Greek Salad Dressing may be purchased by mail in cases of six 16-oz. bottles for $10.75 or twelve 8-oz. bottles for $12.60. Shipping and handling are extra and based on destination.

Joel's Greek Salad

My husband has been known to make this salad for parties of up to 150 people. The salad bowl is amazing! But the salad is even more so.

> 1 head Romaine lettuce, leaves separated
>   and washed
> 2 large vine-ripened tomatoes, thinly sliced
> 1 cucumber, peeled and sliced
> 1 cup cooked chickpeas
> 2 tablespoons chopped fresh parsley
> 8 oz. Feta cheese, crumbled
> ⅓–½ cup Christie's Greek Dressing
> ¼ cup anchovy fillets (2 oz. can)
> ½ lemon, washed and thinly sliced
> ½ cup imported niçoise olives or ripe olives

Gently toss lettuce, tomatoes, cucumber, chickpeas, parsley, and Feta together. Add dressing and mix. Garnish with anchovy fillets, lemon slices, and olives. Serve chilled.

Serves 6–8.

The Green Briar Jam Kitchen

GREEN BRIAR JAM KITCHEN. 6 Discovery Hill Road, East Sandwich, Massachusetts 02537. 508/888-6870.

There is an old adage that says one sunny day does not a summer make, but at Cape Cod's Green Briar Jam Kitchen, a host of sunny summer days makes a lot of jam. Sunshine is the singularly most important ingredient in the unique sun-cooking process used at the Green Briar Jam Kitchen.

The wholesome combination of nature's finest — sun, fresh fruit, and a slow cooking process — results in flavors so intense that one can only respond with, ''Wow, that's a jam!''

Established in 1903, the Jam Kitchen is believed to be the oldest commercial sun-cooking operation in the United States. It still follows many of the methods and recipes of its founder Ida Putnam, who started the business to support herself. Everything is done by hand, using locally grown fruits and produce. Small batches of fruit are sweetened with a light sugar syrup and set outside to bake for up to 5 days under the June, July, or August sun. This process allows the products to retain the texture, color, and full flavor of the fruit. No pectin, preservatives, or artificial ingredients are added.

The Jam Kitchen produces a wide range of jams, jellies, marmalades, pickles, relishes, and sun-cooked fruits. One of the most popular is the Beach Plum Jelly made from native beach plums that ripen to perfection in the sandy soil of the Cape Cod dunes. Other favorites include Cranberry Conserves, Raspberry Jam, Paradise Jelly, Crab Apple Jelly, and Damson Plum Jelly.

The kitchen borders on the Green Briar Nature Center, and today the two are owned and run by the Thornton W. Burgess Society, a nonprofit educational organization dedicated to conserving the natural beauty and wildlife of Cape Cod. The Society operates the kitchen much the same way as it was run back in Ida Putnam's day with turn-of-the-century pots, pans, utensils, cook stoves, and Hoosier cabinets still used to make the jams and jellies. More than 15,000 visitors come to Green Briar every year to see its operation and to buy the products. The proceeds from visitors to this ''living museum'' and an extensive mail order business go toward maintaining the Society and the kitchen.

Thornton Burgess, a Cape Codder, author, and naturalist, roamed the Cape terrain as a boy. His bedtime stories, written for his young son, feature characters such as Peter Rabbit and Old Mother West Wind and habitats such as the Old Briar Patch, Smiling Pool, and Crooked Little Path, where Peter Rabbit nibbled on the sort of native berries that go into Green Briar Jam Kitchen's preserves.

Burgess gave his contemporary Ida Putnam a copy of one of his books with an inscription that still rings true: ''It is a wonderful thing to sweeten the world which is in a jam and needs preserving.''

HOW TO PURCHASE: Green Briar Jam Kitchen products are sold on the premises and are available by mail. Prices range from $3 for most jams and jellies to $4 for Beach Plum Jelly and Raspberry Jam. Gift assortments are available: four or six 6-oz. jars for about $17 to $30. Shipping and handling are included. Visa and MasterCard are accepted. Write or call for the latest prices and extensive product list.

TO VISIT: Visitors are welcome to watch jams and jellies being made at the Green Briar Jam Kitchen. The best time to visit is weekdays from 10 A.M.–4 P.M., June through November. To get to the Jam Kitchen, take exit 3 (Route 6) off the Mid-Cape Highway. Follow Quaker Meeting House Road north for about 1 mile and turn west onto Route 6A. Watch for the sign on the left.

Sea Scallops with Raspberry Butter Sauce

A wonderful appetizer or main course, this recipe is enhanced by the intense flavor of Green Briar Jam Kitchen's Raspberry Jam.

> 2 lbs. sea scallops, washed, feet removed, and cut
>   in half through the center
> Salt and freshly ground black pepper to taste
> 2 tablespoons unsalted butter
> ½ cup fresh raspberries for garnish (optional)

1. Preheat oven to 425 °F. Butter a cookie sheet and line with scallops. Sprinkle with salt and pepper. Butter one side of a large sheet of aluminum foil and lay, buttered side down, over the scallops, leaving a 1-inch opening on one end. Bake 10 minutes or until scallops are opaque and tiny lines appear on the tops.
2. Transfer to 8 plates and drizzle Raspberry Butter Sauce (below) over scallops. Garnish with fresh raspberries.

Serves 8.

Raspberry Butter Sauce

> 2 tablespoons unsalted butter
> 4 tablespoons finely chopped shallots
> ⅔ cup raspberry vinegar
> ½ cup whipping cream
> ½ lb. unsalted butter, softened at room temperature
> 3 tablespoons Green Briar Raspberry Jam, strained
>   to remove seeds

1. In a medium skillet, melt 2 tablespoons butter and sauté the shallots for about 1 minute. (Do not brown.) Add the vinegar and simmer until liquid is reduced to about 2 tablespoons. Add cream and simmer until reduced by about two-thirds.
2. Remove from heat. Whisk in the ½ lb. of butter by tablespoonfuls. Add the jam and blend. Spoon over scallops.

Note: This sauce is wonderful with poached salmon or sole as well.

Specialty Peanut Butter

TROMBLY'S PEANUT BUTTER FANTASIES. 64 Cummings Park, Woburn, Massachusetts 01801. 617/935-6460.

David Thibodeau had a fantasy that he could buy a peanut butter and jelly sandwich for lunch. He came up empty. But it fueled another idea. If everyone was doing fast foods such as hamburgers and fried chicken, why not give Boston something different, tasty, and inexpensive . . . a good peanut butter sandwich?

First he and a friend listed all the ways they could think to use peanut butter—a product list as it were. Then Thibodeau, who was already in the business, did a little marketing research and discovered that New England was second only to the South in peanut butter consumption. He also found out that the peanut market was on his side, the lowest it had been for 2 years. Armed with this information, Thibodeau launched Trombly's Peanut Butter Fantasies.

He picked the name of his great grandfather, who started Trombly Farm and established the precedence for quality that Thibodeau promises to stand by as well.

True peanut butter lovers will find celestial bliss in Thibodeau's fantasy product line: peanut butter cookies, granola bars, peanut butter spreads with honey, raisins, raspberry, Marshmallow Fluff, or cinnamon, and fantasia butters such as chunky maple cashew and chocolate raspberry. Even non–peanut butter lovers will enjoy the sophisticated version of some childhood tastes in the last two. Not to be missed, also, are the chocolate-dipped peanut butter truffles.

Thibodeau, who was 26 when he founded Trombly's, started with a retail outlet in Boston's busy Faneuil Hall Marketplace. Products were made in the small back room of the store. Besides all the peanut butter fantasies imaginable, there was also a take-out counter where the peanut butter czar offered peanut butter and jelly parfaits, banana and peanut butter burritos, peanut butter Reubens, and a sandwich named after Malcolm Forbes of *Forbes* magazine.

Thibodeau recently moved production to a larger facility where the nuts can be roasted and ground as needed. They have also added a mail order business and a whimsical, but slick catalog, and in 1987, Trombly's Peanut Butter Fantasies added a wholesale dimension to the peanut butter business.

HOW TO PURCHASE: Trombly's extensive catalog is fun to read even if you don't order anything. Assortment packages, the Perpetual Peanut Butter Club, and Peanut Butter of the Month Club with a wide range of choices and prices are perfect for those who can't pick just one flavor. Truffles are $16.95 for a 1-lb. box. A 16-oz. jar of peanut butter is $4.35; an 8-oz. jar of specialty butter is $5.55–$6.50, and 8-oz. jars of fantasia butter are $4.95. Prices include shipping and handling. Trombly's accepts credit cards.

Banana Peanut Butter Fantasy

We've kept this recipe appropriately short. When overwhelmed by an incredible urge for bananas, peanut butter, and chocolate, nothing should stand between a person and his or her fantasy! To make this a megacalorie extravaganza, serve with premium quality chocolate or vanilla ice cream and top with a spritz of *real* whipped cream.

> 6 ripe bananas, cut in half lengthwise
> 4 oz. Trombly's Chocolate Raspberry Fantasia Butter
> ½ cup heavy cream
> 5 tablespoons seedless raspberry jam

1. Line a cookie sheet with plastic wrap. Spread the banana slices over the sheet and cover with another sheet of plastic wrap. Freeze for at least 3 hours.

2. Just before serving, warm the fantasia butter, cream, and 2 tablespoons of the jam in a saucepan over medium-low heat. Stir until mixture is smooth. Remove from heat. Heat the remaining jam in a separate pan until it is syrupy.

3. Set 2 banana slices in banana split dishes (or cut each slice in thirds and set in bowls). Spoon fantasia butter mixture over the top of each banana slice. Drizzle a little of the warm jam over the top. Serve.

Serves 6.

NEW HAMPSHIRE

Mustards, Salad Dressings & Herb Mayonnaise

PETER CHRISTIAN'S SPECIALTY FOODS LTD. c/o Gourmet Garden, P.O. Box 1646, New London, New Hampshire 03257. 603/526-6656.

When Murray Washburn and his wife Karen founded the first Peter Christian Tavern in Hanover, Washburn had in mind to serve understated, quality food in a friendly atmosphere. He didn't realize the game plan would include two more Peter Christian restaurants (named for the couple's second oldest son) and a line of versatile gourmet foods, each tasting better than the next.

Washburn, who now considers himself a New Englander, reached the Granite State via a serpentine route. A native of Chicago, he studied international finance at the University of California at Berkley, then took off for Hawaii to work with his father in an import-export business. Evenings saw him moonlighting in a local restaurant. And soon he discovered he enjoyed his night job more than his real profession.

So Washburn, who owned land in New Hampshire, took off for the great Northeast with no money, ''hat in hand,'' to embark on a new life as a restaurateur. He opened the first tavern in Hanover in 1973. A second opened in New London in 1975. Then in 1983, Washburn opened a third eatery in Keene, just as his specialty food business was getting off the ground.

The first in the line of food products was Peter Christian's Original Mustard Sauce, a secret recipe from Washburn's mother using cider vinegar and brown sugar as the principal ingredients. A mainstay at the taverns, this sweet and tangy sauce is at the top of our list of unforgettable tastes and must have been for many others. Diners were always asking Washburn for jars of the rich brown mustard when they left the restaurant, and letters requesting mustard by mail were coming in from everywhere. It seemed natural to package the popular mustard and make it more readily available.

Soon Washburn and his family picked other favorites for the condiment business. Dressings with flavors such as tamari-honey and orange-sesame, mayonnaise laced with tarragon or pesto, and two more mustard sauces are among the delightful additions.

Washburn's next goal is to sell Peter Christian products to supermarkets. Since so many stores have begun to offer a gourmet section, ''it's a lot easier to sell to them and still be associated with quality,'' explains the restaurateur. As for where the Peter Christian company has gone and what lies ahead, ''we're between rinse and spin dry in our business cycle,'' says Peter Christian's father.

HOW TO PURCHASE: Peter Christian's Specialty Foods are available by mail. Original Mustard, Mulled Cider Mustard, and Ginger Honey Mustard are $4.95 each. The three dressings are $4.45 each. Flavors are Tamari and Honey, Orange Sesame, and Peter's Original Mustard Vinaigrette. Herb mayonnaise—New England Pesto, Sweet Tarragon, and Grande Aioli—is sold for $4.95 each. All products come in 8-oz. jars. There is a 10 percent discount for orders of 5 or more jars (your choice of items). Shipping and handling are included. Check or money order should be made out to Gourmet Garden. Major credit cards are accepted.

Bluefish with Mustard Sauce

Peter Christian's Original Mustard and bluefish are a great match. The tangy sauce balances the taste of this strong-flavored fish to produce a divine dish.

3 lbs. bluefish fillets

Marinade

¼ cup Peter Christian's Original Mustard Sauce
⅓ cup soy sauce
3 cloves garlic, crushed
2 teaspoons finely chopped fresh gingerroot
2 tablespoons olive oil

1. Wash the fish and pat dry. Combine the remaining ingredients and whisk together. Set fish fillets in a shallow baking dish and add the marinade. Turn the fish to coat and allow to sit 30 to 60 minutes.
2. Remove the fish from the marinade and grill or broil, 7 minutes on each side.

Serves 8.

Bavarian-style Mustard

COCHON ET CO. Box 210, Rye Beach, New Hampshire 03871. 603/964-7181.

Peter Case is going hog wild in Rye Beach, New Hampshire, producing an irresistible sweet and spicy brown mustard that's enough to make the most pedestrian ham sandwich sit up and squeal.

With the nickname Piggy and a vast collection of miniature pigs of all sizes, it's only natural that Case should carry the theme into his mustard business. He's cleaned up the act, however. Cochon et Co. has a classier ring at the cash register than pork bellies or hog futures. And it's certainly paying off for Case.

Case's mustard is made the Bavarian way, using eggs, sugar, vinegar, and ground mustard cooked together in a double boiler. His secret ingredient, according to the mustard czar, is New England cider vinegar.

Case's early version of Cochon et Co. was marketed in glass jars with a pig-in-profile on the label. Case thought this packaging was more suitable for the gourmet clientele he was courting. But recently the power of the pig has taken over, and his mustard now appears in 6-inch-high plastic piggies with the same face that's on his logo. Perhaps the best part is that Case gets to keep any slightly misshapen containers for his collection!

A former broadcaster who once headed a studio for Talking Books for the Blind, Case started making mustard for a living in 1979 after a friend introduced him to the wonderful tasting condiment during a sailing trip in Nantucket. She gave him the recipe that her sister had found in an old cookbook.

At the urging of friends and family, he decided to start marketing the tangy sauce. He brought his product to a wholesale food show and gave out samples with crackers and cheese. Within a year orders got so big he outgrew his kitchen and had to move to a commercial space. Today he's producing 4 tons of Cochon mustard annually that's carried in many gourmet and specialty food stores around the country. Looking to break into the supermarket trade, Case says Cochon et Co. is "somewhere between trying to get big and the gourmet market." One thing is certain, however. This is litter-ally just the beginning for one pig-headed entrepreneur and his flourishing mustard business.

HOW TO PURCHASE: Case sells a minimum of two 9-oz. plastic piggies filled with his mustard sauce for $4.95. Add $1.50 ($2.50 west of the Mississippi) for postage and handling. A case of Cochon et Co. Mustard (twelve 9-oz. bottles) is $22.50 plus shipping. Send check or money order payable to Cochon et Co.

Chicken in Pita Pockets with Cochon Mustard

The combination of chicken, sautéed onions, Monterey Jack cheese, and a favorite mustard has always been a hit around our house. Tucked in a pita bread, this one's a great Sunday night supper and makes for good eating in front of the football game.

>*1 large onion, thinly sliced*
>*2 tablespoons butter or vegetable oil*
>*4 boneless chicken thighs (about 1 lb. total)*
>*Salt and pepper to taste*
>*¼ cup Cochon Mustard*
>*1 large or 2 medium ripe tomatoes, sliced*
>*3–4 oz. Monterey Jack cheese, sliced*
>*Additional Cochon Mustard to brush on the breads*
>*4 small pita breads, opened to form pockets*

1. Sauté the onion in the butter or oil until light brown. Remove with a slotted spoon and reserve. Place the thighs between two sheets of waxed paper and pound with a kitchen mallet until thin. Sprinkle with salt and pepper and sauté in the same skillet over medium-high heat (about 3 minutes per side).

2. Preheat oven to 400°F. In a baking pan, spread out the thighs in a single layer. Brush with the mustard. Top with onions, then slices of tomato. Cover with slices of cheese. Bake 15 minutes or until cheese is melted.

3. Warm the pita breads briefly. Brush the inside with Cochon Mustard and tuck one piece of chicken in each pocket.

Makes 4 pocket sandwiches.

More Than a Mustard

FOX HOLLOW FARM, INC. R.F.D. #85, Lyme, New Hampshire 03768. 603/643-6002.

With all the mustards being made in home kitchens, it's easy to become blasé and forget that 15 years ago mustard meant that gooey bright yellow stuff that went on hot dogs. But Phyllis Fox is making a mustard that's so rich, smooth, and pungent that it will make even mustard mavens take notice. Fox's "More Than a Mustard" has a unique and memorable taste that comes from an array of exotic ingredients, including balsamic vinegar, fresh garlic, ground mustard, a blend of Oriental and Indian spices, and many years of experimenting on friends and family.

Back in the late seventies, Fox was already trying out her mustard recipe in Chicago where she was teaching cooking classes and selling food in a place called "Foodstuffs." As part of the application for her job, she brought in a blueberry tart and a jar of her mustard sauce. Not only was she hired, but the company wanted to market her mustard. She declined the second part of the offer.

When her husband Neil became marketing director of a Vermont company, they moved to a restored farm in New Hampshire that they named Fox Hollow Farm. Fox was looking for a food-oriented business, and friends' requests for refills of her mustard prompted her to consider starting her own cottage industry. Her husband designed the logo and label, and she found just the right size jars for bottling the by-then-perfected product.

In 1983, she began making mustard in the commercial kitchen of a nineteenth-century inn just across the Connecticut River in Vermont. She used the tiniest food processor imaginable. Seven jars at a time and brown sugar in 5-pound boxes were the scale of her operation.

To give you some idea of the amount of business she does now, Fox is buying 100-pound bags of sugar from a wholesaler and sells to many of the larger specialty food stores throughout the Northeast and on the West Coast. What started as more than a mustard is now more than a tiny operation for Phyllis Fox.

HOW TO PURCHASE: Fox sells her tangy More Than a Mustard in 7-oz. jars for $3.75 each. She sells in packages of 3, 6, 12, c 24 jars, and shipping is $2.60, $2.90, $3.60, and $4.64 respectively Shipping is via U.P.S. Orders must be prepaid, and checks or mone orders should be made out to Fox More Than a Mustard.

Honey-Mustard Glazed Cornish Hens: More Than a Chicken

The combination of honey and the spicy-sweet taste of Fox More Than a Mustard, makes for a flavorful marinade for Cornis Hens. This may be cooked on the grill or baked in the oven.

2 whole Cornish hens

Glaze

3 tablespoons honey
2 tablespoons Fox's More Than a Mustard
2 tablespoons freshly squeezed lemon juice
2 teaspoons good quality curry powder
1 tablespoon vegetable oil
3 cloves crushed garlic

1. Combine glaze ingredients and brush liberally over the hen Allow to stand at room temperature 30 minutes or refrigerated fc up to 2 hours.

2. Prepare a charcoal grill and set up rotisserie. Skewer the bird onto the rotisserie and fasten the legs and wings against the bod of the hens using kitchen twine. Grill over medium flame for 4 to 60 minutes, brushing often with the remaining glaze mixture

Note: Hens may also be baked in a 425°F. oven. Set on the rac of a roasting pan, breast side down, and bake 20 minutes. Turn th hens breast side up and bake another 20 to 30 minutes or until juice run clear when the thigh meat is pierced. Brush frequently wit glaze while the hens are baking.

Serves 4.

Homemade Preserves

EONE'S HOMEMADE PRESERVES. Timber Street, R.F.D.
9, Londonderry, New Hampshire 03053. 603/432-5741.

For Leone Gage, life has revolved around the kitchen for as long
she can remember. She's been cooking jams, jellies, and preserves
r more than 30 years. In 1985, she turned from hobbyist to profes-
onal jam maker, and now she sells her products to gift shops and
untry stores, and via mail to individual customers.

Gage started out by bringing her products to the League of New
ampshire Craftsmen Fair one August. To her surprise and delight,
e completely sold out. Now she is juried with this league, an honor
at's bestowed on only a few specialty food businesses in New
ampshire. And thanks to simple word-of-mouth advertising, Gage
now running a thriving jelly, jam, and preserves business. She loves
ery aspect of what she does, from picking the fruit (she uses most-
locally grown products) to making her preserves and marketing
em.

Gage makes several flavors including Apple Butter, Crab Apple
lly, Cranberry Conserve, Plum, Peach-Plum, Rhubarb, Blueberry,
rawberry, and Strawberry-Rhubarb. She also makes an intensely
vored Banana-Pineapple, Mango, Pineapple-Orange-Rhubarb, and
Lime and an Orange Marmalade. All are made with fresh fruit, and
ey are cooked in small batches. Most are from recipes that Gage
eated as she experimented with various fruits, but some are recipes
nded down from her mother.

While Gage does the cooking, her husband, Ted, who shares her
ve for the kitchen and her business, designs and handcrafts wood-
gift boxes to hold her products. The two package her preserves
the rustic two-, four-, or six-jar-size holders for country fairs. Aside
om helping with this part of the business, Ted and family also help
hen fruit-picking season comes around. And Ted and Leone spend
good part of each summer attending New England country fairs
gether with their handmade wares.

If this isn't a family business, we don't know what is!

OW TO PURCHASE: All Leone's Homemade Preserves are sold
r $4 per 9-oz. jar. Exceptions are Red Raspberry which sells for
5.75, and Mango, Strawberry, Strawberry-Rhubarb, and Strawber-
-Banana which sell for $4.50 each. Add $2.95 for orders up to
3; $3.95 for orders between $13.01 and $25. Shipping is via U.P.S.
rders must be prepaid with check or money order payable to
eone Gage.

Betty Ann's Fruit-filled Pinwheel Cookies

Our neighbor makes these for holiday gift giving, and we've been
the fortunate recipients for several years. Using a variety of preserves
and jams for fillings makes it seem as though you've made several
kinds of cookies.

> *½ lb. unsalted butter, softened*
> *8-oz. package cream cheese, softened*
> *½ cup sugar*
> *Grated rind of a small lemon*
> *2¼ cups all-purpose flour*
> *Pinch of salt*
> *¾ cup finely chopped walnuts*
> *½ cup Leone's Banana-Pineapple Preserves*
> *½ cup Leone's Peach-Plum Preserves*
> *¼ cup confectioners' sugar*

1. Cream butter and cream cheese until smooth. Add sugar and beat
well. Add lemon rind and mix. Stir in flour and salt with a spoon
until texture is a coarse meal. Form into a ball. Divide the dough
in half and wrap each piece in waxed paper and press each into
roughly a 6-inch square. Chill 1 hour.

2. Preheat oven to 350°F. On a lightly floured surface, roll each
piece of dough into a 12-inch square and cut into 2½-inch squares.
Use a knife to cut a 1-inch slit from each corner into the center of
the square. Sprinkle ½ teaspoon of walnuts over squares and press
into dough. Drop a small dollop of the preserves in the center. (Alternate the two flavors.) Fold every other tip to the center like a pin-
wheel. Pinch the edges firmly into the center and set 1 inch apart
on ungreased cookie sheets. Bake 15 minutes or until tips are golden.
Remove from oven and sprinkle with confectioners' sugar. Transfer
to a wire rack to cool.

Yields 50 cookies.

Colonial Pepper Jelly

THE LOLLIPOP TREE, INC. 41 Liberty Common, Rye, New Hampshire 03870. 603/436-8196.

When Lori Lynch's friend needed a food item to sell in her boutique, Lori remembered an old family recipe for spicy pepper jelly. She began making batches of it in her kitchen in 1981. Today she still cooks out of her kitchen, but now the kettles on her stove make pepper jelly in 60-gallon vats and Lori has help.

What began as a home business to provide a second income for a growing family is now a bonafide enterprise. Customers include Neiman-Marcus Department Stores, L. L. Bean, and Dave Maynard, radio personality with WBZ in Boston. The Lollipop Tree started with pepper jelly, because it was unique, especially in New England which was light years from the southern epicenter of red pepper jelly, and because they thought it would sell. They were right. Now their product line is quite extensive—Mustard Fruit, Cape Cranberry Conserve, Strawberry Walnut Preserves, Cranberry Pineapple Walnut Preserves, Clear Mint Jelly, Yankee Citrus Marmalade, and a Downeast Meat and Seafood Sauce. But Pepper Jelly is still their top seller. Their products are all natural, affectionately stirred by hand, and poured, labeled, and shipped with loving care.

The marketing and accounting sides of the company—Lori's husband Bob and MBA graduate student Brian Nicholson—are always on the lookout for new products. Most new items evolve "at the stove," says Nicholson. Who knows what the trio will cook up next?

HOW TO PURCHASE: The Lollipop Tree products are sold in 10-oz. jars. A box of three (your choice of flavors) is $17.95; twelve 10-oz. jars (any combination) is $57. Prices include freight and handling. Lollipop Tree also offers a sampler of twenty-four 2-oz. jars in your choice of flavors for $56. Visa and MasterCard are accepted.

Tarragon Pepper Jelly Aspic with Shrimp

Thanks to Lollipop Tree's Colonial Pepper Jelly, this tomato aspic packs a nice little zing.

> 4 cups V-8 juice
> 1 tablespoon confectioners' sugar
> 2 teaspoons dried tarragon
> 2 tablespoons gelatin (2 packages)
> 5 oz. Lollipop Tree Pepper Jelly
> ¼ cup tarragon wine vinegar
> 3 tablespoons freshly squeezed lemon juice
> ½ lb. cooked shrimp, peeled and chopped
> 1 carrot, peeled and diced
> ½ red onion, minced
> Lettuce leaves for garnish

1. Heat 1½ cups of juice with the sugar and the tarragon. Soften the gelatin in ½ cup of juice. Heat the jelly until melted. Add the gelatin and heat until it has dissolved into the jelly. Remove from the heat and mix with the juice, sugar, and tarragon mixture.
2. Add the remaining V-8 juice, vinegar, and lemon juice to the liquid. Add the shrimp, carrot, and onion and mix. Spray a 6-cup mold with vegetable spray and add the aspic mixture. Refrigerate at least 4 hours but preferably overnight. Unmold on a bed of lettuce leaves that have been arranged on a round serving platter.

Serves 12.

Lucie's Original Peanut Butter

all - natural
Lucie's Original
Peanut Butter
made from unblanched peanuts
· unique texture · no preservatives ·
Oil separation occurs in natural peanut butter.
Stir well.

✓

LUCIE'S PRODUCTS COMPANY. 24 Rayton Road, Hanover, New Hampshire 03755. 603/543-3393.

Lucie Minsk is making peanut butter in New Hampshire that's guaranteed not to stick to the roof of your mouth. In addition, it's an intensely nutty, slightly sweet peanut butter unlike any other you'll encounter.

One bite and most people say, "This is the best peanut butter I've ever tasted." That very statement from one Murray Washburn (Peter Christian's Tavern Specialty Foods in this book) prompted us to seek out the New England peanut butter wizard.

Minsk began making Lucie's Original Peanut Butter for the public in 1985 after producing it for her family for 15 years. Her husband and three sons ate peanut butter every day, and she wanted to serve them a better product than anything they could buy in the store.

When her sons left for college, Minsk began receiving requests for this family treat from all of their friends, too. That provided the impetus for Minsk to take her product to an annual state fair. Soon it was being juried by the League of New Hampshire Craftsmen.

Several things make Lucie's Original outstanding. Minsk uses only dry roasted, unblanched peanuts. Roasted peanuts are usually done in oils other than peanut oil, she says of her choice. Her main secret, however, is that she uses the skins of the nuts, which she believes enhances the flavor. "Because peanuts are legumes, 30 percent of the nutrition and fiber is in the skins."

She adds a touch of honey, molasses, and salt to compensate for any bitterness in the skins and uses just a little peanut oil to bind the butter. Rather than adding chunks of peanuts after she's made the butter, she grinds it in a way that leaves bits of the nut. This accounts for the no-stick factor.

Her product is not homogenized and contains no preservatives. Minsk urges her customers to buy her peanut butter in small quantities as they need it, so that it's always fresh.

Lucie's original is made in small batches in Minsk's state-approved home kitchen—"just the way I would for my own family," she says of her no-cholesterol product. "It takes a little more time that way, but most folks seem to like the results," she says.

HOW TO PURCHASE: Lucie's Original Peanut Butter is sold in 6-oz. jars for $2.25. A 16-oz. jar costs $4.50, and a 4-lb. container is sold for $15. Prices include shipping (via U.P.S.). Send checks or money orders payable to Lucie's Products Company.

Peanut Butter Chocolate Chip Oatmeal Cookies

What could be nicer than a cookie that's laced with chocolate chips, the chewy texture of cooked oatmeal, and the subtle nuttiness of Lucie's Original?

6-oz. jar Lucie's Original Peanut Butter
12 tablespoons unsalted butter, softened at room temperature
1 cup light brown sugar
1 cup white sugar
2 eggs
2 cups all-purpose flour
1 teaspoon baking soda
½ teaspoon salt
¼ teaspoon cinnamon
¼ cup milk
1 teaspoon pure vanilla extract
2 cups uncooked oatmeal
1½ cups chocolate bits

1. Preheat oven to 350°F. Lightly grease 2 cookie sheets. Cream together the peanut butter, butter, brown and white sugar. Add the eggs and beat well. Add the flour, baking soda, salt, cinnamon, milk, and vanilla. Beat to combine. With a wooden spoon, stir in the oatmeal. Fold in the chocolate bits.
2. Scoop up rounded teaspoonfuls of batter and drop onto cookie sheets, leaving about 1 inch between cookies. Bake 12 minutes or until slightly brown and centers are still chewy. Remove from oven, loosen cookies with a spatula, and cool on baking rack.

Makes 4–6 dozen.

New England Peach Chutney

✓

WHITEHOUSE FARM. Foster Center Road, Foster, Rhode Island 02825. 401/397-4386.

Since 1980, Carole Harman has been racing home from her job as a school teacher to make her gardens grow. The moment school breaks for summer recess, she gears up to tend and harvest the vegetables, herbs, fruits, and berries that her rural Rhode Island 15-acre farm puts forth.

And each year she turns her crop into wonderously creative homemade chutneys, relishes, jellies, and jams that are known throughout most of Rhode Island and much of southern New England.

Cranberry Chutney, Raisin and Mint Chutney, and Peach Chutney are among her most popular items. The last — a mild relish chock full of large chunks of peach and red pepper — is a lovely, versatile cooking and eating condiment.

For Harman, food has always been an avocation. But in recent years, as word of her top-notch products has gotten out, cooking has become more of a business than a hobby for this art teacher.

Harman's enterprise took off around 1982 after prompting by friends and acquaintances to bring her homemade condiments to the public. A real boost came from the owners of Al Forno, a trendy Providence restaurant, when they asked Harman to make all the condiments they serve with grilled vegetables and meats. "They've been the prime people responsible for my success," says Harman. It was through the restaurant that Harman linked up with *New England Monthly* magazine, which featured her products in a 1987 article on New England Foods and brought further acclaim.

A native of Manchester, Connecticut, Harman had a fascination for food and herbs even as a youngster. When she got her driver's license, her first trip was to visit an herb farm, Caprilands, in neighboring Coventry. The well-known herbalist and owner Adelma Simmons "is one reason I'm into herbs," she reminisces.

Harman attended school in Rhode Island where she met her husband Matthew. The two decided to stay in the small state and picked a remote setting to call home. Their farmhouse dates back to 1750, as do many of the fruit trees that furnish the basis for Harman's products.

Two large vegetable gardens, an herb garden, and numerous berry bushes complete the sum total of the makings for her business. Harman works every day throughout the summer and the fall "putting up" her bountiful harvest in a small-batch kitchen operation. Recently, she expanded her tiny kitchen into a new, much larger setting designed for canning.

HOW TO PURCHASE: Harman sells her Peach Chutney in ½-pint containers for $4.50 and pints for $8. Shipping is via U.P.S. and depends on destination. Orders must be prepaid with check or money order to Carole Harman.

Sautéed Duck Breast with Peach Chutney

We found Whitehouse Farm Peach Chutney to be a wonderful match with duck breast and a sauce with an Oriental tang.

4 boneless duck breasts, excess skin and fat removed
Salt and freshly ground black pepper
4 tablespoons unsalted butter
2 shallots, minced
½ cup peach wine (a medium-dry white wine may be substituted)
1 cup rich duck or chicken stock
1 tablespoon finely chopped fresh gingerroot
1½ tablespoons soy sauce
4 shiitake mushrooms, caps thinly sliced
8-oz. jar Whitehouse Farm Peach Chutney

1. Sprinkle the duck breasts with salt and pepper. In a large skillet arrange the duck, skin side down, in the skillet and cook over medium-low heat about 10 minutes or until skin is browned and crisp. As fat collects, spoon some of it off and discard. Remove duck from skillet and discard all the fat. Melt 2 tablespoons of the butter and return the duck to the skillet, skin side up. Sear the meat about 2 minutes, then remove to a heated platter and keep warm.
2. Add remaining butter to the skillet and sauté the shallots for 1 minute. Deglaze with the peach wine and simmer until reduced and syrupy. Add the stock and ginger and reduce by half. Add the soy sauce and the mushroom slices and simmer 2 minutes. Add the peach chutney and heat.
3. Cut the duck into thin slices on the diagonal. Loosely reassemble breasts on the platter and spoon the sauce over the duck. Serve at once.

Serves 4.

VERMONT

Seafood Sauce, Barbecue Sauce & Specialty Mustards

ANNIE'S ENTERPRISES, INC. Foster Hill Road, North Calais, Vermont 05650. 802/456-8866.

"But you're out of business," we said with great surprise when we met Ann Christopher selling her food at the New York Fancy Food Show. "It's not me," she protested, having heard repeatedly about "the other Annie's of Vermont" during the show. Indeed, we're glad to report that Ann Christopher of Annie's Enterprises is doing a thriving business in North Calais, Vermont.

Christopher started her business in 1984 when everyone she knew was asking for her barbecue sauce. After attending college in Colorado, the New York native decided to make a career change and went to cooking school at New York Technical College. Her training in classical cuisine left her with aspirations of becoming a chef. At about the same time, she married a Vermont man, and the two moved to his family's vintage 1815 dairy farm. There was just one problem. "The farm is 50 miles from the nearest fancy restaurant," she says.

Determined to do something with her newly acquired credentials, Christopher opened a barbecue stand where she made American food and worked 15 hours a day. Then the erstwhile chef became pregnant and closed the stand. She decided to continue with the barbecue idea which had been such a hit and began to make her sauce at home.

What began with only a sauce on the menu has grown to include a list of products that would fill an entire page. Recently Ann's operation has become too big for her home kitchen, and she's started working out of the facilities at the Cherry Hill Cooperative Cannery in Barre.

Several mustards are part of Annie's repertoire: Bee Sting Honey, lightly sweet and pungent; Raspberry Hot, fruity and zapped with a hint of spiciness; Rosemary Galore, with an herb taste; and Farmhouse Maple, more sweet than pungent and a perfect glaze for ham, carrots, or sweet potatoes. Annie's latest is a full-flavored Seafood Sauce with many uses. She's just come out with a Raspberry Vinaigrette. And the cook-turned-businesswoman is working on a new all-natural barbecue sauce.

It doesn't seem to matter that Ann Christopher is tucked "way way out in the country." Customers seem to find her. Today her products are sought by more than just friends. Her first account was Bloomingdale's, and she counts Balducci's and Four Seasons Restaurant of New York City among her valued customers.

HOW TO PURCHASE: Annie's BBQ Sauce is sold in 16-oz jars. The mustards are packed in 8-oz jars, and the tantalizing Seafood Sauce comes in 16-oz. jars. All products are sold for $4.50. Shipping is extra and determined by destination. To order, send check or money order payable to Annie's Enterprises, Inc. Prices are subject to change. It's advisable to call or write before ordering.

Mussels Marinara

Using Annie's Seafood Sauce, a bit of white wine, and clam broth makes this dish a cinch. All that's needed are mussels or clams, a loaf of good French bread, and a salad, if you wish.

> *16-oz. jar Annie's Seafood Sauce*
> *½ cup white wine*
> *1 cup clam broth*
> *16-oz. can plum tomatoes, drained and chopped*
> *3 dozen fresh mussels, washed and debearded*
>   *(clams may be substituted)*
> *10 oz. fresh linguine, cooked al dente*
> *¼ cup chopped Italian parsley*

1. In a medium pot with tightly fitting lid, combine the Seafood Sauce, wine, clam broth, and tomatoes. Bring to a boil. Add the mussels, lower the heat to medium and cover. Steam 5 minutes or until mussels open.
2. Put linguine in a deep serving dish and top with the mussels and their sauce. Sprinkle with parsley and serve.

Serves 4.

Chunky Ketchup

BLANCHARD & BLANCHARD & SON. P.O. Box 1080, Norwich, Vermont 05055. 802/649-1327 in Vermont or 1/800-334-0268.

What to do after you've created the best fudge sauce in the world? Make a revolutionary ketchup, of course! That is, if you're Melinda and Bob Blanchard. From a tiny cookware shop in 1976 to a major expansion within 6 months, to a children's toy and furniture store that mushroomed into a chain with four locations, the duo discovered they had the Midas touch when it came to business. In 1983, they took a $2,000 tax refund and launched a gourmet-food business, Blanchard & Blanchard & Son. (The "son" was added for their son Justin.)

The two began with fudge sauce, made with Belgian chocolate and pure heavy cream, and created right in their home kitchen. Soon Balducci's, Macy's, and Bloomingdale's in New York became customers. Today an impressive line of salad dressings, mustards, ice cream toppings, cooking sauces, and ketchups appear on the shelves of more than 800 stores throughout the country.

Their fudge sauce was voted first place several times, including in a *Boston Globe* survey. True chocoholics will find their way to nirvana by dunking a spoon into this mixture. But our favorite is a new item, chunky ketchup, which comes either mild or extra spicy. Hailed as "revelatory" by *Newsweek* magazine, this zesty condiment makes a hot dog or a hamburger sing. It's nothing like the generic stuff. This one's a versatile cooking and barbecue sauce as well.

Although the business has grown far beyond a mom and pop operation and employs twenty people, Blanchard & Blanchard & Son still make their products in single batches using the same TLC that gave them their start. The secret to success? Just using the best ingredients, according to the Blanchards.

HOW TO PURCHASE: Blanchard & Blanchard products are available by mail order. Dressings come in 8-oz. bottles for $1.99 each; Chunky Ketchup (Mild and Extra Spicy) is sold in 12-oz. bottles for $2.29; Fudge Sauce in 8.5-oz. jars is $2.99 each. Special gift packages, especially lovely Christmas samplers, are available. Shipping is via U.P.S. and is an additional charge based on destination. All major credit cards are accepted as well as checks and money orders. Write or call for their latest mail order brochure.

Spicy Garlic Shrimp

Blanchard & Blanchard Extra Spicy Chunky Ketchup has a natural affinity for an Oriental dish. Its hot and sour taste makes for a terrific sauce in this slightly New England-ized version of Shrimp with Garlic Sauce.

1 lb. large shrimp (26–30 count), peeled and deveined

Marinade

½ teaspoon coarse salt
¼ teaspoon freshly ground black pepper
2 teaspoons cornstarch
1 egg white, beaten until frothy

Batter

2 egg yolks
3 tablespoons cornstarch
2–3 tablespoons water (enough to make the batter smooth)

½ green pepper, cut into ¼-inch cubes
1 medium onion, chopped
3 cloves garlic, minced

Seasoning Mixture

½ cup Blanchard & Blanchard Extra Spicy Chunky Ketchup
1 tablespoon pure maple syrup

3 cups vegetable oil for deep frying
2 tablespoons vegetable oil

1. Coat the shrimp with the marinade ingredients and let stand in the refrigerator about 1 hour. Combine the batter ingredients and set aside. Prepare the green pepper, onion, and garlic. Combine and reserve.
2. In a wok or a deep saucepan, heat the 3 cups of oil to 375°F. Dip the shrimp in the batter, then deep-fry in the oil for about 2 minutes or until coating is golden brown. With a slotted spoon, remove the shrimp to a paper towel–lined plate and blot.
3. Heat the 2 tablespoons of oil in a wok or frying pan. Add the chopped vegetables. Stir-fry 30 seconds. Add the sauce mixture and simmer 1 minute. Set the shrimp on a plate and pour the sauce over them. Serve at once.

Serves 2.

Applesauce & Apple Butter

CHERRY HILL COOPERATIVE CANNERY. Route 1, Barre, Vermont 05641. 802/479-2558.

Cherry Hill Cooperative Cannery started in 1976 with a dual purpose. Situated in one of Vermont's busiest commercial strips, the coop provided low-cost equipment and space for people to can their garden produce. It was also the commercial facility for many small Vermont cottage industries that would not be in business were this space not available. All these services came together to meet the cannery's objective to stimulate Vermont's agricultural economy by encouraging the use of a variety of locally grown products.

To finance these services, the Cherry Hill coop was also a commercial canning business. But the nine members of the workers' collective that runs Cherry Hill Cannery soon discovered that their altruistic goals of the seventies wouldn't pay the mortgage. "About years ago the interest in community canning just evaporated," says Ken Davis, manager of the coop. "We had to step back from our original ideology and realize that each part had to support itself."

The facilities are still available for noncommercial use and cottage industries, but now the coop's primary business is that of canning and marketing its own products, chiefly applesauces, apple butters, and maple syrup. The ingredients, with the exception of a few spices and the cranberries for cranberry applesauce, all come from Vermont farmers, and everything is packed as though it comes from someone's home kitchen, in simple glass Kerr canning jars.

The Cannery makes Maple Sweetened Applesauce that has the distinctive taste of maple and Cranberry Applesauce that's a luscious rose color and sweetened with maple syrup, but that still retains some of that cranberry tartness. They also produce Raspberry and Strawberry Applesauce with distinct berry flavors and a hint of maple from that sweetener.

In true Yankee tradition, the cannery produces some wonderfully tasty apple butters. (A book about New England foods would not be complete without a mention of apple butter!) These are made in a multitude of flavors: Spiced, Raspberry, Strawberry, and Unsweetened Apple Butter. All are made primarily with McIntosh apples and a few Delicious and Cortlands.

Additionally, this operation produces a popular line of pickles, including Pickled Fiddleheads and Pickled Red Cabbage. The first are made in a brine of vinegar, salt, and spices that results in a slightly hot and wild tasting pickle. The red cabbage is combined with apple cider and maple syrup, beets, caraway, salt, and cider vinegar and makes for unique eating, too.

Cherry Hill Cooperative Cannery sells most of its products through food coops, health food stores, and specialty food stores throughout the East. Products are also available by mail.

HOW TO PURCHASE: An 8-oz. jar of Raspberry or Strawberry Apple Butter is $2.99. Unsweetened Apple Butter sells for $2.59; and Spiced Apple Butter is $2.59. Raspberry, Strawberry, or Cranberry Applesauce sells for $2.89 per 16-oz. jar. Maple Sweetened Applesauce is $2.39, and Unsweetened is $2.19. Shipping is extra and based on destination. Orders must be accompanied by check or money order.

Strawberry Applesauce Harvest Loaf

Not too sweet and not too tart, this is a quick bread and a cake at the same time.

> ¼ lb. unsalted butter, softened
> ½ cup honey
> 2 eggs
> 2 cups all-purpose flour
> 1 teaspoon baking soda
> ½ teaspoon salt
> 1 cup Cherry Hill Cooperative Cannery
>   Strawberry Applesauce
> ¾ cup Vermont cheddar cheese, grated
> ½ cup walnut pieces

1. Preheat oven to 350°F. Grease a 3x5x9-inch loaf pan. Cream the butter with the honey until light and fluffy. Add the eggs and beat well.

2. Sift together the flour, soda, and salt. Add sifted ingredients to the butter mixture and mix to moisten. Stir in the applesauce; then fold in the cheese and the nuts. Turn into prepared loaf pan and bake 50–55 minutes. Remove from pan and cool on a rack.

Yields 1 loaf.

Apple Cider Jelly, Syrup & Concentrate

COLD HOLLOW CIDER MILL. R.F.D. #1, Route 100, Box 430, Waterbury Center, Vermont 05677. 1/800-3-APPLES or 1/800-U-C-CIDER in Vermont.

To sip a glass of freshly made Vermont apple cider is to drink in one of the most satisfying and wholesome delights the Green Mountain State has to offer. Nestled in a valley between two mountain ranges in Vermont's north-central forest region, Cold Hollow Cider Mill is one of the major producers of this refreshing drink, pressing cider all day long during the fall months, for a total of about 3,000 gallons each year.

The mill sells apples in many forms. It is one of only two producers of pure apple cider jelly and syrup in the United States. Using just one ingredient, apple cider, Cold Hollow Pure Vermont Cider Syrup is bursting with apple flavor, and Cold Hollow Original Pure Cider Jelly is completely natural owing to a process that uses no sugar or pectin. High on the list of Cold Hollow Cider Mill's products is Hot Spiced Cider Concentrate which makes this festive beverage available all year long.

The mill also makes its own eat-em-soon-as-they're-ready apple cider doughnuts. It's the only kind of doughnut they produce, and they use a primitive machine to make them. In addition, Cold Hollow sells apple butter, applesauce, and not-to-be-forgotten, large, red, juicy McIntosh apples.

Eric and Francine Chittenden started Cold Hollow Cider Mill back in 1974. At the time they met, Eric was a merchant seaman who was away 6 months a year. These lengthy separations didn't seem conducive to a healthy family life so the two began looking for a way to make a living together and pursue their interest in natural and minimally processed foods. They tried several ideas before the cider mill business clicked. It was perfect. The equipment they needed was available used, and they already had the building.

Now people line up for the Chittendens' cider and doughnuts during ski season. And the mill, which is open year round, sells some 100,000 pounds of apple products each year. The two recently expanded the cider mill operation to include a mail order business. But their reputation has preceded them, and the energetic couple already has amassed 200,000 names for their mailing list.

HOW TO PURCHASE: The Original Pure Cider Jelly and Pure Vermont Cider Syrup (in 8-oz. jars) are $8 to $9 for 2 (your choice of products), depending on destination. Hot Spiced Cider Concentrate is $14.80 to $16.36 for two 20-oz. jars, depending on location. A pack of 12 apples is between $10.95 and $12.75. Prices include shipping. Major credit cards are accepted.

Old-time Vermont Pure Cider Jelly Pie

This wonderful old-fashioned New England pie takes just minutes to make thanks to the Chittendens who have already boiled the cider into jelly for us!

> *9-inch pie crust*
> *1 cup Cold Hollow Cider Mill Cider Jelly*
> *⅓ cup sugar*
> *2 tablespoons melted butter*
> *3 egg yolks*
> *1 cup milk*
> *1½ tablespoons all-purpose flour*
> *3 egg whites, stiffly beaten*
> *1 cup lightly sweetened whipped cream*

1. Preheat oven to 425 °F. Line pie crust with foil and pie weights and bake blind for 10 minutes. Remove the weights and foil and bake 5 minutes or until lightly browned. Raise heat to 450 °F.
2. Beat the jelly with the sugar, butter, yolks, milk, and flour until blended. Gently fold in the whites. Pour into pie crust and bake 10 minutes. Lower the heat to 325 °F. and bake 30 minutes. Remove and cool. Serve with whipped cream.

Serves 8.

Filomena's Marinara Pasta Sauce

D'AGOSTO, INC. P. O. Box 974, Burlington, Vermont 05402. 802/863-1608.

Everyone claims his or her mother's cooking is the best, says Frank Dell'Amore. The only difference is that Dell'Amore has staked business on it. The founder of D'Agosto Inc., he makes and sells marinara sauce using a recipe that was his mother's and his grandmother's and follows a matriarchal line for several hundred years.

Dell'Amore named his sauce for his grandmother Filomena D'Agosto, who brought the recipe with her when she came to the United States from Agropoli, Italy, in 1924. And he's put a picture of this elegant-looking lady on each jar of Filomena's Marinara Pasta Sauce. A beauty in her youth, Filomena is still going strong at 94.

Filomena's grandson makes the sauce in the same time-honored way, using choice ground peeled tomatoes, freshly chopped garlic, olive oil, Italian herbs and spices, no sugar or salt, and lots of simmering.

This versatile marinara sauce was started in 1985, in the kitchen of Dell'Amore's Pizzeria, aptly named Filomena's. (The sauce is still used in several of the restaurant dishes.) In the early days, Dell'Amore would cook the sauce and boil a dozen canning jars at a time using only his four-burner stove.

Then he hooked up with Justin Baker, who had worked for him delivering pizzas while going to school at the nearby University of Vermont. Dell'Amore was impressed by Baker's attention to detail, and soon the two became partners. Today they make Filomena's Marinara Pasta Sauce in 100-gallon batches using the facilities of the Cherry Hill Cooperative Cannery in Barre, Vermont. It still tastes homemade. Filomena's sauce appears on the shelves of many fine stores including Balducci's and Macy's in New York.

HOW TO PURCHASE: Filomena's Marinara Pasta Sauce is sold in many gourmet shops throughout New England and New York. It comes in a mild and a spicy variety and is available by mail in pint jars for $2.75 and quart jars for $4. Shipping is extra and is based on destination. Orders must be prepaid and checks should be made out to D'Agosto, Inc.

Filomena's Zucchini

Don't be deluded by the simplicity of this recipe. Not much is required to enhance the already flavor-filled Filomena's. The combination of fresh zucchini and this well-seasoned sauce makes for a delicious dish — and it's so easy to prepare!

1 medium onion, chopped
2 tablespoons good quality olive oil
6 medium zucchini, peeled and cut into ¼-inch thick slices
1 pint Filomena's Marinara Pasta Sauce (hot or mild)
¼ cup freshly grated Parmesan cheese

In a large skillet with a tightly fitting lid, sauté onion in olive oil until the onion is soft (about 5 minutes). Add the zucchini and sauté 1 minute. Add the pasta sauce. Cover and simmer 30 to 40 minutes or until zucchini is tender. Add the cheese and serve with rice or over fettucine noodles.

Serves 4–6.

Maple-sweetened Jams

GRAFTON GOODJAM

GRAFTON GOODJAM. R.D. #3, Box 247, Grafton, Vermont 05146. 802/843-2276.

Mary Schoener is the chief, cook, and bottle washer at Grafton Goodjam. She's also the creator of a line of seven intensely flavored jams, jellies, and relishes, sweetened with maple syrup. Her one-person business, started in 1982, finds her doing everything from developing recipes to designing her own labels (based on medieval woodcuts) to locating French jam jars for her products and marketing them.

Schoener, who works "all the time," says she probably wouldn't have taken on such a project if she had known what was involved. But looking back, she says, "I'm pleased with myself because I've done it."

Grafton Goodjam grew out of a surplus of fruit from the family berry bushes that Schoener's husband Allon decided to turn into jam. Attracted by the idea of marketing the product more than actually making it (Schoener admits she never really liked to make jam), she started small. Batches were cooked slowly and tested repeatedly until they were just the right consistency.

As for marketing, Schoener, who doesn't advertise or attend food and trade shows, simply went to places she thought would sell her products. Today, while her copper kettles of Goodjam bubble on the big black stove in her kitchen, she ponders just how large she wants to become. Schoener is at a crossroads: she faces the dilemma of remaining a small one-person operation or adding more people so she can expand her lines. She's already buying basic materials and ingredients in quantities that are beyond her one-person capacity, and she expects to need at least one extra pair of hands in the near future.

All Grafton Goodjams are made with 4 ounces of maple syrup to each pound of fruit. And that's it for ingredients. No pectin, sugar, or honey is used. As a sweetener and preservative, the maple syrup allows the fruit flavor to dominate and produces a texture slightly softer than jelly-firm, making for a delightfully spreadable preserve.

There are no plans in Schoener's future to get rich at what she does. "I don't want to get too big. I don't want to make millions," she muses.

HOW TO PURCHASE: Grafton Goodjam is $8.80 per attractively decorated 12-oz. jar. Flavors are Raspberry, Blueberry, Wild Blackberry, Strawberry, Loganberry, Apricot, and Hot Gingered Apricot Chutney. There is a 3-jar minimum. Shipping, additional, is via U.P.S. and based on destination. Orders must be prepaid with check or money order to Grafton Goodjam. Credit cards are not accepted. Grafton Goodjam is also sold through Grafton Village Apple Company, another business included here.

Blueberry Cheese Tart

This yummy cheese tart may be made with any Goodjam preserves. However, blueberry is our favorite, and when they are in season, we sprinkle fresh blueberries over the top.

Crust

1 tablespoon sugar
Grated rind of 1 small lemon
¼ lb. chilled, unsalted butter, in small pieces
¾ cup plus 2 tablespoons all-purpose flour
½ teaspoon baking powder
Pinch salt
½ teaspoon vanilla extract
1 tablespoon cold water

1 cup Grafton Goodjam Blueberry Jam

1. In a food processor fitted with the steel blade, combine the sugar, butter, flour, baking powder, salt, and vanilla and pulse until mixture is a coarse meal. Add the lemon peel and pulse to combine. With the machine running, add the water through the feed tube and process just until dough forms a rough ball.
2. Preheat oven to 350°F. Press over the bottom and 1 inch up the sides of a 10-inch springform pan. Spread cheese mixture (below) evenly over crust. Bake 40 minutes. Remove from oven and cool completely. Top with an even layer of jam. Refrigerate. Remove sides of springform when ready to serve.

Serves 8.

Cheese Filling

6 oz. cream cheese, softened at room temperature
½ cup ricotta cheese
¼ cup sour cream
2 teaspoons grated lemon peel
½ cup sugar
1 tablespoon vanilla extract

Place all ingredients in a medium mixing bowl and beat until smooth. Pour into crust above.

Marinades, Cooking Sauces

✔

JASMINE & BREAD, INC. R.R. #2, Box 256, South Royalton, Vermont 05068. 802/763-7115.

Sherrie Maurer specializes in the great beyond—Beyond Catsup, Beyond Belief, Beyond Horseradish Mustard. Six addictive combinations make up the Jasmine & Bread line to date, and Maurer is always on the lookout for more. It all started in 1983 with a surplus of tomatoes from her own garden, apples from a neighbor's farm, and a strong desire to market her own creation, Beyond Catsup, which developed from the bumper crop. In true Vermont fashion, about fifteen friends and neighbors showed up at the cannery the first year to help with production. With 4 tons of tomatoes and an army of helpers, Maurer produced 6,000 jars of her catsup condiment that year.

First-time customers were delighted with the thick, tangy blend of tomatoes, apples, vegetables, cider vinegar, and spices that she had created. They kept demanding more. Jasmine & Bread has grown at least five-fold since that time and now faces challenges such as procuring 20 tons of good tomatoes for Maurer's products. Despite the popularity of her products, Maurer remains steadfast in using only the best ingredients in her sauces. Because the Indianapolis native comes from a long line of great cooks, for Maurer the best compliment is to be told that her condiments taste "just like Grandma used to make them."

Her product list reads like the menu from a trendy café: Beyond Catsup—a gourmet blend of fresh tomatoes, apples, and vegetables; Beyond Belief—a zesty, spicy, tomato, pear, chili pepper condiment; Plum Perfect—a sassy plum, mint sweet and sour sauce; Beyond Horseradish Mustard—not for the faint of heart; White Lightning!—Maurer's own horseradish sauce; Sweet Lightning—a horseradish jelly that's sweet but packs a punch.

Maurer took the name for her company from a line in a Middle Eastern fable: "I give you jasmine for your soul, and bread for your body." Her success story indeed sounds like a fairy tale come true.

HOW TO PURCHASE: Beyond Catsup, Beyond Belief, Plum Perfect, Sweet Lightning, or Beyond Horseradish Mustard are sold in any combination of 2 jars for $8.50. Two jars of White Lightning prepared horseradish cost $5.50. Shipping is included. Orders must be accompanied by check or money order.

Braised Brisket from the Great "Beyond"

This simple but succulent dish can be completely done ahead.

3½-lb. brisket, flat cut
1–2 teaspoons seasoned salt
4 large onions, thinly sliced
13-oz. bottle of Jasmine & Bread Beyond Catsup

1. Set a heavy cast iron pot over medium-high heat until it is hot. Add the brisket and brown. Turn and brown the other side. Lower the heat to medium. Sprinkle both sides of the meat with the seasoned salt. Add the onions and continue cooking until lightly caramelized, stirring frequently to prevent meat and onions from burning.

2. Preheat oven to 350°F. Add ½ cup of water and stir, loosening the juices that have collected in the pot. Add the Beyond Catsup, stir, and bring to a simmer. Cover and bake 2 hours or until meat is tender when pierced with a fork.

3. Remove the meat to a carving board and slice. Arrange the slices on a serving platter and top with the cooking liquids.

Serves 8.

Salsa Cruda

MIGUEL'S. Stow-Away Lodge, Mountain Road, Box 1360, Stowe, Vermont 05672. 802/253-7574.

Michael "Miguel" Henzel makes a southern salsa that's getting plenty of northern exposure, and it all happened really by accident. Henzel didn't plan on running a popular forty-five-seat Mexican restaurant in the tiny ski village of Stowe, Vermont, nor did he intend to become the king of salsa. But Stow-Away Lodge's authentic Mexican fare has become a favorite in this little south-of-the-Canadian-border town and so, too, has his Salsa Cruda.

The Mexican theme came about in 1977 when Henzel came up to Stowe to help his parents. Retired school teachers from the Philadelphia area, the two had bought the 1930 vintage ski lodge 7 years earlier.

Henzel and a friend arrived to cook for house guests and decided to see if they could interest locals in dining at the lodge's restaurant. Stow-Away Lodge was already well established in these parts, known as one of the oldest ski lodges in the area and the first home for the famous Trapp Family when the Trapps moved to Stowe. To stir up business, Henzel and his friend thought they would offer a different type of cuisine each night. Mexican was the first evening's choice, and they never got to do any other.

Soon everyone who came to Stow-Away Lodge's restaurant was served a bowl of salsa and a basket of tortilla chips when they sat down. So many of them began asking for a jar of salsa "to go" when they had finished eating that Henzel decided to bottle it.

He started out making his salsa in the kitchen of the Stow-Away Lodge restaurant. Soon he outgrew that kitchen and moved to a nearby cannery. Now Miguel's has moved to yet a larger operation, the Cherry Hill Cannery in Barre where he turns out some 30,000 pounds of hot and regular Salsa Cruda each year. All natural with fresh tomatoes, tomatillos, onions, chilis, serrano peppers, coriander, lime juice, apple cider vinegar, and fresh garlic, this versatile sauce is great with nachos, omelettes, just about anything Mexican, and all sorts of seafood.

Today, Henzel's folks are semiretired and living in Burlington, and Henzel operates the lodge, restaurant, and a rapidly expanding cottage industry. In 1987, he introduced bags of crispy tortilla chips to accompany his salsa. Both are decoratively packaged in brightly labeled jars and bags depicting Miguel's Hacienda (we suppose) on the front of them. And, after all, what goes better with a jar of New England Salsa Cruda than a bag of chips brought to the Northeast by the Stow-Away Lodge?

HOW TO PURCHASE: A 9-oz. jar of hot or regular Salsa Cruda is $3; 16-oz. jars sell for $4.50. An 8-oz. bag of Tortilla Chips is $2. Shipping is an extra charge and is via U.P.S. Send checks or money orders, payable to Miguel's.

Mousse of Summer Squash with Salsa

This light summer dish makes a wonderful appetizer, salad, or elegant lunch.

> *2 tablespoons olive oil*
> *1 small onion, minced*
> *1 lb. yellow summer squash, chopped*
> *1 clove garlic, minced*
> *¼ teaspoon ground coriander seed*
> *Pinch of cayenne*
> *½ teaspoon salt*
> *Ground black pepper*
> *2 cups chicken stock*
> *1 tablespoon unflavored gelatin*
> *1 cup heavy cream*
> *1 cup Miguel Salsa Cruda (regular is best)*

1. In a medium sauté pan, heat the oil and sauté the onion until soft, but not browned. Add the squash and the garlic and sauté briefly. Add coriander, cayenne, salt, pepper, and 1 cup of the chicken stock. Cover and simmer until very soft. Meanwhile, simmer the remaining cup of stock until reduced to ¼ cup. Sprinkle the gelatin over the broth and mix to dissolve.

2. In a food processor, combine the cooked squash (and liquid) and the gelatin mixture. Purée until smooth. Cool to room temperature. Whip the cream until it forms stiff peaks. Fold into squash purée. Turn into a large bowl and chill 2 hours.

3. Place about 2 tablespoons of the salsa on each of 8 small plates. Spoon 2 dumpling-shaped scoops of mousse onto the salsa and serve.

Serves 8.

Vegetable Marmalades

POULTNEY PRESERVES. P.O. Box 206, Poultney, Vermont 05764. 802/287-9163.

Everybody makes strawberry or raspberry jam. But only Floyd and Peggy Kerber at Poultney Preserves make Strawberry Beet Jelly, Raspberry Beet Jelly, and Carrot and Zucchini Marmalade. These unlikely combinations make for delightful tasting condiments that are just as spreadable on an English muffin as a piece of chicken.

Floyd was working as a chef at an inn in Killington when he met Peggy, an unemployed artist who was waitressing there. Peggy had read an article on cottage industries in Vermont and how helpful the state Department of Agriculture was in assisting small food businesses to get started. She related all this to Floyd who, at the time was "just a friend." Peggy encouraged this job burn-out candidate to come up with a twist and start his own company.

Little did she know she was carving out her own future with her suggestions. Today Peggy and Floyd are husband and wife, and Poultney Preserves is a joint adventure. The two use recipes that have been in the family for many years and have adapted them by adding their own vegetable ideas to the traditional fruit jams and jellies. They grow most of their own produce. What they don't raise, they buy locally.

They have their own zucchini patch which furnishes the necessary ingredient for Zucchini Marmalade and Relish. (The latter makes a terrific thousand islands dressing.) And many neighbors' rhubarb patches supply the tart-tasting stalks for the Kerbers' wonderful Rhubarb Jam and Strawberry Rhubarb Jam.

The two are currently working on a Raspberry Beet Jelly and a Black Cherry Beet Jelly. All products are cooked in two 80-quart kettles and jarred and labeled by hand.

What began in 1986 as little more than a dream is now a reality for Peggy and Floyd. Poultney Preserves appears on many specialty food store shelves and serves a growing number of mail order customers. The whole family helps out on those many occasions when orders must be filled and there's more than the two can handle. In fact, these newlyweds and their relatives have been known to be up until the wee hours of the morning making jam for a business that's become a family affair.

HOW TO PURCHASE: Poultney Preserves are sold in 11 oz. jars for $4 per jar. Gift packs of 3 jars (a Strawberry Jam, a Beet Jelly, and a Marmalade) come in natural wooden crates and sell for $15. Shipping is via U.P.S. Postage is extra and depends on destination. Payment is by check or money order payable to Poultney Preserves. Call or write for the latest price list and shipping charges.

Poultney Preserves Carrot Cake with Carrot Marmalade

What an ingenious way to use a marmalade!

> 2¼ cups all-purpose flour
> 2½ teaspoons cinnamon
> 1 teaspoon salt
> 1½ teaspoons baking soda
> 4 eggs
> 1 cup sugar
> Two 11-oz. jars Poultney Preserves
> Carrot Marmalade
> 1½ cups vegetable oil

1. Preheat oven to 350°F. Grease a 9x13-inch cake pan. Combine the dry ingredients except the sugar in a mixing bowl and reserve.
2. In a large bowl beat the eggs with the sugar until fluffy and light lemon color. Add the marmalade and the oil and mix well. Add the flour mixture and mix to moisten. Pour into prepared cake pan and bake 45 minutes or until a toothpick comes out clean. Turn onto a wire rack and cool completely. Frost with cream cheese frosting below.

Serves 12.

Cream Cheese Frosting

> 3-oz. package cream cheese, softened
> ¼ cup unsalted butter, softened
> 2¼ cups confectioners' sugar
> 1 teaspoon grated lemon peel

Combine the frosting ingredients in a medium mixing bowl and beat until fluffy and of spreading consistency.

Yields enough frosting to frost a 9x13-inch cake.

Chutney

PUTNEY CHUTNEY. R.F.D. #3, Putney, Vermont 05346. 802/387-4297.

Part of why Deborah Stetson decided to make chutney was surely the name. How could anyone miss with a label that says, "Putney Chutney?"

Stetson, a vegetable farmer in the small southern Vermont community, saw the chutney business as a natural outgrowth for her garden-fresh produce. And the desire to work for herself at home and raise her family made it that much more attractive. She and husband Leon Cooper have been working their 80-acre farm since 1980.

Stetson started making chutneys to complement her own home-cooked vegetarian curries. "It was so good, I went public," says Stetson. "With a name like Putney Chutney, I knew I had to make it available."

Following the traditional chutneys made in England and India, Stetson's chutney is both sweet and pungent. Permeated with the bite of fresh ginger, it also embodies the old New England recipes using apple, cucumber, and green tomato balanced with the tang of citrus and pineapple.

Eight ingredients in all (besides sugar and vinegar) go into Putney Chutney which Stetson makes entirely by hand. There are no tools for shortcutting the many steps required in this labor-intensive project. Stetson slices the oranges and cores the apples herself. Many ingredients require two steps each in the preparation, such as peeling the skin, then seeding the cucumbers, and peeling the citrus rind before it's cut into thin strips.

"It's really a labor of love," says Stetson, who began her business in 1983. Now people write to her praising her product and asking for more.

Stetson's selection of just-the-right photo of Putney for her label was done with the same love and detail. The final choice was a photo of downtown Putney in the late 1800s that was gleaned from the Putney historical archives. In addition to depicting a horse-drawn milk wagon, it also shows the local general store which stands nearly unchanged after all these years. There's one change, however. Today it carries Putney Chutney!

HOW TO PURCHASE: Putney Chutney (one flavor) is sold in 17-oz. jars. A 2-jar package is available by mail through the Vermont Country Store, Mail Order Office, Manchester Center, Vermont 05255, or through Stetson. (Stetson and her family are not at the farm from January to March.) The cost is $9.95 plus shipping, which is $3.50 (U.P.S.) in New England. Stetson will mail order a half case (6 jars) for $16.50 or a full case (12 jars) for $33 plus the $3.50 shipping charge.

Putney Chutney Chicken

This yummy recipe was created by another entrepreneur in this book, Ivy Darrow, for a column called the "Instant Gourmet" that appears regularly in the *Brattleboro Reformer* in Brattleboro, Vermont.

3–4 lbs. chicken parts
¾ cup Putney Chutney
3 tablespoons prepared mustard
1½ tablespoons Worcestershire sauce

1. Wash the chicken and pat dry with paper towels. Line a large dish with the parts. In a blender or a food processor, combine the chutney, mustard, and Worcestershire sauce and pulse just until chutney is well chopped but not puréed. Pour mixture over the chicken and turn the pieces until well coated with the chutney sauce. Marinate in the refrigerator several hours or overnight.
2. Preheat oven to 400°F. Spread the chicken, skin side down, in a baking dish and bake 30 minutes. Turn the pieces and bake 15 minutes or until skin is golden brown.

Serves 6.

Dr. Shah's Indian Spice Concentrates

SPICES OF VERMONT. Route 7, P.O. Box 18, North Ferrisburg, Vermont 05473. 802/425-2555.

Dr. Navin Shah came to the United States in 1972 as a renowned oceanographer on a Fulbright Fellowship to study science, not cooking. Soon his compulsion to feed people overtook his thirst to study, and he exchanged that profession for one behind the stove.

In 1976, Shah and his wife Neeta opened The Spices Restaurant in North Ferrisburg, Vermont. For 10 years, the two ran the forty-four-seat dining room in the small town 70 miles south of the Canadian border. People traveled for miles to eat at the establishment. Customers were positively devoted to the small eatery; one man is reputed to have dined there 218 times!

The Shahs ran the entire operation by themselves. But their lives were tied up with the 6-day-a-week business. Gradually the couple realized they could feed more hungry people with less back-breaking work by packaging cooking sauces from favorite restaurant recipes and selling them.

Their marketing approach was appropriately scientific. On the eighth anniversary of the restaurant, the industrious couple gave out jars of curry spice paste as gifts to their diners. There was a string attached, however. Customers had to use them and give the Shahs feedback on the prodcts. Meanwhile, Shah was testing his spice mixture for shelf life and making variation upon variation until he found the right combination. "It's not an overnight process from the kitchen to the jar," explains the good doctor, who has logged thousands of hours of entertaining between his home and restaurant.

In 1986, much to the dismay of their loyal customers, the Shahs closed The Spices Restaurant. They started selling curry-style spice concentrates (hot and mellow) as a full-time business. Billed as "a thousand years of tradition in 20 minutes," the flavorful hand-blended spice pastes need only sour cream and shrimp, fish, pork, or boneless chicken to make nearly instant, exotic-tasting curry entrées.

The two also bottled the perfect accompaniment to this kind of meal, Mrs. Shah's popular Vermont Apple Chutney and Pear Chutney. The tangy, single-fruit relishes follow a recipe from her native Bombay. Once again, the reception to their cooking has been overwhelming. During the first year, business grew considerably. By the second year, it had a healthy 40 percent growth.

The Spices of Vermont products are made without salt or preservatives. Although "instant" is the operative word for Dr. Shah's spice pastes, these sauces reach their maximum potency when allowed to mellow with long-cooking meats such as bone-in chicken, lamb, or beef. That's not really much extra work even for a cook who's in a rush. Shah has already prepared the spices that are so time-consuming in Indian cooking.

HOW TO PURCHASE: Dr. Shah's 8-oz. jars of Indian Spice Concentrates (Hot or Mellow) and Mrs. Shah's 9-oz. Apple Chutney and 8-oz. Pear Chutney are available by mail. Cost is $10.50 for 2 jars (any items); $14.50 for 3; and $18.50 for 4. There is a 2-jar minimum, and prices include shipping. There is a 50¢ charge for gifts. Gift enclosures and addresses should be included with orders. Send check or money order payable to Spices of Vermont.

Lamb Curry with Dr. Shah's Indian Spice Concentrate

Longtime fanciers of Indian cuisine, my husband and I have found numerous ways to enjoy Dr. Shah's spice concentrates. One of our favorite is this lamb curry. Served with saffron rice and Indian tomato relish, it's a delightful Eastern meal.

1 tablespoon unsalted butter
1 tablespoon vegetable oil
2 lbs. boneless lamb, trimmed of fat and cut
  into cubes
1 medium onion, chopped
¼ teaspoon ground cardamom
4 oz. Dr. Shah's Spice Concentrate (Hot)
½ cup coconut milk
½ cup chicken broth
⅓ cup yogurt
2 oz. sliced almonds, toasted in a 350°F. oven
  for 15 minutes
Salt and pepper to taste, if desired

1. In a large skillet, heat the butter and oil over medium-high heat. Add a few cubes of lamb at a time, searing the cubes then removing them until all the lamb has been cooked in this fashion.

2. Add a little more oil if necessary and sauté the onion. Add the cardamom, Dr. Shah's sauce, coconut milk, and chicken broth and mix into a smooth paste. Heat; then add the lamb cubes and stir to coat them in the mixture. Cover and simmer 1 hour.

3. Remove the cover, add salt and pepper, and whisk in the yogurt. Warm then transfer to a serving platter. Cover with almonds. Serve with rice.

Serves 8.

Gourmet Cooking Sauces

TASTE MATTERS, INC. P.O. Box 17, Monkton, Vermont 05469. 802/453-4238.

Dorothy Rankin had been a well-known Vermont caterer for many years. (She had even catered for a former governor of the state.) Then she experienced the proverbial "burn out" and decided to start what has become one of the booming cottage industries in Vermont. What to make was not a problem for Rankin. She simply picked out the five most popular sauces she'd been using in her catering operation.

Then Rankin, who also writes cookbooks, gave up all but a tiny catering clientele and began mixing, cooking, and bottling exotic-sounding sauces. She picked special blends that were designed to become instant, elegant cuisine. The addition of meat, vegetables, rice, or pasta would transform each sauce into an innovative main course without hours of planning and preparation. And Rankin gathered a multitude of serving hints and had them printed to help the dabbling cook reach instant success.

Rankin brought some of her most popular products to a major food show and, she says, "Everyone loved them." So she came back to Vermont, and in July 1985, she opened Taste Matters, a wholesale and mail order business specializing in cooking sauces.

Rankin features five sauces from Oriental to Mediterranean in flavoring. Her Thai Marinade and Stir Fry Sauce with ginger, soy, and cilantro makes the perfect, quick marinade for chicken, pork, or seafood. The well-drenched meat can then be grilled or stir-fried with vegetables for a complete menu.

A slightly spicy and pungent Madras Dressing, flavor-filled with curry and ginger, is recommended for fruit and chicken salads or spinach salad with oranges, raisins, and cashews. Rankin also makes an Apricot Dipping Sauce that she serves in her own catering business as a dip for Chinese dim sum and chicken nuggets or as a sweet and tangy glaze for chicken.

A Mediterranean Marinade with a lemon juice and olive oil base and a generous helping of ginger, garlic, and other spices makes a grand marinade for lamb shish kebob.

Rankin's most popular sauce, however, is her medium-hot Peanut Sauce. Spicy and nutty at once, this is equally wonderful as a satay sauce for pork or chicken or as a topping for hot or cold spicy Oriental noodles. It's also great over steamed vegetables or as a dip for raw veggies.

All of Rankin's products are made in small batches to make the most of their unique blend of fine, natural seasonings. No stabilizers or preservatives are used.

Chinese Noodles with Taste Matters Peanut Sauce

This filling dish is simplified by using the already flavor-packed peanut sauce. Vary the spiciness by adding more or less of the red pepper than called for below.

10-oz. package fresh egg noodles, lo mein noodles, or linguine
2 tablespoons vegetable oil
1 lb. boneless pork loin or beef sirloin cut into paper-thin slices
½ teaspoon crushed red pepper flakes
Salt and pepper to taste
6½-oz. jar Taste Matters Peanut Sauce
1 cup chicken stock

Toppings

1 bunch green onions, washed, trimmed, and sliced (discard top third of stalks)
¼ cup crushed peanuts

1. Cook the pasta in salted boiling water 1–3 minutes or until soft but slightly chewy. Drain and keep warm.

2. In a wok or skillet, heat the oil and sauté the meat 2 minutes over high heat. Add the pepper flakes, salt, and pepper and toss. Add the peanut sauce and the chicken stock and mix to combine. Add the cooked noodles and toss to coat with the mixture. Transfer to a serving platter and top with the green onions and crushed peanuts.

Serves 4.

VERMONT'S CLEARVIEW FARMS, INC. R.R. #1, Box 5070-TNE, Enosburg Falls, Vermont 05450. 802/933-2537.

Caroline Longe of Clearview Farms is living out a dream in the tiny village of Enosburg Falls, Vermont, less than 10 miles from the Quebec border. She's carved out a thriving business making her sweet Farmstead Zucchini Relish, her grandmother's delectable sweet and sour Piccalilli, Apricot Date Chutney, and unusual chunk-style mixes of fruit preserves.

The idea for starting a business of her own took root in 1984 when Longe, on encouragement from the Vermont Department of Agriculture, decided to diversify her dairy farm and grow a vegetable garden on some extra acreage. With just four canning kettles in her basement kitchen, Longe's enterprise blossomed.

The business began simply. Longe was canning pickles, jams, and relishes to feed her husband, four children, and thirty hired men who often stayed for dinner after haying on their prosperous dairy farm. Summer residents who stopped by to purchase her handmade quilts would catch her canning and ask to taste her jams. They loved the old-fashioned flavor and were delighted to find whole strawberries in the strawberry jam and large chunks of identifiable fruits in her other preserves. Soon Longe was taking orders, and even local stores were asking to carry her products.

It seemed as though she'd better get a license to sell this food, so Longe contacted the Department of Agriculture. With their help, she set up labels and began marketing her products. Deliveries were made right out of the back seat of her car. Stores kept reordering and she just kept canning and selling.

Today, Clearview Farms could fulfill Longe's original desire to become a major employer and still make home-grown, old-fashioned products that do not pollute the Vermont air. But Longe likes working 2 or 3 days a week and having time to spend with her family. And she's become ''sort of friends'' with many of her customers. ''Now it's still fun,'' says the jam lady, who feels growing any bigger would mean sacrificing some of those luxuries.

Meanwhile, she's added a 20-gallon kettle to her basement kitchen supplies, but that's hardly cause to call hers a commercial operation. The 22-quart kettles are also still in use. Most of her items are sweetened with honey or 100 percent pure maple syrup also made on the Longe farm. No salt is added to any but her Sweet Zukes pickles. And everything is cooked in small batches without using a pressure cooker, so fruits stay nice and chunky. The last is a trademark of Clearview products that we suspect will be as enduring as the Green Mountain State's fresh air.

HOW TO PURCHASE: An 8-oz. jar of Zucchini Relish or Piccalilli costs $2.50. Appreci-Date (apricot-date chutney) in an 8-oz. jar is $3.50. Braisin Raisin (brandied raisin sauce) is $3.50. Maple Cranberry-Orange Relish is $3.10. Shipping is extra, and all orders are via U.P.S. To order, send check or money order to Vermont Clearview Farms, Inc. or send Visa or MasterCard information.

Clearview Fruit Bars

These bars are a favorite with kids of any age. Any kind of preserves may be used, but Clearview's chunky relishes are particularly wonderful.

> *¼ lb. unsalted butter, softened*
> *1 cup firmly packed dark brown sugar*
> *½ teaspoon almond extract*
> *1 cup all-purpose flour*
> *1 teaspoon baking powder*
> *1 cup quick-cooking oats*
> *½ teaspoon cinnamon*
> *Pinch of salt*
> *½ cup Clearview Maple Cranberry-Orange Relish*

1. Preheat oven to 350°F. Grease an 8-inch-square pan. Cream the butter with the sugar until fluffy. Add the almond extract and mix. In another bowl, combine the flour, baking powder, oats, cinnamon, and salt.

2. Add the dry ingredients to the butter mixture and mix until crumbly. Remove 1 cup of the mixture and reserve. Firmly pack the remaining mixture into pan. Cover with an even layer of preserves, leaving a ¼-inch border on all edges. Top with reserved crumbs and pat down lightly. Bake 30–35 minutes. Remove and cut into squares. Allow to cool in the pan before removing.

Yields 9–12 squares.

Maple Basting Sauces, Dressings & Baking Mixes

VERMONT FARE. Dodd Enterprises, Inc., Dodd Road, East Fairfield, Vermont 05448. 802/827-3271.

Linda Dodd was marketing the maple products produced by her husband, a third-generation maple sugar maker, when she discovered she had yet another product line to sell, her maple basting sauces, salad dressings, and maple baking mixes.

A home economist by training, Dodd and her family had always reached for the maple syrup and sugar when they wanted a sweetener. It was no surprise then, when Dodd began developing her products, she chose maple as the basis for sweetener and flavoring.

Out of her Vermont farm kitchen, Dodd came up with three superb basting sauces: Mustard, a blend of mustard, pineapple, and spices that's 50 percent maple syrup; Sparerib Basting Sauce, maple and molasses with spices; and a Sweet & Sour Sauce that's great on chicken. She put together two dressing recipes, a versatile Apple Lemon made with honey and a French Dressing with maple and herbs. A Maple Nut Muffin Mix, Maple Cornbread, and Maple Apple Pancake Mix are also sold under Dodd's Vermont Fare label.

Vermont Fare became a bona fide business in 1985. Today it no longer operates out of Dodd's turn-of-the-century farmhouse kitchen. Instead, a remodeled corner of the homestead has been dedicated to the Dodd Enterprises operation, where sauces and dressings are packaged in sterilized jars with automatic filling equipment. However, mixes are still sifted and bagged by hand.

Despite distribution that sees the Vermont Fare label in many of the big-time New York gourmet and specialty stores, Dodd's approach to her products has not waivered from the initial, fine quality, family-style flavor.

HOW TO PURCHASE: Basting sauces in 8-oz. jars are $3.19 each. Dressings (also 8 oz.) cost $2.39 each. Maple Nut Muffin Mix in a 4-oz. bag is $1.99. The Maple Cornbread & Muffin Mix (4 oz.) is $2.39; and Maple Apple Pancake Mix (8-oz. bag) is $2.59. Shipping is extra and varies with destination. Orders must be prepaid with check or money order made out to Dodd Enterprises, Inc.

Mustard Scallop Kebobs

Try this with vegetables for an entrée, or place two or three bacon-wrapped scallops on short skewers and grill or broil for a delightful appetizer.

> 1 lb. extra large sea scallops (about 20 per lb.), washed and defooted
> 4 oz. Vermont Fare Mustard Basting Sauce
> 10 slices of bacon, cut in half
> 1 sweet yellow pepper, washed, seeded, and cut into eighths
> 1 sweet red pepper, washed, seeded, and cut into eighths
> 1 large onion, quartered and parboiled for 2 minutes
> 8 cherry tomatoes
> Four 12-inch bamboo skewers (soaked in water for 30 minutes)

1. Marinate the scallops in the mustard sauce for 1 hour. Drain the scallops, reserving the marinade.

2. Wrap each scallop in bacon and assemble on the skewers, alternating with the peppers, onion, and tomatoes. Brush the kebobs with the reserved marinade liquid and grill or broil 7 minutes. Turn, baste with more marinade, and broil another 5 minutes or until bacon is cooked through and tiny lines appear in the scallops.

Serves 4.

Adult-flavored Conserves

VERMONT HARVEST PAN HANDLER PRODUCTS. R.R. #2, Box 399, Stowe, Vermont 05672. 802/253-8683.

In 1983, Patty Girouard went to the Vermont Department of Agriculture and asked for help in marketing her line of homemade jams. Girouard, an executive secretary with a background in business management, was growing restless and had an "urge to create something of my own." She had a favorite recipe for strawberry conserve that she had been making as a hobby. When the Department of Agriculture suggested that she switch to something that Smuckers and Kraft were not already doing, Girouard threw in some booze. That was the beginning of her plan to make "stylish" preserves. Today her Strawberry Amaretto conserve has become the backbone of an 8,000-jar a month business.

Girouard developed a business plan and a few more flavors. She came up with heady-tasting conserves such as Blueberry Bourbon, Apple Rum Walnut, and Brandied Peach and a few nonalcoholic items such as Apple Cranberry Maple and Apple Blueberry. (Conserves are similar to jams, but fancier and chocked full of raisins, nuts, and good-size pieces of fruit.)

Girouard headed for the bank, and despite the fact that she had no track record, she convinced them she had thoroughly researched her product and her market. She cooked all winter, and when the snow melted, she had a basement full of jars. She called everyone in the specialty foods business that she could think of and gave them samples of her products.

Her marketing technique worked. During the first year, she sold 17,000 jars of spiked conserves under the Vermont Harvest label. (Pan Handler Products is the official name of her company and gives Girouard room to add new product lines in the future.)

Vermont Harvest conserves are all made by hand and without additives, preservatives, or pectin and with twice as much fruit as sugar. Despite the impressive growth and a staff of four, Patty Girouard still hand delivers orders around the state of Vermont. She likes to "get around this beautiful state" and wants to see how her products are being displayed and to check on the competition.

HOW TO PURCHASE: A package of four 8-oz. jars of any combination of Strawerry Amaretto, Blueberry Bourbon, Apple Cranberry Maple, Apple Blueberry, Brandied Peach, Apple Rum Walnut, Raspberry Apple, or Peach Melba conserves costs $21.00; a 3-pack is $16.50. Pineapple Pepper Jelly, Jalapeno Pepper Jelly, Banana-Berry Jam, and Blackberry Jam come in 7½-oz. jars. A 4-pack is $21.00; 2 jars are $12.00. Prices include shipping, which is primarily via U.P.S. Payment is by check or money order payable to Pan Handler Products, Inc. Visa and MasterCard are accepted.

Baked Butternut Squash and Apples with Apple Cranberry Conserve

This holiday-sounding dish is just that. Serve it with your Thanksgiving turkey, Christmas roast goose, or baked ham.

> 2-lb. butternut squash, peeled, seeded, and cubed
> 2 large apples, peeled, cored, and cut into chunks
> ⅓ cup pure maple syrup
> 1 cup apple juice
> ½ teaspoon ground cinnamon
> ¼ teaspoon ground cloves
> Salt and pepper to taste
> 1 jar Vermont Harvest Apple Cranberry Maple
>   Conserve
> ¼ cup pecan halves

1. Preheat oven to 425°F. In an oven-proof baking dish, combine the squash, apples, syrup, and apple juice and mix. Add the cinnamon, cloves, salt, and pepper and toss. Partially cover and bake 30–40 minutes or until squash is tender.
2. Uncover and spread the conserves over the mixture. Sprinkle pecans over the top. Bake 15 minutes.

Serves 8.

Cider Jelly, Boiled Cider & Cider Syrup

Wood's Cider Mill
RFD #2, Box 477
Springfield, Vermont 05156

WOOD CIDER MILL. R.F.D. #2, Box 477, Springfield, Vermont 05156. 802/263-5547.

An old-fashioned white cape, several barns, and a sign that says, ''Apple Cider,'' let you know that you've reached the home of Willis and Tina Wood. Amid the tall maples and open meadows is the Wood homestead, which dates back to 1798.

Although this business is as diversified as maple syrup to sheep's wool, fame has come to Willis and Tina via a longtime favorite, Apple Cider Jelly. They produce about 30,000 pounds of it each year. This thick, sweet concentrate, made by boiling apple cider until it's one-ninth of its original volume, is made with no added sugar or preservatives and requires no refrigeration.

Wood's Apple Cider Jelly is nearly an institution in Vermont. Willis's great-great uncle started the cider jelly operation back in 1882. Willis and his bride Tina returned to the homestead in 1970, right after college, to buy the family-run operation from his cousin. Like so many return-to-the-land entrepreneurs we interviewed, these two also sought ''something different from the professional 9-to-5 work hours of most of our contemporaries.'' ''And we never regretted it,'' says Willis Wood.

The Wood's farm is open the year round, producing maple syrup and raising sheep and cows, along with making their Apple Cider, Cider Syrup (a blend of cider and maple syrup), and Apple Cider Jelly. Willis and Tina also sell lamb, sheep's wool, and cow's milk, and operate a sawmill on the property.

HOW TO PURCHASE: Many Wood's Cider Mill products are available by mail including the Cider Jelly, Maple Syrup, Boiled Cider, and Cider Syrup. Cider Jelly comes in packs of four or twelve 8-oz. jars for $8 or $19 respectively. Boiled Cider is $4 per pint and $6 per quart. Cider Syrup is $4 per ½ pint, $6 per pint, and $8 per quart. There is an additional charge for shipping (by U.P.S.). Write or call for an up-to-date price list which includes shipping costs, too.

TO VISIT: Visitors are welcome weekends during the fall season (Columbus Day through Thanksgiving) when the apples are being pressed and the Cider Jelly is being made. Traveling north on I-91, take exit 7 through Springfield, Vermont. Turn right on Valley Street. The farm is about 5 miles north on this road. Don't be alarmed; Valley Street becomes Wethersfield Center Road before you get there.

Linzertorte with Cider Jelly

This is adapted with permission from a recipe by New York Pastry Chef and Baking Teacher Nicholas Malgieri for a classic Viennese Linzertorte. In place of hazlenuts, we've added walnuts. Wood's Cider Jelly is substituted for the more traditional raspberry preserve to produce a wonderful New England variation on this pastry.

> 1½ cups flour
> 1 cup ground walnuts
> ¾ cup sugar
> 1 teaspoon cinnamon
> 1 teaspoon baking powder
> 12 tablespoons butter, softened at room
>   temperature for 1 hour
> 1 egg
> 1 yolk
> 4 oz. Wood's Cider Jelly
> 1 egg, beaten
> ¼ cup coarsely chopped walnuts
> Confectioner's sugar

1. Mix all the dry ingredients together in a bowl. Rub in the butter by hand until pieces of butter are very fine. Beat the egg and yolk together and stir into the dough with a fork. Mass the dough together.
2. Spread half the dough in the bottom of a buttered and paper lined 8-inch cake pan. Spread cider jelly over the dough leaving a 1 inch margin around the outside. Using the remaining dough and a pastry bag, pipe a diagonal lattice over the preserves using a ½-inch tip. Pipe a border of large dots around the outside edge. Paint the lattice and border gently with beaten egg and strew with coarsely chopped walnuts. Bake in a preheated 350°F. oven for about 35 to 40 minutes or until the top is slightly brown. Cool completely, unmold, and dust with confectioner's sugar.

Serves 12.

DAIRY PRODUCTS

CONNECTICUT

Farmstead Gouda Cheese

CONNECTICUT FARMHOUSE CHEESE COMPANY. Route 7, Falls Village, Connecticut 06031. 203/824-5878.

Connecticut Farmhouse Cheese is the only farmstead cheese-making business in Connecticut. That is, it's the only operation where both the milk and the cheese are produced on the same farm. This small company is a newcomer to the list of cheesemakers in New England, but already it's leaving its mark with a creamy, rich, high-butterfat Gouda that practically melts in the mouth.

The company began in 1986 in a rather complicated arrangement. Robert Reid purchased a 200-year-old farm in a hilly part of northwestern Connecticut as a future retirement spot. (Having grown up as a farm boy, he hoped to retire to a profitable, working farm.) He met Mark Burdick, an agriculture teacher at a nearby high school, who had wanted to buy the farm but couldn't afford it. The two shared the belief that small farms are the future of farming in Connecticut and that they can be viable and profitable. Reid sold Burdick the farmhouse and a small amount of acreage with the understanding that Burdick would turn it back into the working farm they both wanted.

After several ventures, Burdick discovered that cheese-making was the business that could make the farm profitable. After all, it was a perfect way to use the milk produced by the farm's Jersey and Holstein cows, and it gave them a product to sell.

Burdick got the business off the ground, then returned to teaching. And Reid's daughter Kathy, who was an unemployed artist at the time, took over. Burdick taught her everything he knew, and she studied further and made some of her own improvements.

Connecticut Farmhouse Cheese Company philosophy is to make a high-quality product that will stand out on the grocery shelves. About 10,500 pounds of cheese is made per year following a technique that a Dutch farmer's wife taught Reid's brother and Burdick when they visited the Netherlands on a fact-finding trip.

The cheese is made 2 days a week. It's carefully cultured, and the curds are packed into molds so they can be pressed. Then it sits out in a drying room and ages about a month before it's dipped in a flexible wax coating. The aging process continues for a few weeks before the cheese is ready for market. Reid contends that about 3 months total aging produces the best flavor.

Connecticut Farmhouse Cheese Company sells a plain Gouda, one with garlic and onion, and one with nettles. Herbs are imported from Holland. And sometimes there's cheddar for sale, too.

HOW TO PURCHASE: Mild and aged Gouda, Gouda with nettles, Gouda with onion and garlic, and cheddar cheese are sold at the farm store and are all available by mail order. A 2-lb. wheel is $15 including shipping and handling. To purchase, send check or money order payable to Connecticut Farmhouse Cheese Company.

TO VISIT: Visitors are welcome to visit the farm, watch the cheese making (2 days a week), and purchase cheese on the premises. To get to the farm, take Route 118 from Litchfield until it intersects with Route 63. Bear right onto Route 63 north and follow until it intersects with Route 7. Take a left (south) and stay on this road about 2 miles. A black and white sign for the farm is on the left. The store hours are 12–5, Thursday, Friday, and Sunday; 10–5, Saturday.

White Pizza with Broccoli and Farmstead Gouda

We'd never considered Gouda a topping for pizza until we met Connecticut Farmhouse Cheese. This one's so creamy that it effortlessly drapes over the pizza and leaves a luscious taste in your mouth. Use any fresh vegetables you have on hand.

Pizza Dough

1¼ cups warm water
1 teaspoon sugar
1 package active dry yeast
1 teaspoon salt
1 tablespoon olive oil
3½ cups flour

1. Combine ¼ cup warm water, sugar, and yeast in a large mixing bowl and let rest for 5 minutes. Add remaining water, olive oil, salt, and flour and mix well. Turn dough onto a lightly floured surface and knead until the dough is smooth and elastic, about 10 minutes. Cut dough in half and reserve half in the freezer or refrigerator for a later use. Allow remaining dough to rise in a covered bowl until doubled in bulk, about 1 hour.
2. Preheat oven to 425°F. Punch down the dough to release air bubbles and knead briefly. Roll or press out to a 12-inch circle. Place on a 12-inch pizza pan that has been dusted lightly with cornmeal. Top with the broccoli and cheese topping below.

Yields one 12-inch pizza.

Topping

2 teaspoons extra virgin olive oil
2 cloves of garlic, crushed
2 teaspoons dried basil leaves
½ teaspoon salt
½ lb. Italian sausage (hot or mild), crumbled, cooked, and drained
3 cups broccoli florets, cut into 1-inch flowers and steamed 3 minutes
6 oz. Connecticut Farmhouse Aged or Mild Gouda, grated
¼ cup freshly grated Parmesan cheese

Combine the first four ingredients and brush over dough. Sprinkle with sausage, then broccoli. Top with an even layer of grated Gouda and sprinkle top with Parmesan cheese. Bake 15–20 minutes or until edges of crust are golden brown.

Yields topping for one 12-inch pizza.

MAINE

Air-dried Goat Cheese (Petit Chèvre) & Chèvre

Peacefield ✔

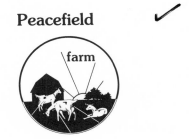

PEACEFIELD FARM. R.F.D. #1, Box 268, Bear Hill Road, Dover-Foxcroft, Maine 04426. 207/564-3031.

Our first encounter with Sherri Hamilton's goat cheese was via Madeleine Kamman, who used the cheese in a cooking demonstration we attended. We made note of the supplier and the fact that this notable cooking teacher thought Hamilton's product was akin to the cheeses of her native Loire Valley. Soon we discovered that, indeed, the entire Peacefield Farm operation is in the French style, where goat herdsmen, following centuries of tradition, produced most of the country's chèvre on their small farms.

Wanting to develop a self-sustaining cottage industry, but facing conditions much like those of France where small farms are marginally suited for food crops, Sherri and her husband Danny chose goats as an adaptable alternative agriculture.

The couple began their enterprise rather innocently in the 1970s when they moved to Maine for peace and quiet. They first bought a small farm near Bangor and bought two goats since cows produced too much milk for their small family.

Then, in 1977, the two bought Peacefield Farm, a rambling 120-acre farm in tiny Dover-Foxcroft (on the way from Bangor to Baxter State Park). Hamilton started making fresh and aged goat milk cheeses as a business in 1980, and her French-style, air-dried chèvre caught Kamman's interest. (Hamilton is one of the few cheesemakers in the country making an aged goat cheese.)

Peacefield Farm's herd of thirty to forty-five Saanen goats, a hardy Swiss breed known to be good milkers, produces enough milk for 150 pounds of cheese a week. This goat herder has the capacity, but not the time, to make twice that amount. ''I'd be swimming in milk if I took all the babies off the mothers,'' says Hamilton. Peak production occurs from the time the goats freshen in late spring until midsummer. In the late summer, the goats' milk production drops, but the butterfat content increases.

A small portion of the cheese, the Petit Chèvre, is air dried as the process requires a separate aging and refrigeration system. The product is a slightly tangy, rich-tasting cheese. It's dry as a chèvre should be yet retains enough moisture to make a creamy product. The remainder is a moist chèvre flavored with herbs, garlic, or is sold plain.

Hamilton also makes and sells goat's milk Feta cheese that's less salty and more delicate tasting than that sold commercially. Her goat milk mozzarella and farmhouse cheddar never escape to the outside world, such is the demand from family and neighbors.

The Hamiltons have arrived at the French success story with a farm that's self-sufficient. The goats graze and browse all summer requiring only the purchase of grain as a supplement to their diet.

And the couple grows and puts up some 2,000 bales of hay each year for winter feeding.

In addition to Kamman, Hamilton's customers include Inglenook Vineyards and Kristina's Restaurant in Bath, Maine.

HOW TO PURCHASE: Chèvre (plain, garlic, or herb) in 4-oz. packages sells for $2; 8-oz. pieces are $4. Petit Chèvre is $2 and comes plain or with herbs. Feta cheese is sold for $7 per lb. Add $1 for every $4 in orders. Packages are shipped U.P.S. Next Day Delivery on the East Coast, and Federal Express to locations farther west. During the summer months, however, shipments are limited to the East Coast. Hamilton will make cheeses without salt on request. Make checks payable to Peacefield Farm.

Fettucine with Maine Chèvre & Scallops
Recipe from Mindy Silver, chef, Kristina's Restaurant

When we found out that Kristina's Restaurant in Bath, Maine, buys its goat cheeses almost exclusively from Sherri Hamilton, we went to the upscale Down East eatery for cooking ideas. They gladly shared this grand recipe with us. With salad and French bread, it's a full meal.

> 1 lb. fresh fettucine, cooked al dente
> 2 cups broccoli florets
> 2 leeks, trimmed, well washed, and finely chopped
> 2 tablespoons unsalted butter
> 3 cups heavy cream
> 1 teaspoon dried thyme
> 1 lb. fresh Maine sea scallops, cut in thirds horizontally
> 8 oz. Peacefield Farm Chèvre
> ¾ cup sun-dried tomatoes cut into strips (if packed in oil, drained)
> Salt and freshly ground black pepper to taste
> ½ cup pine nuts, toasted in a 350°F. oven for 15 minutes
> ½ cup chopped fresh parsley

1. Blanch the broccoli in boiling water 2–4 minutes until cooked but still crunchy. Drain and rinse under cold water.

2. In a large sauté pan, cook the leeks in the butter until soft, about 5 minutes. Add the cream and thyme and simmer until liquid is reduced by one-third. (If using dehydrated tomatoes, add while liquid is reducing.) Add the scallops and heat for 1 minute. Crumble the chèvre and add, stirring constantly until melted. Add broccoli and sun-dried tomatoes and mix well. Add salt and pepper to taste. Toss with cooked fettucine, divide among 4 serving plates, and garnish each with pine nuts and parsley.

Serves 4.

Maine Cheddar Cheese

STATE OF MAINE CHEESE COMPANY. 75 Front Street, Rockland, Maine 04841. 207/596-6601.

Taylor Mudge, owner of the State of Maine Cheese Company, might as well be a native for all the Yankee ingenuity he's used in pulling together his cheese-making operation. Mudge came to Maine first as a visitor, then as the owner of a sheep farm in Lincolnville. But it wasn't until a group of investors became interested in a farm-related project that Mudge started to think about making cheese.

For nearly a century and a half Maine's milk had been shipped out of state to be processed into cheese, and there was nary a morsel of hard cheese being made in the Pine Tree State. Mudge felt certain the people of Maine would buy a Maine product first, particularly a good tasting cheddar, if there was one. He also thought he might be able to capture a bit of Maine's pride and richness of natural resources in his products. He was right on both counts. Now people in Maine and beyond are consuming half a million pounds of State of Maine cheese each year in eight varieties named for geographic locations in Maine. There's Penobscot Cheddar, Katahdin Cheddar, Cumberland Smoked (smoked with hardwood), Aroostook Jack (delicate and light), Sebago Gold (a full-bodied cheddar), Allagash Caraway, Kennebec Dill, and Saco Jalapeno.

Mudge started on a shoestring. New ready-made equipment for a small cheese-making plant did not exist, and if it had, there was no money to buy it. Mudge picked up a machine that vacuum seals the vinyl packages of cheese from a Yarmouth canning factory. He bought a cheese-making vat from a used equipment dealer in Ohio and the milk pasteurizer came from a small dairy in Biddeford. He also bought their 50-horsepower boiler for $100 just before they hauled it off for scrap. Mudge, who had repaired motorcycles while in graduate school, used that talent to bring the boiler back to life.

The business began in 1983 in a leased building in Rockland that had been an insulated shell built for a fishing cooperative that never got off the ground. A jack-of-all-trades, Mudge restored the facility. As a bonus, the building happened to be located in a deserted section of Rockland's waterfront with a spectacular view of Penobscot Bay.

Peter Kress, who was a principal at a local school, joined Mudge as his general manager. The two set up the plant, then Kress traveled to Wisconsin and Vermont to learn the art of cheese-making from the masters. The cheese is made using time-honored methods such as English hand cheddaring. Cheddaring is the process of stacking and restacking the blocks of cheese to drain off the whey.

The milk for the cheese is bought from area farms. It's made into 40-pound blocks that are aged up to a year, depending on the type of cheese (jack requires much less time). Then it's cut into 10-ounce sticks that are packaged for shipping. It's all-natural and all-Maine.

HOW TO PURCHASE: State of Maine Cheese Company puts together a wooden box of three 10-oz. bars of cheese (your choice of flavors) that's an ideal gift from Maine. Cost is $14 including shipping which is usually via U.P.S. A 5-lb. pack of all 8 choices is sold for $19.50, and shipping is included. To order, send check, money order, or Visa or MasterCard number.

Cheddar-stuffed Baked Potato

What could be more appropriate with State of Maine Cheddar Cheese than state of Maine potatoes? We used Sebago Gold because of its robust flavor, but any cheddar cheese would work nicely in this recipe.

> *4 large Maine potatoes*
> *1 tablespoon olive oil*
> *3 oz. bacon, chopped*
> *1 tablespoon butter*
> *¼ cup chopped onion*
> *½ cup each, chopped red and green bell pepper*
> *¼ cup heavy cream*
> *1 cup grated State of Maine Sebago Gold Cheese*
> *(reserve 2 tablespoons to top the stuffed potatoes)*
> *Salt and pepper to taste*

1. Wash the potatoes and brush with the olive oil. Bake in a 350°F. oven until soft. Remove and cool until they can be handled.
2. Preheat oven to 350°F. In a skillet, sauté the bacon until cooked, but not crisp. Remove the bacon and drain on paper towels. Discard the bacon fat. In the same skillet, melt the butter and sauté the onion and peppers over medium-low heat for 15 minutes or until soft. Slit the top of the potatoes and scrape the pulp into the skillet. Mix with the onion and peppers, breaking up any large pieces of potato. Add the bacon and heavy cream and mix until blended. Add all but 2 tablespoons of the cheese, then salt and pepper as needed. Scoop the mixture into the skins and sprinkle the tops with the remaining cheese. Bake 15 minutes.

Serves 4.

Aged and Soft Goat Cheese

THE SQUIRE TARBOX INN. R.R. #2, Box 620, Wiscasset, Maine 04578. 207/882-7693.

For Karen and Bill Mitman, innkeepers and owners of the Squire Tarbox Inn, "pampering" is the operative word. Goats and guests are equally indulged at the historic inn on remote Westport Island, just south of Wiscasset, Maine.

The Mitmans came to the Squire Tarbox Inn in 1983 seeking a simple life in the country and the space and environment in which to raise dairy goats. Soon after, they began converting their rich goat's milk into delicious products that could be served at the inn. Today they serve their soft herbed chèvre, an aged Caerphilly with dill, and goat salami at informal tastings. The Mitmans also invite guests to help them milk the goats, if they are so inclined. The Nubian goats delight in having visitors, and many of the guests enjoy this new experience.

Karen makes the cheese in an absolutely sterile little room beneath the inn's kitchen. It is here that she developed the fine cheeses from the goats' high butterfat milk. These cheeses have won the Mitmans blue ribbon prizes from the American Cheese Society.

Transplanted Bostonians who left high-pressure jobs at the Copley Plaza Hotel, the Mitmans purchased the already operational inn with the intention of raising some sort of livestock. They decided on goats almost by default, becoming quickly captivated with the intelligence, production, and demeanor of the floppy-eared, Roman-nosed Nubian goats. "Goats have personality," says Karen. They're affectionate, curious, and fastidious."

HOW TO PURCHASE: Dill Caerphilly, a waxed and aged cheese, is $8 per lb. Soft Herb Chèvre is $4 per 8-oz. container. Tellicherry Crottin (aged for several days and rolled in cracked tellicherry pepper) is $2.50 per 3-oz. roll. Chevon (goat) Salami is $4 each. Shipping is $4. There's an additional $10 charge for Second Day Air (outside the Northeast). Orders must be accompanied by check or money order payable to the Squire Tarbox Inn.

TO VISIT: Take Route 1 north from Bath toward Wiscasset until it intersects with Route 144. Follow Route 144 about 8½ miles to the inn.

Goat Cheese Salad with Walnuts and Raspberry Vinaigrette

The delicate combination of ingredients in this salad makes it one that can be served after a sumptuous meal.

> 1 medium head radicchio, leaves separated, washed, and patted dry
> 1 medium head red leaf lettuce, leaves separated, washed, and patted dry
> ½ lb. fresh young green beans, boiled 3 minutes, drained, and cooled
> ¾ cup walnut halves, toasted 15 minutes (350°F. oven)
> 8-oz container Squire Tarbox Soft Herb Chèvre

Dressing

> ⅓ cup raspberry vinegar
> ⅓ cup olive oil
> Salt and freshly ground pepper
> Pinch of sugar

1. Arrange the radicchio and red leaf lettuce on 8 salad plates. Divide the beans and arrange over the lettuce. Sprinkle some of the walnuts and the chèvre over each salad.
2. Whisk the dressing ingredients together and drizzle a tablespoon over each plate. Top with additional freshly ground pepper and serve with any remaining dressing.

Serves 8.

Hard Aged Goat Milk Cheese

YORK HILL FARM. York Hill Road, New Sharon, Maine 04955. 207/778-9741.

On a 10-acre farm situated on York Hill in central Maine, Penny and John Duncan raise thirty-five goats that produce rich, high-quality milk ideal for cheese-making. Since starting their business in 1984, the couple now turns out about 2 tons of cheese, with their goal set on making 10,000 pounds of cheese a year very soon.

Their first cheese, a hard aged York Cheese, is a combination of cheddar texture and goat milk flavor. Slightly nutty and easy to slice, this cheese is pale yellow since goat's milk does not contain carotene. The Duncan's also make a full-flavored Capriano Romano with a sharp piquant taste reminiscent of a good Parmesan. This one is crumbly in texture and should be grated.

York Hill also makes fresh chèvre—one with garlic and herbs, one coated with pepper, and discs of chèvre rolled in tarragon. A Chèvre Rolle with Pepper is another specialty for the Duncans. It has won two blue ribbons from the American Cheese Society, and is affectionately referred to as the "Jelly Roll."

The Duncans have not always been cheesemakers. The two were working in the medical field in Greenwich, Connecticut, when they decided to try homesteading in Maine. The barn was initially a little "Noah's Ark" with just about two of every creature, explains Penny. "The goats and I got along the best," she says of their decision to raise these affectionate, fastidious creatures. The desire to pursue an economically viable agricultural enterprise, coupled with the ease of handling goats, made them decide to go into cheese-making.

The two enjoyed the alchemy of cheese-making. Like medicine, it was a combination of science and art that fascinated them. Because of the gourmet quality associated with these specialty cheeses, they knew they could turn the rich goat milk into a valuable commodity. And they've done just that.

For about 2 months during the winter, the goats take a break from producing milk. But the Duncans do not. They make a second line of cheeses, a goat and cow blend that takes up the slack. Instead of milking the curious goats, the two spend their January and February months tending a flock of well-behaved milk cans!

HOW TO PURCHASE: York Cheese and Capriano Romano are sold in waxed 2-lb. wheels that are available by mail throughout the year. The cost is $15 per wheel. Fresh Chèvre products are also sold by mail from April through December. A 1-lb. Chèvre Roll with Pepper is $9. York Hill features a $19.25 sampler that contains 1 lb. each of Cheddar and Capriano, a Garlic and Herb Chèvre Disc, and a Pepper Chèvre Disc. Cheeses are packed in reusable styrofoam boxes with ice packs. There is a $4 shipping charge for each address. South of Virginia and west of Ohio, add $10 more per address.

Risotto with Porcini Mushrooms and York Hill Cheese

What a lovely combination this makes with wild mushrooms, a hint of Marsala and brandy, and the piquant taste and the luxurian texture of York Hill Cheeses.

> *1 oz. dried porcini mushrooms, rinsed*
> *¼ cup Marsala wine*
> *4 tablespoons unsalted butter*
> *1 medium onion, chopped*
> *1 large clove garlic, minced*
> *1 cup Arborio rice, rinsed and drained*
> *¼ cup brandy*
> *3-4 cups hot chicken stock*
> *2 oz. York Hill York Cheese, grated*
> *2 oz. York Hill Capriano Romano, grated*

1. In a small saucepan, simmer the mushrooms with the wine and ½ cup water for 5 minutes. Remove from heat and drain, reserving the liquid to add to the rice. Chop the mushrooms and reserve.
2. In a medium saucepan, melt 2 tablespoons of the butter and sauté the onion and garlic until the onion is opaque, but not brown. Add the rice and sauté until the edges of the rice begin to turn clear. Add the brandy and deglaze. The liquid will evaporate quickly, so have the stock on hand. Add ½ cup of stock and the mushroom liquid and simmer until nearly evaporated. Continue adding stock this way until the rice is creamy and soft, but slightly chewy. Swirl the pan occasionally to loosen the rice but do not stir it while it cooks. Cooking time will be about 30 minutes.
3. Remove from the heat and gently stir in the two kinds of cheese, the remaining 2 tablespoons of butter, and the mushrooms. Serve hot.

Serves 4.

MASSACHUSETTS

Camembert Cheese

CRAIGSTON CHEESE COMPANY. Box 267, 45 Dodges Row, Wenham, Massachusetts 01984. 617/468-7497.

American cheeses are beginning to steal the international spotlight for excellence from their European counterparts. Right on top is a Massachusetts cheese made in an on-farm plant from the farm's own herd of Jersey cows. Remembering that "fresh" and imported are mutually exclusive when it comes to soft, ripened cheeses, it's a safe bet that most of us have never tasted as wonderful a Camembert as Craigston Cheese in this hemisphere.

It started more than 10 years ago when Susan and Timothy Hollander, owners of Craigston Cheese Company, bought a single family cow, "Mistletoe," along with 15 acres of land, four sheep, and twelve chickens. Their goal was to become "totally self-sufficient." Initially, selling milk and cream directly from their farm was going to be their means of income. So, more cows joined the barnyard crew until there were fourteen.

Like so many others, the Hollanders quickly discovered that selling milk on a small scale was not lucrative. Turning their country-fresh milk into creamy Camembert cheese, however, was. Since few were making Camembert in this country, and since the brief shelf life of this product makes it difficult to import, it seemed like the natural choice for the Hollanders. "We wanted to prove that a small dairy herd could still work in New England with some innovative thinking," explains Susan.

Finding equipment for their on-farm cheese-making operation was their biggest obstacle. And locating people to help set up the plant and curing room to their needs was tough since there were few role models around, recall the Camembert specialists. To learn more about the process, Susan and her grown daughter Lisa took a trip to France to tour Camembert plants and learn all they could about making this special kind of cheese.

Craigston cheese is made using a centuries-old method first developed in France and hours-old milk from the Hollander herd (that's grown to twenty-eight). The cheese-making is meticulously supervised from vat to curing room. It cures for 21 days before it's sold. Much of it is shipped to restaurants and specialty food stores in nearby Boston or into the New York market. But the Hollanders have an extensive list of customers including mail order clientele.

HOW TO PURCHASE: A 10-oz. wheel of Camembert is sold for $6.75. Shipping and handling are extra. Prices are subject to change, so call before ordering.

Fried Camembert with Lingonberry Preserves

When it comes to textures and tastes, fried cheese is the next best thing to pizza. Making this recipe with creamy Craigston Camembert and adding the tang of lingonberries produces a unique and delightful combination.

> *10-oz. wheel Craigston Camembert Cheese*
> *1 cup flat beer*
> *1 cup all-purpose flour*
> *1 egg, beaten*
> *¼ teaspoon salt*
> *1 cup unseasoned bread crumbs*
> *3 cups vegetable oil*
> *Lingonberry preserves*

1. Cut the Camembert into 12 equal size wedges and chill while making the beer batter.
2. Whisk the flour with the beer until smooth. Add the egg and salt and mix well. Spread the bread crumbs over a plate. In a medium saucepan heat the oil to 375°F.
3. Dip the cheese wedges in beer batter. Then roll each wedge in bread crumbs. When oil is hot, add 2 or 3 pieces of cheese at a time and cook 40 to 45 seconds or until outside is brown. Remove with a slotted spatula or spoon and drain on paper towels. Spoon a little of the preserves onto the center of 4 plates and surround with 3 wedges for an attractive and delicious appetizer. Or serve hot with a dish of preserves for a lovely hors d'oeuvre.

Serves 4.

Cellar-aged Cheddar Cheese

THE GRANVILLE COUNTRY STORE. Granby Road Cut Off, P.O. Box 141, Granville, Massachusetts 01034. 1/800-356-3141 or 413/357-8555 in Massachusetts.

For more than a century, a cheese-making tradition has been taking place at the rustic white Granville Country Store that's nestled in a small hill town in western Massachusetts. It began in 1851 when John Murray Gibbons first developed a recipe and a unique room temperature aging process for what has become known as Granville Cellar-aged Cheddar. Back then, it was called Gibbons Cheese. Its fame was limited to New England, and folks dropped by to pick up their blocks of cheddar.

Today, the process for making Granville's well-known cheese has not changed one bit. It's still aged at room temperature in one of four aging rooms in the cellar beneath the country store. And while most cheeses are aged under refrigeration, Granville cheese applies the principle that warmth increases bacteria growth which produces a sharpness that cannot be achieved otherwise.

Blocks of cheese are each wrapped in cellophane, set in cardboard boxes, and stored on wooden shelves in one of the aging rooms. The boxes are turned twice a week. When gases from the aging process cause the boxes to bloat, they are pierced, but the cheese itself is not touched until the aging process is complete. Sometimes that's a full year or more, depending on sharpness desired.

While the cheese-making process hasn't changed, many other things have at Granville Country Store. For one, there's a new owner. In 1971, Roland Entwistle bought the operation from its second owner Paul Nobbs, who in turn had bought it from Gibbons's sons in 1935.

For another, the second-floor office now houses a computer to handle Entwistle's growing mail order business. He conceals the automated aspects of the business as best he can, but it's difficult to disguise success.

When the Entwistle family bought Granville Country Store, about 30,000 pounds of cheese were sold each year. Now Entwistle sells about 200,000 pounds a year, much of it through his mail order business which sees cheese distributed to all corners of the world.

The store's history, according to Entwistle, is that Gibbons developed his creamy, piquant cheese in the 1850s, making it and selling it from the store. The country store burned to the ground in the 1930s and was rebuilt on the same site. At about that time, Entwistle says, the owners decided to have the cheese made in a plant in upstate New York, as it had outgrown the milk supply from the local dairy. They continued aging it themselves. Entwistle uses the same plant whose name is kept secret.

Because of the aging process, a Granville "medium" tastes like most extra sharp cheese. Sharp and extra sharp are proportionately stronger, where stronger means wonderfully robust. All are delightfully full-flavored products, and that's something that hasn't changed for the well-aged cheese-making country store.

HOW TO PURCHASE: A 2-lb. brick of Granville Cheddar Cheese (medium, sharp, extra sharp, or super sharp) is $14.95, east of the Mississippi; $15.45 to points west; and $17.95 to Florida, Texas, Oregon, and California. A 3-lb. wheel of cheese is $21.95, $22.45, or $25.50 depending on destination. Prices include shipping. To order send check, money order, or Visa or MasterCard information, or use credit card and toll-free number.

TO VISIT: The Granville Country Store welcomes visitors. From Route 90 (the Mass Pike), take exit 3, marked Westfield. Follow Route 10/202 into Southwick where it intersects with Route 57 west. Take this about 6 miles. Store is on the left just past the town green, tucked away in a triangle made by the intersection of Route 189.

Summer Squash and Cheddar Cheese

Jimmie Booth, chef and owner of the bucolic Golden Lamb Buttery in Brooklyn, Connecticut, serves a similar casserole of summer squash in a heavy cheese sauce. A woman who never measures anything, she waves her hands with lots of "you knows." I inspired this.

> 2 lbs. zucchini and yellow squash, washed and cut
>   into julienne slices
> 1 large onion, minced
> 3 cloves of garlic, minced
> 4 tablespoons butter
> 5 tablespoons flour
> 2 cups milk
> 2 cups Granville Country Store Extra Sharp
>   Cheddar Cheese
> Salt and freshly ground pepper to taste

1. Preheat oven to 425°F. Butter the bottom and sides of a large oven-proof casserole. Line the casserole with the squash, alternating colors. Sprinkle with onion, garlic, salt, and pepper.
2. In a medium saucepan, melt the butter and whisk in the flour. Cook over medium heat for 2 minutes but do not allow the flour to brown. Add the milk slowly, whisking continuously. Cook over medium heat until the sauce thickens. Remove from the heat and add the cheese and salt and pepper to taste.
3. Mix until the cheese has melted and pour it over the squash. Cover the casserole with aluminum foil or a cover and bake 20 minutes or until the mixture is bubbly. Remove the cover and bake another 40 minutes or until squash is tender. Brown the top lightly under the broiler and serve.

Serves 8.

Monterey Chèvre

RAWSON BROOK FARM. P.O. Box 345, New Marlboro Road, Monterey, Massachusetts 01245. 413/528-2138.

When Wayne Dunlop and Susan Sellew started their business, they didn't even know what a goat was. Today, in the shadow of the Berkshire Mountains, the couple raises an entire herd of French and American Alpine goats and annually produces more than 10,000 pounds of a smooth and mild-flavored chèvre that might well be a viable contender for top cheese honors here or abroad.

Their story begins in the late sixties when the couple bought two goats and brought them to a farm in northern New York in the back seat of their car. Like so many others who have made a commitment to agriculture as a way of life, the two wanted to see if they could support their chosen life-style. Initially, breeding and showing their stock was their only revenue. Then Sellew and Dunlop met a French woman named Martine Gadbois who wanted to pass on the French style of making cheese. She also gave them an incurable enthusiasm for goat cheese that propelled the two into the cheese-making business.

In 1983, Dunlop and Sellew moved to Monterey, Massachusetts, in the foothills of the Berkshires and Sellew's old stomping ground, to start making cheese. Dunlop built a dairy using lumber he milled from trees on the property. It was not just a rustic, throw-together place. Because they were operating a dairy, the facility had to meet stringent state regulations. It met them so well that the state health inspector has taken pictures of the Rawson Farm dairy to show people who want to start their own business.

Sellew and Dunlop import a freeze-dried culture from France and make only a soft-curd-style cheese which was traditionally the trademark of French goat cheese. While most goat cheese suffers from a pronounced taste of goat, Rawson Farm's product does not. The couple has come up with a formula that leaves only the faintest "tang."

They make several varieties of chèvre. The chive and garlic is made with their own organically grown ingredients, as is the wild thyme and olive oil chèvre. The pepper log, chèvre coated with cracked peppercorns, won a blue ribbon at the 1987 American Cheese Society Annual Meeting in Boston.

Not to leave the impression that life has become easy for the people at Rawson Brook Farm; the hours are "ridiculous" by their own estimation—somewhere between 80 and 100 hours a week. They also work hard at staying small. But it seems a small price for a life-style they enjoy.

HOW TO PURCHASE: Rawson Farm Monterey Chèvre may be purchased at the farm and by mail. Minimum order is $20 and orders may be mixed—plain, chives and garlic, wild thyme and olive oil, and no salt. Price is $2 per 4-oz. cup. Twelve 4-oz. cups are $20; a full case (24 cups) is $36. A 1-lb. tub is $6.50; a case

of 6 tubs is $35. A 6-oz. log is $3; an 8-oz. log coated with ground pepper, $4. Prices include shipping. However, there is a $4.50 charge for the insulated box and ice packs in which the cheese is shipped. Shipping is by U.P.S. Second Day Air or ground delivery, depending on time of year and distance it is being sent. These cheeses freeze well, so many people buy in quantity.

TO VISIT: Rawson Brook Farm encourages visitors. "We feel that it is important for people to see how and where their food is produced," says their brochure. From Great Barrington, follow Route 23 to Monterey and turn right (south) on New Marlboro Road. Follow it about 2 miles to the farm.

Chocolate Chèvre Cheesecake

Our friend Becky, whose addictions to chocolate and cheesecake are well known among her acquaintances, calls this the "richest and most decadent of them all."

Crust

2 cups ground vanilla or chocolate macaroons
3 tablespoons melted unsalted butter

Combine ingredients. Spray a 9-inch springform pan with vegetable spray and press the cookie mixture into the bottom and sides of the pan.

Filling

½ lb. good quality semisweet chocolate, cut into
  small pieces
4 tablespoons heavy cream
1½ lb. plain Monterey Chèvre
1½ cups sugar
3 eggs plus 2 yolks
1 tablespoon vanilla extract
1 teaspoon almond extract
Strawberries or raspberries to garnish

1. Preheat oven to 325°F. Add water to the bottom of a double boiler. In the top, combine the chocolate and the cream and set over medium heat until chocolate has melted. Set aside to cool to room temperature.
2. Combine the cheese and the sugar and beat well. Add the eggs and yolks and beat again until smooth. Add the extracts. Fold the chocolate mixture into the cheese. Pour into prepared pan and bake for 1 hour. Allow the cake to cool in the oven with the door open and the heat off. Chill at least 3 hours, but preferably overnight. Serve with sliced strawberries or raspberry or strawberry purée.

Serves 8–10.

Farmstead Gouda Cheese

SMITH'S COUNTRY CHEESE. 20 Otter River Road, Winchendon, Massachusetts 01475. 617/939-5738.

Cheesemaker David Smith decided to specialize in making Gouda cheese because it's versatile, relatively easy to produce, and considered a specialty cheese. He also picked the business as a good way to market some of the milk from his dairy farm.

Smooth and wonderfully fresh tasting with no sharp aftertaste, Smith's Country Gouda is made from raw milk that goes directly from the cows to cheese. Colorings and preservatives are never used, and each wheel of cheese is handcrafted.

Although Smith thinks Gouda is simple to make, the process doesn't sound easy to a non-cheesemaker. First the milk is heated. Then Smith adds the starter culture and rennet which causes the curd to coagulate. After the milk has set, the curds are washed, cooked, and placed into forms for pressing. After about 4 weeks, the cheese must be brined, dried, and waxed. Finally, it is aged for 60 days. All this is done on the Smith's farm in an operation that began in 1985.

Gouda cheese, which originated in the Netherlands, is famous for its mild flavor and ease with which it can be melted. Smith's Farmstead Gouda comes in three delightful ways, a subtly smoked gouda, the plain, and one with caraway seeds. They also make three spreads: Creamy Gouda, Gouda with Wine, and Gouda with Bacon.

HOW TO PURCHASE: Smith's plain Country Gouda is $3.98 per lb., caraway is $4.08 per lb., and smoked is $4.58 per lb. Gouda spreads in 8-oz. containers are $2.25 each. Spreads come in three flavors: Creamy Gouda, Gouda with Wine, and Gouda with Bacon. Shipping is by U.P.S. and ranges from about $1.75 for small orders to $4.80 for large orders and zones that are west of the Mississippi River. Write or call for their latest price list and a mail order form. Payment is by check or money order, and they accept MasterCard and Visa.

Leek and Gouda Cheese Quiche

Of all the combinations that have been cooked up in a quiche we have always been fondest of leeks with cheese. This one's particularly wonderful owing to Smith's silky textured Gouda.

> *3 oz. Smith Plain Country Gouda*
> *2 oz. bacon, coarsely chopped*
> *2 medium leeks, washed thoroughly and chopped*
> *2 eggs*
> *1 egg yolk*
> *1 cup heavy cream*
> *¼ teaspoon freshly grated nutmeg*
> *Salt and pepper to taste*
> *1 uncooked 9-inch pie shell*

1. Preheat the oven to 375°F. Grate the cheese and reserve. In a medium skillet, sauté the bacon until cooked through but not crisp. Remove with a slotted spoon. Drain and reserve. In the bacon fat, sauté the leeks until soft (about 5 minutes). Remove with a slotted spoon and cool slightly.

2. In a large mixing bowl, combine the eggs, yolk, cream, nutmeg, salt, and pepper. Mix well. Prick the bottom of the pie shell several times with a fork. Spread bacon and leeks over the bottom of the pie shell. Sprinkle cheese over the top and add the liquid. Bake 40 minutes or until set.

Serves 8.

Goat's Milk Blue & Camembert Cheeses

WESTFIELD FARM CAPRI CHEESE. 28 Worcester Road, Route 68, Hubbardston, Massachusetts 01452. 617/928-5110.

In the central hills of Massachusetts, Bob and Letty Kilmoyer are producing superb farmstead cheeses, handmade from pure goat's milk. The couple tend a herd of sixty primarily white Saanens and a few floppy-eared Nubians on their 20-acre farm located near Worcester. The milk is used to produce a host of tangy fresh goat cheeses under the Capri (Latin for goat) label.

Cheeses are made in the Old World tradition of European farmstead cheeses. First the milk is pasteurized (a legal requirement for any cheese that is not aged at least 60 days), then made into fresh and mold-ripened cheeses.

The fresh cheese is ladled into cheese baskets lined with cheesecloth and hung to drain. It yields a soft, spreadable cheese that comes plain, coated with coarsely ground black pepper (Pepper Capri), and filled with herbs and great for cooking (Herb-Garlic Capri).

More unique are the Kilmoyers' two molded cheeses that almost no one else is making. They produce a Hubbardston Blue, a surface-ripened goat cheese—delicate within and sprightly flavored from a luxuriant growth of blue mold that's completely edible. This one was awarded a first place blue ribbon by the American Cheese Society in June of 1986. Although it uses the same type of penicillin mold that makes blue cheese, it doesn't have the veins that are a trademark of the cow's milk blues.

Westfield Farm's goat milk Camembert is rich flavored and creamy and "the only Camembert of its type in the East, so far," says Letty. At refrigerator temperature, the Camembert and the Hubbardston Blue will continue to soft ripen from the surface toward the center during a 4- to 6-week period.

The Kilmoyers bought Westfield Farm initially with the idea of growing vegetables. One day a friend asked Bob, who is also a professor of math at Clark University, to take care of his goats and a cow. The friend never took them back, and the couple found themselves with a ready-made herd of friendly animals to tend.

The two tried their hand at making cheese from the abundance of fresh milk that their goats were producing. The fact that goat cheese is a specialty item and that it could be totally produced on their farm was appealing to the Kilmoyers. In 1981, they began making Capri cheese in earnest. Today the talented cheesemakers are among the largest producers of goat cheese in the state. They supply some of the finest restaurants in Boston with their cheeses, and Capri cheeses appear in specialty shops in many parts of the United States.

HOW TO PURCHASE: The Capri and Herb Garlic Capri (soft cheese) are $5.50 per lb. for 16-oz. logs. An 8-oz. log sells for $2.90, and 4-oz. logs are $2. The round Capri is $2.10; Pepper Capri is $2.30; Herb Capri sells for $2.30; Hubbardston Blue is $2.35; and Capri Camembert is $3.75. All but the Camembert weigh about 5 oz. The Camembert weighs about 8 oz. Cheeses are shipped with ice in insulated containers. Handling is $3 per container. Shipping is an additional $3 but is free for orders over 3 lbs. going to northeastern states. For areas where packages must be sent Second Day Air, there is an additional charge. Orders must be prepaid with check or money order payable to Westfield Farm Cheese.

Roast Stuffed Chicken Thigh with Goat Blue Cheese Sauce

This splendid recipe was created by Chris Pardue, a good friend and chef-owner of the three-star L'Americain Restaurant in Hartford, when we asked him for a suggestion for cooking with Westfield Farm's Hubbardston Blue goat cheese.

The Filling

6 boneless chicken thighs, skin left on
¼ cup olive oil
¼ cup thinly sliced green onions
2 cloves garlic, minced
1 teaspoon crushed black peppercorn
2 teaspoons fresh sage, julienne
4 teaspoons sun-dried tomatoes, julienne
½ cup cooked whole wheat berries
¾ cup steamed and julienned spinach
Salt and pepper to taste

1. Place the thighs skin side down on a flat surface, so each lays flat. Heat the oil in a small sauté pan and add the green onion and the garlic. Toss 30 seconds. Add the peppercorns and sage and sauté briefly. Remove from heat and add remaining ingredients.
2. Preheat oven to 400°F. Sprinkle salt and pepper over both sides of each thigh. Divide the mixture among the thighs and roll the meat around it, tucking in loose edges. Encase each stuffed thigh in aluminum foil to hold the thigh in place but do not cover the top. Set in a heavy metal pan and bake 15 minutes. Remove chicken from the aluminum boats and keep warm. Reserve the cooking juices for the sauce below.

The Sauce

1 cup heavy cream
2 tablespoons unsalted butter
2 cups red onion, julienne
¼ cup red bell pepper, finely diced
¼ cup yellow bell pepper, finely diced
2 teaspoons fresh thyme leaves
½ cup sherry wine
¼ cup sherry wine vinegar
Salt and pepper to taste
1 tablespoon sherry wine vinegar
5-oz. wheel Hubbardston Blue goat cheese
4 sage sprigs and 4 red pepper fans for garnish
(optional)

1. In a small saucepan, combine the cream and the cooking liquid and simmer until thick enough to coat the back of a wooden spoon. Reserve.
2. Melt the butter in a medium skillet. Sauté the onions until they begin to soften. Add peppers and thyme. Sauté briefly; then add the sherry and ¼ cup vinegar and deglaze the pan. Add the cream mixture and remaining vinegar. Season with salt and pepper. Spoon sauce into a pool in the center of 4 plates. Slice the chicken and arrange slices over the sauce. Cut the cheese into thin wedges and arrange around the chicken so that it partially melts in the sauce as it's being served. Garnish with sprigs of sage and red pepper fans, if desired.

Serves 4.

Fruit and Herb Butter Spreads

DRAKE'S DUCKS. R.D. #2, Box 810, Keene, New Hampshire 03431. 1/800-53DUCKS or 1/800-533-8257.

''Drake's Ducks'' might lead you to think that Marie and Chris Drake's business involves our fine feathered friends. But there are no ducks, geese, or even chickens at the Drake Farmstead these days. Nevertheless, the food that Marie and Chris make is worth quacking about: wonderfully creamy and smooth fruit and herb butters. Packages of vibrant color and flavor—wild blueberry, cranberry and orange, and red raspberries—they're easily devoured by the spoonful.

This husband and wife team began working in restaurants years ago but never cooked for a living until they went into business for themselves. They started as farmers, raising their own ducks and chickens, collecting the eggs, and processing their own butter.

As an avenue for using their products, the two started making pastries until they were making more than 200 baked items. Finally, in 1985, it occurred to the Drakes that they were earning more with their pastries than they could possibly earn running a farm. Bad weather could ruin an entire growing season, but the two could still bake pies and cakes even if it rained for 5 days straight. Soon they were selling off all their farm equipment to raise money to build a commercial kitchen in their basement.

They phased out the bakery line, and they added their flavored butters and a wonderful pesto sauce which became overnight sensations. They've also introduced a line of frozen entrées: Seafood Mornay, Shrimp à L'Orange, Eggplant Parmesan, among them.

''Absolutely the best'' is the way most of their customers describe their products. Although they no longer have their own eggs and butter, the two still purchase only farm-fresh ingredients. And they are always developing new flavors for their butter spreads and new items for their frozen food line. ''We don't want to turn down success,'' say the Drakes whose products are selling in no fewer than forty stores already.

HOW TO PURCHASE: Drake's Ducks will mail order a sampler package of 6 items for $25.95 including shipping. The sampler includes Herb Cheese, Herb Butter, Pesto, Raspberry Butter, Blueberry Butter, and Cranberry Orange Butter. Orders must be prepaid with a check to Drake's Ducks.

Chocolate Raspberry Cream Torte

This heavenly combination of chocolate, raspberry, and butte[r] can't miss. But it's especially tasty (and easy) when you use Drake['s] Ducks Raspberry Butter.

> *1 chocolate génoise or other sponge cake*
> *8 oz. good quality semisweet chocolate*
> *4 tablespoons unsalted butter*
> *¼ cup orange-flavored liqueur or light rum*
> *6-oz. container Drake's Ducks Raspberry Butter*

1. Cut the cake into 3 layers, setting each layer aside as it's cu[t]
2. In the top of a double boiler, melt the chocolate and the butt[er] over low heat.
3. Brush the bottom layer of the cake with half the liqueur. Sprea[d] half the raspberry butter over the layer and carefully replace th[e] center layer of the cake. Brush with the remaining liqueur and th[e] raspberry butter. Center the top layer of the cake over the fillin[g.] Spread the chocolate mixture over the cake allowing it to drip ov[er] the edges. Refrigerate at least 1 hour before serving.

Serves 8.

VERMONT

Vermont Cheddar Cheese

CABOT FARMERS' COOPERATIVE CREAMERY. Main Street, Box 128, Cabot, Vermont 05647. 802/563-2231.

Many New Englanders find it difficult to say "Vermont Cheddar" without saying "Cabot" first. Despite the many other fine cheddar cheeses to pick from these days, Cabot cheese is a well-established Yankee tradition backed by a taste that's unquestionably among the best.

Since 1919, a cooperative of Vermont dairymen has been producing its top-quality cheese in the Green Mountain countryside. The cooperative began with the founding farmers assessing themselves $ per cow to finance the creamery's start-up costs. More than half a century later, descendants of the original Cabot farmers—more than 500 strong—are hard at work keeping the Cabot name foremost among distinguished cheesemakers of the world.

Cheddar Cheese has had its place in history, too, and not just as a pantry staple. A 1,400-pound cheddar cheese was given to President Andrew Jackson and sat aging in the White House vestibule for 2 years before dignitaries in Washington accepted an invitation to "dig in." It was devoured in 2 hours, and Old Hickory had only a small wedge. Following suit, in 1937, Cabot presented the New York State Fair with an awesome 17-ton cheddar cheese. Needless to say, it was a main attraction of the fair!

Today farmers of the Cabot cooperative produce 12 million pounds of "the best cheddar in the world," say the 200-plus employees of Cabot Cheese. That claim is echoed by thousands of impressed customers. Despite a $30 million a year business, Cabot's still keeps that personal touch. All cheeses are cooked in large vats, then handmade, salted, and aged carefully for 3 to 18 months. The cheese is aged slowly without additives or preservatives.

The aging process is the determining factor in the final taste of the product. Cabot Mild is aged about 3 months to produce a delicate, pleasing flavor that appeals particularly to young cheese lovers. It pairs nicely with fruit. The sharp cheese is a bit more full flavored, having aged nearly a year. Extra Sharp Cabot Cheddar ages from 12 to 24 months, producing a distinctive cheddar taste that lingers after it's eaten. And the Cabot Private Stock, akin to a vintage port wine, ages at least 18 months.

In addition to cheddar, Cabot makes cottage cheese, sour cream, yogurt, and butter. The manufacture of these high-quality dairy foods provides farmers a chance to profit from their milk production beyond the sale of just the farm milk. And it's keeping the cows in Cabot, Vermont, quite busy, too.

HOW TO PURCHASE: Cabot has an extensive mail order catalog that includes mild, sharp, extra sharp, and private stock cheddar cheeses in several sizes. Other creamery products are not sold via mail, but the catalog carries a host of other Vermont-made products. A 1-lb. waxed brick of Cabot is sold for $6.50 (sharp); $7.25 (extra sharp); and $7.95 (private stock). A 3-lb. brick is $12.75 (mild); $13.95 (sharp); and $14.95 (extra sharp). There is a small discount per brick when buying 2 or more. A variety pack of five 8-oz. waxed cheeses, including a sage and a smoked cheese, is $17.50. Shipping and handling are included except for express service. Check or money order payable to Cabot Farmer's Co-op or Visa or MasterCard are accepted.

Very Cheddar Spoonbread

Light and airy like a souffle, but hearty like a corn bread, this is wonderful with a bowl of chili, a big salad, or a cup of New England clam chowder.

> 3 cups milk or light cream
> 1 cup cornmeal
> ½ teaspoon salt
> ¼ teaspoon freshly ground pepper
> 4 tablespoons unsalted butter
> 2 cups grated Cabot Vermont Cheddar Cheese
> 5 room-temperature eggs, separated
> 1 cup fresh or frozen corn, cooked 5 minutes

1. Preheat oven to 375 °F. Butter a large shallow casserole (a 9x13-inch pan is ideal).
2. In a medium saucepan, bring milk or cream almost to a boil. Sprinkle cornmeal over milk, whisking continuously as mixture begins to thicken. Reduce heat and stir in salt, pepper, butter, cheese, and corn. Remove from heat and stir in the egg yolks. Mixture should be smooth and thick.
3. Beat the egg whites until stiff. Gently but thoroughly fold them into the corn mixture. Turn into casserole and bake 35 minutes or until puffed and golden.

Serves 8.

Vermont Colby Cheddar Cheese

CROWLEY CHEESE, INC. Healdville, Vermont 05758. 802/259-2340.

What's new at the Crowley Cheese Factory isn't much. In fact, it's that dogged resistance to change that's earned Crowley Cheese its reputation as a premium Vermont cheese. This unique cheddar variant is made entirely by hand, just the way it has been since Winfield Crowley founded the business out of his kitchen more than 100 years ago.

Nearly 100,000 pounds of rich, light yellow Colby cheese, a first cousin to the cheddar but moister and less acidic, are produced each year in the same wooden, three-story barn that was built by Crowley in 1882.

Believed to be the oldest continuously operating cheese factory in the United States, the cheese company is on the Register of National Historic Places. People arrive by the bus loads to see the factory and the cheese being made.

Only whole raw milk, bacterial cultures, and salt are used, and they are paddled in big stainless steel tubs to separate the curds. The curd is cut, and the curd and whey are stirred by hand. The cheese is rinsed with cold spring water which, some say, gives it a slightly sweet taste. Then it's packed into old crank presses. The cheese is aged just to the right point. No preservatives or chemicals are used to hasten the aging process. Most food enthusiasts enjoy its sweet, mild taste, and it has brought rave reviews from magazines such as *Bon Appetit*, *New York*, and *Yankee*.

Four generations of Yankee ingenuity went into Crowley cheese. Then Robert, the last of the Crowleys, died in 1967 leaving no one to take over the company. Randolph Smith, a summer resident of Healdville, stepped in. He knew nothing of cheese-making, but he was retiring as the director of a private school in New York and wanted something to do that carried with it an important tradition. His quest for holding on to old values, coupled with the energies of several employees who didn't want the factory to close, kept the Crowley tradition alive. The cheese company is now in its second generation of Smith management, with Randolph's son Peter continuing to uphold the longtime tradition.

HOW TO PURCHASE: Colby cheeses are available in 3 ages: mild, medium, and sharp; sage-flavored and smoke-flavored cheese is also sold. A 2½-lb. wheel is $13.75 to $14.75, depending on destination. A 5-lb. wheel is $25.25 to $27. Send check, money order, Visa, or MasterCard information, and orders will be filled promptly. Call or write for the latest brochure which includes a chart of prices by region of the country.

TO VISIT: Visitors are welcome to visit the factory and watch cheese being made most weekdays before 2 P.M. Factory hours are Monday through Saturday, 8 A.M.–4 P.M.. The factory is located between Rutland and Ludlow, 2 miles south of Vermont Route 103, 5 miles north of Ludlow, and 20 miles south of Rutland.

Cheddar and Sausage Brioche

Make this dough ahead and store in the refrigerator overnight so you can have freshly baked brioche in the morning. It's the quintessential breakfast treat.

- ¼ cup lukewarm water
- 2 packets active dry yeast
- ¼ cup sugar
- 3¾ cups unbleached flour
- 2 teaspoons salt
- 7 eggs
- ¾ lb. unsalted butter, softened
- ¼ lb. Crowley cheddar cheese, grated
- ½ lb. sage sausage, crumbled and browned lightly, drained on paper towels
- Vegetable spray or vegetable oil for oiling pans
- Egg wash (1 egg yolk beaten with 1 tablespoon water)

1. In a large mixing bowl, combine water, yeast, and sugar. Add ½ cup of flour and mix. Cover mixture with 1 cup of flour and set in a warm place away from any draft. Allow to rise until flour begins to show cracks (about 30 minutes).

2. Turn into mixing bowl of a heavy duty mixer, fitted with a dough hook. Add remaining flour and salt. Add eggs and beat for 10 minutes or until dough becomes smooth and shiny. Add the butter in tablespoon-size pieces and beat just until most of the butter is incorporated. Remove and combine any lumps of butter with your fingers. (Mixture will be quite loose at this point.)

3. Cover and allow to rise until doubled in size (about 1 hour). Punch down and turn into a plastic container. Cover tightly and refrigerate for 2 to 24 hours. (Dough may be stored in the refrigerator for up to 3 days or frozen for up to a month at this point. If frozen, allow to thaw in refrigerator overnight before proceeding.)

4. Remove from refrigerator and add cheese and sausage. Mix well using your fingers to stretch and pull the dough until ingredients are blended.

5. Spray 24 brioche tins with vegetable spray. Roll out twenty-four 2-inch balls and set in tins. Cover with oiled plastic wrap and allow to rise in a warm place until the dough has reached the top of the tins.

6. Preheat oven to 350°F. Place tins on a cookie sheet for ease in handling. Brush with an egg wash. Bake 20 to 25 minutes or until golden brown. Serve warm.

Makes 24 brioche.

Covered Bridge Cheddar Cheese

GRAFTON VILLAGE CHEESE COMPANY, INC. P.O. Box 87, Townshend Road, Grafton, Vermont 05146. 802/843-2221.

Five out of six guests at our dinner table named Grafton cheddar as their favorite Vermont cheese. So, the very next day, we made a beeline for the Covered Bridge label. Our lips smacked as we dug into the piquant cheddar. Aged a full year before it's sold, Grafton cheddar leaves a pleasant cheddar nuttiness on the palate and an urge to eat more.

Grafton Village Cheese had its beginnings around 1890 when the original Grafton Cooperative Cheese Factory was making cheese for the village and surrounding homesteads. That craft died out for a time and was resurrected in 1966 with a generous trust from a woman who loved this southern Vermont location and wanted to see it restored in much the fashion of the old Grafton Village. Today Grafton Cheese is made in a new plant that's housed in a reproduction New England Cape with attached barn in the old village area.

That trust money and the historic district are administered by the Windham Foundation (named for Windham County, in which Grafton is located). Frank Dickison was appointed president of the cheese-making operation in 1977 and, as such, he managed the production of some half a million pounds of cheddar cheese each year. After his death in 1988, Stephan Morse was appointed to head the company.

Cheese is made using the historic Grafton Cheese formula. But, unlike the old days, milk arrives at the plant in large steel tank trucks rather than directly from a herd. The milk is tested for butterfat content upon arrival and, before it's heated, cooled and pumped into cheese vats. The culture is added, and the milk solids begin to separate. At this point, almost 90 percent of the milk is pumped off and used as cattle feed. Then the curd is bonded, and the resulting slabs of cheese are turned several times. This last is the cheddaring process. After the cheese is pressed into bricks, it sits under pressure for 14 to 16 hours. Then it's cooled and aged before being cut and shipped to customers via a large mail order, wholesale, and on-site retail business.

An old Yankee tradition filled with pride in high standards of workmanship, Grafton Cheddar is a rich reminder of the past.

HOW TO PURCHASE: Grafton Covered Bridge Cheddar Cheese is available in several sizes: 1 lb. for $6.85; 2 lbs., $11; 3 lbs., $15; 5 lbs., $21.50. Shipping and handling are included; however, west of the Mississippi there is an additional charge of $1.75. All orders must be prepaid. Make checks payable to The Grafton Village Cheese Company, Inc.

Smoky Vermont Cheddar Cauliflower Soup

When there's a blizzard swirling all about, it's time for fortitude, the kind that comes from a big bowl of hot soup. Grafton Cheddar Cheese gives even more substance to this already robust dish.

> *2 oz. smoked bacon (about 4 slices)*
> *2 medium leeks, trimmed, washed thoroughly, and chopped*
> *2 large potatoes, peeled and diced*
> *1 medium head of cauliflower, in florets*
> *4 cups chicken stock*
> *1 cup grated Grafton Covered Bridge Cheddar Cheese (plus ¼ cup for garnish)*
> *½ cup light cream*
> *Salt and freshly ground pepper to taste*
> *¼ cup chopped fresh parsley*

1. In a medium saucepan, cook the bacon but do not let it brown. Remove with a slotted spoon. Sauté the leeks in the rendered fat over low heat, until soft. (Add butter if necessary to prevent sticking.) Add the potatoes and sauté 3 minutes. Add the cauliflower and stir. Add the stock and simmer, covered, 20 minutes or until vegetables are soft.

2. Transfer contents to a food processor or blender and purée. Return the mixture to the saucepan. Add cheese and cream and stir until cheese has melted. Add salt and pepper to taste. Garnish with parsley and ¼ cup grated cheese and serve.

Serves 8.

French-style Brie & Camembert

GUILFORD CHEESE COMPANY. R.D. #2, Box 420, Guilford, Vermont 05301. 802/254-9182.

A red barn on a country road just outside Brattleboro is home for two dozen jersey cows who contribute their rich Vermont milk to a small innovative family-run cheese company, Guilford Cheese. John Dixon, a Brattleboro surgeon, and his wife Ann started the company as a hobby in 1984 with hopes of becoming a commercial venture. Their only products in those days were the soft-textured Verde-Mont cheeses, soft, spreadable, low-fat products. One version was a blend with several herbs and spices to make a boursin-style spread. The other, unflavored, had many uses in the kitchen.

Today, cheese-making is more than a hobby for the Dixons. The entire family is involved. Stepson Sam tends their herd of cows. His brother Peter makes the cheese. Ann is the marketing person, and John helped design the original cheese-making plant.

A new plant and processing room were added in 1987, and the Dixons are now buying additional milk from a neighboring farm to supplement their own supply. Much of this growth is the result of an arrangement with a French cheesemaker to develop French-style Brie and Camembert in Vermont. "No other cheesemaker has such an agreement," says Ann, who adds that few American cheese-makers make exotic cheeses such as Brie and Camembert.

The outcome is that Guilford Cheeses are now appearing in some of the finest restaurants in the Northeast—An American Place in New York, Jaspers in Boston, and Panache in Cambridge. Blooming-dale's and many well-known food writers are counted among their regular customers.

With the new plant in place, Guilford Cheese Company is producing 100,000 pounds of cheese a year and expects to continue growing. And Ann Dixon, who plays an active role in the American Cheese Society, sees her company's success as a role model for other dairy farmers in Vermont. She's proving that the state's small, family-run farms can process their milk into new products, and what's more, there's a market for them. "I would love to see the day when Vermont is known for farm-produced products—a sort of mini Switzerland," she says.

HOW TO PURCHASE: Guilford Cheese has an extensive mail order business. A 5¼-oz. package of Verde-Mont (plain or herb) is $1.75. An 8-oz. wheel of Camembert (Mont-Bert) is sold for $3.60; the 6-oz piece, called Mont-Petit, is $2.50. Mont-Brie in 2½-lb. wheels, their version of Brie cheese, sells for $3 per pound. Guilford Cheese Company also makes its own Mozzarella (Montarella), which costs $4 per pound. Shipping is extra and is via U.P.S. Payment is by check or money order payable to Guilford Cheese Company.

Pat Tabibian's Spicy Brie Wrapped in Puffed Pastry

Although Guilford Cheeses are almost too good to be baked, Mont Brie is truly wonderful in this recipe (created by cooking school director Pat Tabibian) which is always a hit with company. It's so easy to make, but the preparation can be done a couple of days ahead.

> 2½-lb. wheel of Guilford Cheese Company Mont-
> Brie (9-inch wheel)
> ¼ cup minced fresh parsley
> 1 clove garlic, minced
> 1 teaspoon dried rosemary, crushed
> 1 teaspoon dried thyme, crushed
> 1 teaspoon dried marjoram, crushed
> 2 oz. hard salami, finely chopped
> 1 sheet puff pastry (available in freezer sections of
> the supermarket)
> 1 egg, lightly beaten

1. Set the cheese in the freezer for 30 minutes. Meanwhile, combine the parsley, garlic, rosemary, thyme, marjoram, and salami in a small bowl and reserve.
2. Slice the brie in half horizontally. Spread the herb and salami mixture over the cut side of one slice of brie and cover with the other slice. Press gently and return to the freezer. Roll the puff pastry into a rectangle measuring about 15x17 inches.
3. Preheat the oven to 425°F. Spray a baking rack and a jelly roll pan with vegetable spray. Set the chilled cheese in the center of the puff pastry. Gather the edges and crimp and twirl them into the center of the circle so that the cheese will not leak from the pastry as it cooks. Cut off any excess pastry and turn the package over and set on pastry rack. Cut small slits in the top. Brush top and sides with beaten egg. Decorate with cut outs from the leftover dough, if desired, and brush again with the egg mixture. (At this point, the cheese may be refrigerated for up to 2 days, wrapped tightly in plastic.)
4. Set the cheese and rack in the center of the pan. Bake 20 minutes or until pastry is golden brown and slightly puffed. Remove from oven and allow to stand 15 minutes before serving. Serve with crackers, bread, or wedges of fruit.

Serves 12–20.

Vermont Farmhouse Cheese

ORB WEAVER

RB WEAVER FARM. Box 75, Lime Kiln Road, New
aven, Vermont 05472. 802/877-3755.

We grew up with a watercolor of an old Maine lumberjack that
e affectionately nicknamed "Molunkus Harry" after a tiny town-
ip in Maine where this character was said to have originated. He
as a salty-looking cuss with a long scraggly beard that perfectly
into the features of his thin, angular jaw. When we were searching
ut Orb Weaver, I vaguely expected to find him looking much like
at picture.

Instead, to our surprise and delight, it turned out that Orb Weaver
eese is made by Marjorie Susman and Marian Pollack, two young-
h women who run a 30-acre dairy farm in New Haven, Vermont.
d Orb Weaver is not a weathered, rough-hewn man at all, but
e name of a delicate spider that weaves beautiful round, intricate
ebs. "We sort of work like spiders—busy every minute," says
sman.

Pollack was a family therapist and Susman was a classics major
college when they met and decided to go into something agricul-
ral together. They started dairy farming with a herd of twenty Jer-
y cows. Like so many dairy farmers, they wanted to increase the
lue of their milk. In 1982, they began turning their milk into a
ch Colby cheese that could be sold for much more than the going
rice of milk.

Unlike many cheesemakers, however, they make their cheese
clusively with milk from their own herd, making it truly a farm-
ouse cheese. (Their milk was chosen by the Department of Agricul-
re in Vermont as having the best flavor in the state.) This at least
rtially accounts for the wonderful, creamy taste of Orb Weaver
eese. Add to that the fact that the cheese is made entirely by hand
d in small batches in their spotless cheese-making facility.

The cheese is sold at the farm and through many specialty stores
well as via the mail. Among Orb Weaver cheese fans are Vermont
overnor Madeleine Kunin and several fine Vermont restaurateurs.
sman and Pollack and their Orb Weaver cheese are included in
book by cheese expert Laura Chenel.

HOW TO PURCHASE: Orb Weaver Vermont Farmhouse Cheese
is available in 2-lb. and 5-lb. waxed wheels. Cost is $12 and $25,
respectively. Prices include shipping and handling. Send check payable to Orb Weaver Farm. Credit cards and C.O.D. are not accepted.

Chicken, Broccoli, and Cheese Quiche

Orb Weaver Vermont Farmhouse Cheese makes a wonderful addition to this already tasty quiche.

> *2 tablespoons unsalted butter*
> *4 green onions, chopped*
> *1 medium onion, chopped*
> *10-oz. package frozen, chopped broccoli, thawed,*
>   *and thoroughly drained*
> *3 eggs*
> *1½ cups heavy cream*
> *½ teaspoon salt*
> *Freshly ground black pepper*
> *1 cup cooked and cubed chicken breast*
> *¼ lb. Orb Weaver cheese, grated*
> *1 uncooked 9-inch pie shell*

1. Preheat oven to 375 °F. In a medium skillet, melt the butter and
sauté the green onions and onion until transparent but not brown.
Add the broccoli and sauté 1 minute. Remove from heat and cool
slightly. Beat the eggs with the heavy cream, salt, and pepper until
well combined.

2. Prick the bottom of the pie shell, then set on a baking sheet.
Spread the broccoli-onion mixture over the bottom. Sprinkle the
chicken over the broccoli, then cover with the cheese. Gently pour
the eggs and cream over the filling. Set in the middle of the oven
and bake 40 minutes or until browned and firm to touch. Remove
from oven and let stand at room temperature about 10 minutes. Cut
and serve.

Serves 6–8.

Old-fashioned Vermont Granular Curd Cheese

THE PLYMOUTH CHEESE CORPORATION. P.O. Box 1, Plymouth, Vermont 05056. 802/672-3650.

If any cheesemaker has a place in history, it's surely the Plymouth Cheese Company. In business since 1890, this firm was started by Col. John C. Coolidge, father of President Calvin Coolidge, and a few neighbor farmers. It ceased operation in 1934 but was revived in 1960 by John Coolidge, the president's son.

The cheese, an old-fashioned, granular curd cheese that's like a cheddar, but less compact, is made just as it was in the nineteenth century. It's hand stirred and kneaded so that the curds are loosely formed and the blocks of cheese have little crevices running through them. The cheese is salted, pressed into molds, wrapped in cheesecloth, and dipped in four coats of wax before aging.

A light yellow color, owing to the all-natural product, the cheese is moist, slightly sour, and rich tasting. The package that arrives by mail is a perfect representation of the frugal Coolidge "waste not, want not" image. Wrapped first in foil, it's finally padded with newspaper before it's sent out to customers. Plymouth Cheese also makes a sage, pimento, and a caraway version of their cheese.

In recent years, the Plymouth Products Division has been added to the business. It makes a number of other fine, traditional Yankee products, such as baked beans, brown bread, corn and pepper relish, mustard and watermelon pickles, and Indian pudding.

The cheese factory is open daily (except Sunday), and visitors are always welcome to see the cheese being made. About 120,000 pounds of the granular cheese are made here each year. And much of it is sold right on the premises with the remainder going to a large list of mail order customers.

HOW TO PURCHASE: A 3-lb. wheel of Plymouth Cheese is $14.50 including shipping to any address east of the Mississippi ($15.50 to points west of the Mississippi River). For sage, pimento, or caraway prices are 15¢ higher. Cheese is also sold in 5-lb. wheels for $24.50 and $26; add 25¢ per wheel for flavors. (Also specify age: mild or medium sharp.) Shipments are via U.P.S. For P.O. Boxes or R.F.D., use Parcel Post and add 50¢ for eastern addresses, $1 for addresses west of the Mississippi. Orders must be accompanied by check or money order payable to The Plymouth Cheese Corporation.

Cheese Puffs

This old standby appetizer is made even better with the distinctive flavor of Plymouth Cheese.

⅔ cup water
⅓ cup milk
6 tablespoons unsalted butter
1 cup all-purpose flour
Dash of salt
4 eggs
¼ teaspoon cayenne
¼ cup finely chopped parsley
1 teaspoon Dijon mustard
4 oz. Plymouth Cheese, grated
1 egg, beaten with 1 teaspoon water for egg wash

1. Preheat oven to 350°F. Line baking sheets with cooking parchment or grease and lightly flour. Combine water, milk, and butter in a large saucepan and set over medium-high heat until butter is melted. Add the flour and salt and mix briskly with a wooden spoon until mixture is dry and pulls away from the side of the pan.

2. Remove from heat and transfer to a mixing bowl. Add the eggs, one at a time, beating on high while they are being added. Beat until mixture is smooth. Fold in the cayenne, parsley, mustard, and cheese.

3. Using a pastry bag or 2 teaspoons, form small balls about 1½ inches apart on prepared baking sheets. Brush with egg wash and bake 20–25 minutes or until light brown and puffs feel light and dry. Serve warm or cool on racks and store in airtight containers in refrigerator or freezer.

Yields 30–40 puffs.

Farmhouse Cheddar

5HELBURNE FARMS. Harbor Road, Shelburne, Vermont
5482. 802/985-8686.

Cheesemaker William Clapp compares his cheese to fine chateau
nes. Like the variations in flavor from chateau to chateau, the taste
each batch of Shelburne Farms cheddar cheese varies depending
the subtle changes in the milk from day to day and season to
ason. Since the cheese is produced solely from milk from the Shel-
rne Farms herd—and the herd grazes only on farm property—
ose subtle differences might be noticed only by a master like
app. Clapp's been making cheese for many years, having studied
e art in France and most recently in Scotland. It's under his watch-
l eye that this time-honored farmhouse cheese-making process
kes place.

He begins at 5:30 A.M. when nearly 4,200 pounds of milk rush
rough the pipe and into the tank in the Shelburne Farms cheese
om. The herd of prize-winning Brown Swiss cows is being milked.
can't be any fresher than this!

The cheese, creamy, moist and full of flavor, not dry and crumbly
e many cheddars, is handmade in the traditional English method.
e milk is converted into cheddar through use of cultures and ren-
t. After the rennet is added, the resultant curd is cooked to develop
e acid. Then it's packed together, and Clapp cuts it into blocks.
r the next 2 hours, he stacks and restacks the flabby, stretchy
ocks to drain off the whey, a process called "cheddaring." The
al product is hand-dipped in a wax coating that preserves its de-
htful texture. Then it's aged slowly under cool conditions. (Even
the curd stage, the temperature is never allowed to exceed 102 °F.)
e length of aging is over 6 months for medium; more than 1 year
r sharp; and over 2 years for extra sharp cheese.

About 425 pounds of cheese are made daily, 5 days a week at
elburne Farms, a 1,000-acre picturesque farm in northwestern
rmont, at the edge of Lake Champlain. The pastoral setting is also
me to a unique, nonprofit organization that's dedicated to the
ewardship and conservation of land and its natural resources.

The cheese-making operation began in 1982 as an economic
easure that has tripled the value of the farm's milk. All the profits
om the cheese and an extensive mail order business are turned
ck into running the organization.

Originally owned by the Webb family, hard economic times and
gh taxes forced them to look at breaking up the farm. Fifteen years
o, a determined group of Webb ancestors, rather than sell off the
nd, decided to dedicate it to the stewardship project. Today three
the family members help run the operation which includes walk-
g trails, a visitors center, and an inn.

HOW TO PURCHASE: Shelburne Farms has a glossy mail order
catalog that includes not only their cheese but the products of
others food producers in the state of Vermont. Shelburne Farms
Cheese is sold by the 1-, 2-, and 4-lb. block. Medium-aged cheese
is $7, $13 and $24; sharp adds $1 to the prices above; and extra
sharp adds $2 to those prices. Shipping and handling are included.
Credit cards are accepted. Call or write for the latest catalog.

TO VISIT: Visitors are welcome to view the cheese-making operation and other aspects of Shelburne Farms. The best time to visit
is between June 1 and October 15. To reach Shelburne Farms, take
Route 7 to the village of Shelburne (near Burlington). Route 7 intersects with Harbor Road in the center of the village. Go 1 mile west
on Harbor Road to the farm.

Norwegian-style Meat Pie

This recipe is a favorite at our house. The combination of extra
sharp cheese, smoked ham, and ground beef in a rich crust is yummy
on a chilly night. Serve with a horseradish and sour cream sauce.

> *2 tablespoons butter*
> *1 medium onion, chopped*
> *1½ lbs. lean ground beef*
> *¾ cup chopped smoked ham*
> *¼ cup chopped fresh parsley*
> *1 teaspoon chopped fresh thyme*
> *1¾ cup grated Shelburne Farms extra sharp*
> * cheddar cheese*
> *Salt and pepper to taste*
> *1 recipe of quiche dough (enough for a 9-inch crust)*
> *1 egg beaten with 2 tablespoons milk*

1. In a medium skillet, melt the butter and sauté the onion until
soft. Add the ground beef and sauté until meat is brown. Drain off
any excess fat. Add the ham, parsley, and thyme and sauté for 2
minutes. Add the cheese and toss to melt. Remove from heat and
add the salt and pepper, if needed. Cool while rolling out the dough.
2. Preheat oven to 375 °F. Cut the dough in half and roll one half
to about ⅛-inch thick. Set on a greased cookie sheet. Mound the
meat mixture in a loaf in the center of the dough. Roll out the remaining dough to the same thickness. Cover meat with the dough.
Crimp the edges with a fork to seal. (After dough has covered meat,
there should be only a little extra dough around the edges.) Trim
away excess dough and roll and cut into strips. Crisscross the top
with these to make an attractive pattern. Brush with the milk and
egg mixture. Bake 30 minutes or until golden brown. Remove from
oven and serve.

Serves 8.

Waxed, Aged Cheddar Cheese

SUGARBUSH FARM. R.F.D. #1, Box 568, Woodstock, Vermont 05091. 802/457-1757.

Jack Ayres came up with an idea to make Vermont cheese more accessible to tourists when, after World War II, people became more mobile and visitors began flooding into Vermont. In those days, most cheese was cut into wedges from large wheels, and it didn't travel well. The wedge shape was also awkward for packaging and had a tendency to dry out and grow mold because so much of the surface was exposed.

Ayres thought if he could cut the cheese into cracker-shaped bars, seal them in foil, then coat them in wax, they would have great appeal. He was absolutely right. That was back in 1945, and the originator of cracker-sized cheese bars has been selling fine waxed cheeses ever since.

Betsy Ayres Luce, Jack Ayres daughter, now heads the family operation housed in an addition to a Civil War–era farmhouse. She grew up with her father's cheese business, starting out as a child helping to cut the wheels of Vermont cheddar into bars.

Things are still done just about the same way they were back when her father started the business, with one major difference. Ayres created a small cheese business. Today's operation sees some 80 tons of cheese handled at Sugarbush Farm each year, and Luce and her staff of three often work overtime. Nevertheless, Luce hand types a letter complete with typos to accompany each and every order. This is no small task. Sugarbush Farm now has more than 8,000 mail order customers. "We've built up a lot of faithful customers on our list," says Luce. "In fact, now we are selling to many of the children of the original list!"

The family has never made cheese themselves. Instead, Ayres started traveling around the state to small cheesemakers, tasting and selecting from their products. He'd bring his finds back to Sugarbush Farm where the young cheeses would be aged, then packaged. Determining which 6-month-old cheeses would be best aged for anywhere from 12 to 26 months became an art that Luce has inherited from her father.

The farm produces a Sharp Cheddar (aged 19 to 26 months), Vermont Medium Cheddar, Vermont Sage, Green Mountain Jack, and Green Mountain Bleu. Another of Ayres's innovative ideas was to smoke cheese. Sugarbush Farm sells a Hickory and Maple Smoked Cheese and a Smoked Cheese with Sausage as well. The family also operates a large sugar house that dates back 150 years. Sugaring is Luce's husband Larry's job.

Truly a cottage industry, Sugarbush Farm now has four generations of Ayres on the property, including toddler Elizabeth Ann Luce who'll be learning the business as soon as she's able.

HOW TO PURCHASE: Four half–size bars (about ½ lb. each) an assortment of flavors, is $14.50 plus $2.65 for postage and handling A box of 6 bars (same size) costs $20.90 plus $3.45 for postage and handling. A 2-lb. block of sharp cheddar (aged about 2 years) i $13.20 plus $2.65. A gift sampler with 2 blocks of cheese, ½ pin of maple syrup, and maple candy is $15.55 plus $2.80 for shipping and handling. Major credit cards are accepted. Orders are shippe the same day they are received.

Ken Haedrich's Three-Grain Cheddar Onion Crescents

Ken Haedrich, a well-known New England cook, food writer, and cookbook author, makes these special rolls for special occasions We'd be more apt to say these rolls make every occasion special Here's his recipe. The dough can also be shaped into loaves.

> *1 tablespoon active dry yeast*
> *¾ cup lukewarm water*
> *2 tablespoons sugar*
> *1 cup lukewarm milk*
> *1 teaspoon salt*
> *1 egg, lightly beaten*
> *1 cup cornmeal*
> *1 cup rolled oats (not instant)*
> *4 tablespoons unsalted butter, melted*
> *3½–4 cups unbleached flour*
> *2 tablespoons unsalted butter*
> *2 cups finely chopped onions*
> *1½ cups grated Sugarbush Sharp Cheddar*
> *1 egg yolk mixed with 1 tablespoon milk*
> * for egg wash*

1. Mix yeast with water and sugar and allow to sit until it become bubbly (about 10 minutes). Add milk, salt, and egg and whisk briefly
2. Whisk cornmeal, oats, and melted butter into this mixture. Usin a wooden spoon, beat in flour, 1 cup at a time, until dough is dens and can be kneaded. Turn onto floured surface and knead 10 minute or until dough is smooth and elastic. Add additional flour as neces sary to prevent sticking. Place dough in a large, greased bowl, cove with oiled plastic wrap, and let sit in a warm spot until it has double in size.
3. While dough is rising, melt 2 tablespoons of butter in a larg skillet and sauté the onions over medium heat until golden brown Remove from heat and reserve.
4. Sprinkle the cheese over the risen dough and punch down Divide in half and knead each briefly to incorporate the cheese Cover loosely with plastic wrap and let dough rest 10 minutes.
5. Roll each half into a 13-inch circle on a floured surface. Sprinkl half the onions over each circle, leaving a 4-inch circle uncovere in the center. Cut the dough into 8 even pie-shaped wedges.
6. Starting at the wide end, roll each wedge up snugly, leaving th very tip barely exposed. Gently pinch the surface into the tip. Pu the ends down in an exaggerated crescent and set on a buttered bak ing sheet, leaving about 2 inches between each for expansion. Cove with plastic wrap and allow to almost double.
7. Preheat oven to 375 °F. Brush the crescents with the egg wash Bake 25 minutes or until golden. Cool on a rack, if not serving a once.

Yields 16 rolls.

Crème Fraîche/Fromage Blanc/Chèvre

VERMONT BUTTER AND CHEESE COMPANY, INC.
Pitman Road, P.O. Box 95, Websterville, Vermont 05678.
802/479-9371.

Ladies in Des Moines and men in Galveston were writing to Allison Reisner and Robert Reese, owners of Vermont Butter and Cheese Company asking where they could get their Crème Fraîche, Fromage Blanc, and their blue ribbon Chèvre. Meanwhile Vermont Butter and Cheese was getting mentioned in publications from the *New York Times* and *Boston Globe* to *Country Journal.* Suddenly, it seemed the whole world knew about Vermont Butter and Cheese Company and wanted their products.

It's not accidental that this partnership has put together an exemplary small business with a tidy profit picture in the matter of just a few years. Reese and Reisner, former employees of the state Department of Agriculture, had watched many other companies get their start. Realizing there was a need for high-quality cheeses and applying the techniques learned while working in the department's marketing office, the two launched their own cottage industry in 1984.

Inquiries from chefs for goat cheese and crème fraîche gave them the clue to exactly what kinds of cheeses would sell. And Reisner, a New Jersey native, had once lived in France, where she remembered eating Fromage Blanc with Crème Fraîche as a daily breakfast. A natural combo over there, she thought it would work as well here.

The business started out as a wholesale supplier to restaurants and shops, mainly in New York and Boston. As word of their products traveled and people began learning to cook with their products, Vermont Butter and Cheese added a direct mail business as well.

The only licensed manufacturer of goat dairy products in Vermont, Vermont Butter and Cheese Company's business has been growing at a rate of 15 percent a month. Each week, the company's six employees turn out about 3,000 pounds of chèvre and two cow's milk products—Crème Fraîche (a fresh ripened cream) and Fromage Blanc (a lightly whipped skim milk cheese).

Until recently the company manufactured all its dairy products in a modest 400-square-foot East Brookfield barn, but now it is located in a new 5,000-square-foot facility in Barre Town's Wilson Industrial Park.

The two principals don't get too carried away with success, however. Having seen it all during their stints in the Agriculture Department, Reisner and Reese realize that the more cheese they sell, the more they open up a market and invite a big company to come in and take over producing the cheese at a lower cost.

While that's something they may have to contend with in the future, the cheesemakers have a concern that's much more immediate—keeping up with today's demand for their products.

HOW TO PURCHASE: Vermont Butter and Cheese Company ships Crème Fraîche in 8-oz. containers for $2.89 each and Fromage Blanc in 6-oz. containers for $2.69. They plan to add an 8-oz. container of the latter at $2.99 in the near future. Chèvre comes in a 6-oz. log for $5 and in a crottin for $3. Shipping is extra and is via U.P.S. Add $5 for 1–5 lbs., $6 for 6–10 lbs. for ground service in the Northeast. In other parts of the country, service is via Second Day Air. Add $10 for first 5 lbs. and $15 for 6–10-lb. orders. Payment is by check or money order.

Cold Broccoli Soup with Curry and Crème Fraîche

Refreshing and rejuvenating, a cup of this soup is splendid when the New England weather turns balmy.

3 tablespoons butter
1 medium onion, chopped
¾ lb. broccoli, stems and florets cut into small pieces
2 teaspoons good quality curry powder
3½–4 cups chicken stock
Juice of ½ lime
Salt and pepper to taste
¾ cup Vermont Butter and Cheese Crème Fraîche
Freshly snipped chives (for garnish)

1. Melt butter in a large, heavy saucepan. When butter begins to foam, add onions and sauté on low heat just until onions soften and become opaque. Add the pieces of broccoli and sauté for about 1 minute. Crumble a sheet of cooking parchment or wax paper, moisten, and spread over the cooking broccoli. Turn the heat to the lowest setting and cover the pan with a tight-fitting lid. Sweat the vegetables in this fashion for 10 minutes. Vegetables should not take on any color during this process.
2. Remove the lid and discard the paper. Add the curry powder and sauté until you begin to smell the aroma of the curry. Add the chicken stock and simmer 15–20 minutes or until broccoli is very soft.
3. Remove pan from the heat and stir in the lime juice. Check seasonings and add salt and pepper as needed. Allow mixture to cool to room temperature. Whisk in the crème fraîche or the yogurt. Chill at least 2 hours before serving. Serve topped with chopped fresh chives.

Serves 6.

Wylie Hill Farm

TIM & AMELIA FRITZ
Craftsbury Common, VT 05827
802-586-2887

WYLIE HILL FARM. P.O. Box 35, Star Route, Craftsbury Common, Vermont 05827. 802/586-2887.

Wylie Hill Farm is one of those cottage businesses that was created out of happenstance. Quite a few years ago, Tim Fritz, a builder by trade, took a job on Nantucket Island. He and his wife Amelia planned to stay just a few years. But they fell in love with New England and decided to remain. They searched for a spot "in the middle of nowhere" to settle and bought a 75-acre farm 20 miles south of the Canadian border in Craftsbury, Vermont.

As part of that dream, Tim was looking for a way to stay home, make a living, and spend a little more time with his young children, Molly and Jacob. While living on Nantucket, the Fritzs met Stephen Swift, who owned a pheasant farm. His inspiration set them on the track of running a bird farm. Wylie Hill Farm (named for the ridge on which part of the property sits), with 5 open acres for growing and 70 acres of forest and meadow, was the perfect spot for birds.

Tim and Amelia began by raising turkeys for their own use. Then they added ducks and geese, which are still raised for the Fritz family's personal menu. Their interest in poultry was already established by the time they decided to try their hand at a commercial venture.

Swift suggested quail for their first attempt. The bird is known to be easier to raise than many of the larger game birds because quails have fewer health problems. The Fritzs have been raising 10,000 of the sweet, tender birds a year since 1984.

Then they added pheasant, a more popular bird and easier to sell, but harder to handle. And most recently, the Fritzs introduced a few partridge (about 400), mostly as "an afterthought."

The fortunate by-product of the bird business is the multitude of beige and brown speckled quail eggs that are sold to cooks and restaurants each week. Freshly killed birds are too perishable to mail order, but Fritz packs the quail eggs in special styrofoam thirty-egg containers for mailing.

The couple has also purchased a smoker and vacuum-sealing machine. As we were about to go to press, the Fritzs announced that Wylie Hill Farm is now smoking pheasant and that product is also available by mail.

HOW TO PURCHASE: Quail eggs are sold in 30-egg containers. The minimum order is 4 cartons or 120 eggs and price is $22, which includes shipping and handling. Smoked pheasants (2-plus lbs. each) are $22 including shipping charges. Payment is by check or money order made payable to Wylie Hill Farm. Quail eggs and dressed birds are sold at the farm. It's best to call for directions upon arrival in Craftsbury.

Golden Coin Quail Eggs

This well-known Oriental hors d'oeuvre is a natural for quail eggs which are already bite-size.

30 Wylie Hill Farm quail eggs
1 teaspoon salt
⅓ cup cornstarch
2 tablespoons vegetable oil

Sauce

4 tablespoons minced onion
2 teaspoons minced fresh gingerroot
2 teaspoons Oriental sesame oil
½ teaspoon chili flakes
⅓ cup water
½ teaspoon sugar
1½ tablespoons rice wine vinegar
1½ tablespoons soy sauce

1. In a medium saucepan, add eggs and salt and cover with water. Bring to a boil and simmer 8 minutes. Remove from heat, drain, and run under cold water until eggs feel cool. Tap each egg gently against the side of the pan and let sit in cold water for 1 hour, or remove from water and refrigerate overnight.

2. Peel, rinse, and pat eggs dry. Cut each egg in half lengthwise. Spread cornstarch over a plate. Roll each half egg in cornstarch to coat. Heat the oil in a large skillet. Add the eggs and brown on both sides. Add more oil if necessary to prevent sticking. Remove to paper towels, then transfer to a serving platter.

3. Heat onion and ginger in the oil for 30 seconds. Add remaining sauce ingredients. Stir to warm. Pour over eggs, just to moisten. Serve.

Yields 60 pieces.

MEATS, FISH & SEAFOOD

CONNECTICUT

Smoked Meats, Fish & Sausage

NODINE'S SMOKEHOUSE. Route 63 North, Goshen, Connecticut 06756. 203/491-3511 or 1/800-222-2059 outside Connecticut.

In the late sixties, Ron Nodine decided he was tired of working as a computer engineer. He wanted to be his own boss, and he wanted to get out of the "rat race." He laughs at the last part, because operating the smokehouse has become a big business, and the 9-to-5 routine has easily become the 18-hour-day.

When Nodine was looking for a change, he discovered that a small, custom smokehouse in Goshen was for sale. The owner promised to stay and teach him the business but died just after the sale was final. So Nodine learned how to smoke meats through trial and error. Today, Nodine's Smokehouse processes more than 200,000 pounds of meat, poultry, fish, and sausage each year and ships to individuals and restaurants in every part of the country. Nevertheless, Nodine's remains a family business with offices in the home and a smokehouse in the yard. Computers have taken over the dining room and baskets for gift packaging have invaded the living room.

Plans call for a major expansion. As Khoury Mubarek, sales manager and a relative newcomer to the business, puts it, "we have to expand or die." However, Nodine's first attempt to expand by building a modern plant behind his house was met by neighborhood resistance. Now Nodine's is constructing its facility in a commercially zoned section in nearby Torrington.

Ron Nodine still oversees all of the smoking, a practice that he says accounts for the fine quality of his products. Indeed, Nodine's smoked boneless chicken, duck, and goose breast are true finds. Remarkably moist and delicately smoked, it's no surprise they appear under "gourmet" in specialty stores. Nodine's has an impressive list of products, and that repertoire is always growing. Trout, scallops, salmon, whole turkeys, geese, and hams, several varieties of bacon and sausage are included. Most recent additions to the line of smoked goods are their spicy andouille sausage, smoked peppered bluefish, chicken and duck sausage, and a smoked crown pork roast.

Many things have changed since Ron Nodine started a little smokehouse back in 1968. But following the tradition started by his predecessor, Nodine's continues to custom-smoke any meat brought in by a customer.

HOW TO PURCHASE: Nodine's retail shop on the premises is open from 9 A.M.–5 P.M., Monday to Saturday; 10 A.M.–4 P.M. on Sunday. All products may be purchased by mail. Items are sold by the pound as well as in gift packages and platters. Sample prices are crown pork roast, $110; whole goose, $54; whole smoked pheasant, $32; 1 lb. of andouille, $5; a side of cold-smoked salmon is $23. There is an extra charge for shipping (via U.P.S. unless otherwise requested). (Prices will vary with destination as some locations will require Second Day Air to insure the quality of the food.) Orders must be prepaid, and Nodine's accepts checks as well as all major credit cards. Write or call for a current price list.

TO VISIT: Visitors are welcome anytime during the shop hours. Tours of the smokehouse can be arranged, but call ahead and try to avoid the pre-Thanksgiving to post-Christmas season when they are frantically trying to keep up with holiday orders. From Litchfield, take Route 63 north to Goshen. Nodine's Smokehouse is 1. miles past the center of Goshen on the left.

Victoria Scott Spear's French Market Soup

This spicy and hearty soup comes from Ms. Spear's Southern Roots Company. It was first introduced to us by the folks at Nodine's who often sell Ms. Spear's bean mix along with all the necessary smoked products.

> *16 oz. of mixed dry beans and peas**
> *3 quarts water*
> *1 tablespoon salt*
> *1 Nodine's smoked ham hock*
> *3 sprigs of parsley*
> *2 bay leaves*
> *28-oz. can tomatoes, undrained*
> *2 medium onions, chopped*
> *6 stalks celery, chopped*
> *2 large cloves garlic, minced*
> *Salt and pepper to taste*
> *1 lb. Nodine's andouille sausage, thinly sliced*
> *1 Nodine's whole boneless smoked chicken*
> *   breast, sliced*
> *½ cup chopped fresh parsley*
> *½ cup dry red wine*

1. Rinse the dry beans. Add to the water and bring to a boil. Skim off the surface and allow beans to sit 1 hour off the heat. Add the tablespoon of salt, ham hock, sprigs of parsley, and bay leaves. Bring to a boil and simmer covered about 2½ hours or until beans are tender.
2. Add tomatoes, onion, celery, garlic, and salt and pepper and simmer, uncovered, for 1 hour or until creamy. Add the andouille and the chicken breast and simmer 30 minutes. Add parsley and red wine and simmer another 15 minutes. Flavor improves if this is made a day ahead.

Serves 10.

---

*Include any combination of kidney, lima, navy, pinto, pink, garbanzo, and lentil beans; blackeye, yellow, and green split peas, and barley.

Naturally Grown Lamb

THE STERNLIEBS

SUGAR HILL FARM INC.™
ALL NATURAL FARM PRODUCTS

SUGAR HILL FARM, INC. Smith Hill Road, P.O. Box 50, Colebrook, Connecticut 06021-0050. 203/379-9649.

When Moe Sternlieb purchased Sugar Hill Farm, there was nary a lamb on the property and the one-time dairy farm hadn't seen a cow in 50 years. The 270 acres of pastureland were completely overgrown, and local residents waited anxiously, expecting the white-haired man to put in a subdivision.

That was the furthest thing from Sternlieb's mind, however. This was a man with a boyhood dream of having his own farm, and although adult responsibilities had gotten temporarily in the way, he was about to do just that. In addition to managing his own accounting firm in Hackensack, New Jersey, Sternlieb now spends nights and weekends as a sheep farmer.

Still, things started slowly until Sternlieb crossed breeds of sheep to develop a market lamb that was far superior to any other lamb being sold. The breed, a cross of Dorset and Finn ewe with Suffolk ram, produced a lamb that grows faster and results in tastier and leaner meat. Today Sugar Hill Farm has some 200-plus ewes grazing over 150-acres of land, making it one of the larger sheep farms in the Northeast.

All the sheep are raised naturally, using no hormones, chemicals, or additives. They eat only the best feed, then the meat is quick-frozen to preserve its delightful quality and texture that's a head, two shoulders, and a resounding ''ba-a-a'' above store-bought lamb.

Sold as whole or half lambs, these are cut to order and packaged for freezer storage before being frozen.

Besides lamb, Sternlieb now raises capons, pheasant, and turkeys on a sister farm that's nearby (he ran out of room at Sugar Hill Farm). During the holiday season (November and December), Sternlieb sells some 600 flash-frozen, ready-to-thaw-and-cook turkeys. He hopes to increase the flock to include partridge and Muscovy duck.

''They thought I was crazy to get into farming at my age,'' says Sternlieb. But this strong-willed man with a childhood dream had no doubt he could do anything he put his mind to doing. Now that he's put Sugar Hill back on the map as farmland, he's hoping to gain national recognition for his operation. We have no doubt he'll do exactly that.

HOW TO PURCHASE: A whole lamb weighs about 60 lbs. before butchering. It includes 2 legs, 2 racks, rib chops, loin chops, riblets, and the balance in shoulder chops, stew meat, and ground meat. Charge is $149.95. Half a lamb (same cuts) weighs about 30 lbs. before butchering and is sold for $79.95. There is an additional charge for shipping and handling: add $7.50 per whole lamb and $5 per half lamb. Orders must be prepaid with check or money order. Sugar Hill Farm does not take credit cards.

Boneless Stuffed Leg of Lamb with Spinach and Hazelnut Stuffing

This is a wonderfully elegant and exotic company meal.

> 5-lb. Sugar Hill Farm leg of lamb, boned
>   and butterflied
> Salt and pepper
> Kitchen twine

Spinach and Hazelnut Stuffing

> ½ cup unsalted hazelnuts, toasted and skinned
> ¾ lb. good quality sausage, preferably with herb
>   seasoning
> 2 tablespoons butter
> 1 medium leek, washed carefully and chopped
> 1 lb. fresh spinach, washed, stemmed, and leaves
>   coarsely chopped
> 2 tablespoons fresh sage, minced, or 2 teaspoons
>   dried
> 2 teaspoons fresh marjoram, minced, or
>   ½ teaspoon dried
> Salt and pepper to taste
> 2 eggs, lightly beaten

1. Trim any large pockets of fat from the center and skin side of the meat. Sprinkle both sides with salt and pepper and spread the roast over a flat surface, skin side down. Finely grind the nuts and reserve.

2. In a large skillet, crumble and brown the sausage over medium heat. Remove and drain. Wipe out the skillet and add the butter. Lower the heat and sauté the leek until soft, about 5 minutes. Add the spinach and toss about 2 minutes, or until soft. Add the herbs and sauté for 30 seconds. Add the toasted, ground hazelnuts, salt, and pepper. Stir and remove from heat. Add the eggs and mix well. Cool briefly.

3. Preheat oven to 375°F. Spread the mixture over the entire piece of lamb, filling in pockets where bones were removed. Cut twine into three or four 1-foot lengths and two 2-foot lengths. Starting at one of the shorter ends of the roast, roll it tightly. Don't worry if some of the stuffing falls out. You can poke it back in or simply discard it. Place the short pieces of twine under the roast and tie them tightly around the meat at intervals. Use the longer pieces of twine to tie the roast end to end. Set on a rack in a roasting pan and roast for 1 to 1¼ hours for a medium-rare roast or 1½ to 1¾ hours for well-done meat. Remove from the oven and allow to sit for 10 minutes before cutting. Slice and serve with pan gravy (below) and your favorite vegetables.

Serves 8.

The Sauce

> ¼ cup dry vermouth
> 2 tablespoons butter
> 1 shallot, minced
> 1 carrot, peeled and finely chopped
> 1 cup chicken stock
> Salt and pepper to taste

Discard any fat from the pan in which the roast cooked. Add the vermouth and deglaze the pan. Reserve this liquid. In a small saucepan, melt butter and sauté the shallot and the carrot 5 minutes. Add the stock and simmer until carrots are very soft and easy to mash. Purée the mixture and add the pan juices, salt, and pepper. Moisten the slices of lamb with a little sauce and serve the rest on the side.

MAINE

Exotic Seafood

CASPIAN CAVIARS. Mitchell and Winter, Highland Mill, P.O. Box 876, Camden, Maine 04843. 207/236-4436.

Man does not live by lobster caviar alone, especially if he's Rod Mitchell. The co-owner and president of the upscale Caspian Caviars makes it his business to locate the most unusual seafood for his very particular clientele.

Live Maine sea urchins, encrusted in spiny cases; tiny succulent cold-water Maine shrimp; and live scallops still in their shells (many say they're sweeter that way) are just a few of the items that Caspian Caviars stocks.

Mitchell does handle Beluga caviar from the Caspian Sea. But the busy entrepreneur gambled that Maine's equally exotic delicacies—lobster caviar (also called coral or roe) and other gustatory extravagances such as monkfish livers and giant Maine sea snails—would appeal to the burgeoning American epicurean market. His instincts were right. The result has been impressive.

Mitchell has peddled his offbeat palate teasers to hotels, the Cunard cruise line, Air France, and fine restaurants such as Jean-Louis at the Watergate in Washington, D.C., Le Cirque and La Bernadin in New York, and the Chicago Fish House.

Part of Mitchell's business strategy is his ability to harvest, collect, and ship delicacies to his nationwide list of customers almost always on the same day. Caspian Caviars hires Maine fishermen who moonlight as divers to search out urchins and scallops hiding in rocky coves. Sometimes their catch comes in at three in the morning. Mitchell and his three employees are all waiting to lend a hand at packing the seafoods in ice and styrofoam containers for same-day air delivery.

After Mitchell began his business importing caviar, he found a photo of his grandfather posed with a sturgeon caught from the Kennebec River in Maine. He'd also been in the caviar business, it seems. Although sturgeon are considered a threatened species in Maine, Mitchell is involved in a pilot program to grow and harvest this fish in a closed water system. One day he believes this will lead to repopulating the Kennebec River. Someday Mitchell hopes to follow in his grandfather's footsteps and once again market Maine Kennebec caviar.

HOW TO PURCHASE: It's always best to call Caspian Caviars before ordering their products. They are too perishable to let them wait on a doorstep. Prices, too, change, depending on availability. Costs range from $1 for a pound of sea urchins to $40 for a pound of lobster caviar. A pound of Maine shrimp with shells on and heads removed is $5.95; peeled shrimp sell for $6.95. Shipping is usually via Federal Express and is an additional charge. Mitchell accepts checks, money orders, credit cards, and will bill for products if desired.

Potatoes Stuffed with Baby Maine Shrimp and Lobster Mousseline with Lobster Coral Sauce

This dish was recently featured on the menu at Jean-Louis Restaurant. Jean-Louis Palladin, executive chef and owner of the upscale Washington, D.C., eatery, graciously permitted us to publish the tantalizing recipe here.

> 6 large baking potatoes
> Coarse salt
> 2 Maine lobsters (about 1 lb. each)
> 1⅓ cups heavy cream for the mousseline
> Salt and freshly ground pepper
> 5 large potatoes, for boiling
> 3 tablespoons unsalted butter
> 3 tablespoons extra virgin olive oil
> ½ cup heavy cream
> 48 Maine shrimp, peeled
> 5 tablespoons olive oil for frying shrimp
> Fresh chopped chives, to garnish

1. Cover the potatoes with aluminum foil and set on a bed of coarse salt. Bake 375 °F. until soft to touch (about 1½ hours). Remove from oven and reserve.

2. Plunge the lobsters in boiling water for 15 seconds. Remove and immediately plunge into ice water. Remove the meat from the shell and purée the meat in a food processor. Pass the purée through a fine sieve and return it to the food processor. Add the 2 cups of cream, salt, and pepper and purée just until blended. Do not over process as cream will curdle.

3. Boil the 5 potatoes until soft. Drain, run under cold water, and peel. Pass through a fine sieve and add 3 tablespoons each of butter and olive oil and ½ cup heavy cream. Season with salt and freshly ground pepper. Mix well over heat and reserve.

4. Cut the baked potatoes in half lengthwise, scoop out the pulp and reserve it for another use.

5. Heat 5 tablespoons of olive oil in a medium sauté pan. Add the shrimp and heat for 1 minute. Remove the shrimp with a slotted spoon and reserve.

6. Preheat oven to 350 °F. Set the potato skins on a baking sheet. Spoon a 1-inch layer of the lobster mixture into the bottom of each. Bake 15 minutes or until mousseline is set. Pipe sufficient potato mixture over the top of the lobster to fill the potato skins. Top with shrimp and cover with lobster coral sauce (below). Sprinkle with chives.

Serves 6.

Lobster Coral Sauce

> 4 oz. lobster caviar (roe)
> 10 tablespoons unsalted butter, softened to room
>   temperature
> 1 oz. fish consomme or clam broth
> Fine sea salt
> Freshly ground black pepper

In a food processor blend the lobster caviar with the butter until smooth. Transfer mixture to a small saucepan, add the consomme, salt, and pepper, and whisk vigorously over low heat until sauce turns bright red. (Do not stop whisking or sauce will curdle. If this happens, pass the sauce through a sieve and reheat.) Add salt and pepper to taste and spoon over potatoes. Serve immediately.

Ocean Fresh Lobster, Scallops & Crab

DOWNEAST SEAFOOD EXPRESS. Box 138, Route 176, Brooksville, Maine 04617. 1/800-556-2326 or 207/326-8246 in Maine.

What can we say about a Maine lobster that comes out of Penobscot Bay one evening and arrives ready for the lobster pot the next morning, except, "Get the melted butter!"

Downeast Seafood Express supplies the world with some of the freshest seafood—lobster, scallops, and crabmeat—that we've ever tasted. It's reminiscent of this author's childhood in Maine when the lobster boat would haul in the traps, we'd pick up our lobsters, and within 4 hours, we'd be feasting on them. The only difference is that Downeast Seafood's products are a little tamer. Claws are pegged so that even the tenderfoot can handle them.

Bill Tomkins and his wife Sally are the sum total of the small Downeast Seafood Express in Brooksville, a tiny town in the heart of lobster country, between Castine and Ellsworth on Penobscot Bay. They have some part-time employees, but mainly it's Bill catching the lobsters and Sally handling the orders.

A New Jersey native, Bill came to Brooksville after college to take a job growing coho salmon. The company closed, and he became a fisherman, buying his own lobster boat which he named "Kokadjo" and enough traps to become a serious lobsterman. The couple decided there was a market for fresh lobster outside northern New England, and in 1984, they opened their own business to express this seafood to other parts of the country.

With lobster traps now numbering from 200 to 300, Bill catches nearly all the lobster his company sells except in the winter months when he buys the local catch from other lobstermen. Spring, summer, and fall he's out 12 hours a day placing and pulling up his traps, but in the winter, he fishes only for sea scallops. "It's a full-time job just keeping a boat in the water in a Maine winter," he says.

Lobsters come well packed in seaweed and ice. (Steam the lobster with some of the seaweed to give it a real Down East flavor.) The crustaceans arrive still lively, the definitive test of freshness.

The Tomkins also sell sweet and succulent Maine crabmeat from cold-water crabs that have been carefully picked over. From November to April, they sell equally sweet Maine sea scallops. Jumbo and tender, these are only offered as a seasonal delicacy.

Although they are not native Mainers, the Tomkins have certainly hit upon a market for one of the state's finer treats—and that's fortunate for all of us who have moved "away," and those who have just visited.

HOW TO PURCHASE: Four 1½-lb. lobsters are $79.50 (2 cost $52.95). Four 1¾-lb. lobsters cost $93 (2 cost $58.75). Two lobsters (1½ lbs. each) and two 8-oz. containers of Maine crabmeat are sold for $61.95. Four 8-oz. containers of crabmeat are $43.95; the same quantity of Maine sea scallops costs $42.95. All prices include the cost of guaranteed overnight air delivery to any point in the U.S. MasterCard and Visa are accepted. Discounts are available when 5 or more orders are placed within a month.

Lobster Pie

Once in a while, someone in a group of guests doesn't like lobster. In that case, confiscate his or her portion before the other guests notice that there might be extra and use it to make a lobster pie. Don't, however, sacrifice your own helping for this wickedly rich dish.

> *4 tablespoons unsalted butter*
> *1 tablespoon flour*
> *1 cup heavy cream*
> *1 egg yolk*
> *1 tablespoon lemon juice*
> *Salt and pepper to taste*
> *2 cups cooked, chunked lobster meat*
> *½ teaspoon paprika*
> *¼ teaspoon cayenne*
> *⅓ cup dry sherry*

Cracker crumb topping

> *¾ cup crumbled oyster crackers*
> *5 tablespoons butter*
> *1 tablespoon freshly grated Parmesan cheese*
> *½ teaspoon paprika*

1. Melt 1 tablespoon of the butter in a saucepan. Add the flour and mix. Cook 2 minutes. Add the cream and whisk until it thickens. Remove from the heat and whisk in the egg yolk. Beat well. Add the lemon juice and salt and pepper. Reserve.
2. In a sauté pan, melt remaining 3 tablespoons of the butter. Add the lobster meat and sauté 5 minutes over medium-low heat. Add the paprika and cayenne and mix. Add the sherry. Simmer 2 minutes. Add the cream sauce and combine. Transfer to a shallow baking dish.
3. Preheat the oven to 375°F. Mix the cracker crumb topping ingredients together and sprinkle over the lobster. Bake 10 minutes or until topping is slightly brown and mixture is bubbly. Serve at once.

Serves 4.

Smoked Fish

DUCKTRAP RIVER FISH FARM, INC. R.F.D. #2, Box 378, Lincolnville, Maine 04849. 207/763-3960.

How a young biology major from Harvard ended up raising trout and running a prosperous fish smoking business in Lincolnville, Maine, is a story in itself. Desmond ''Des'' FitzGerald was smitten with the coastal community when he was a kid and came to Maine with his folks for vacations.

During a year off from school, FitzGerald worked on an Alaskan shrimp boat, a salmon boat off Kodiak Island, and for a man in California who raised trout. While in Alaska, he and a friend caught three Alaskan king salmon and smoked one of them in an old refrigerator-turned-smoker. ''It was delicious,'' he recalls. That hooked him on smoked fish.

After college, he studied fisheries and aquaculture at the University of Washington, then headed east to set up his own trout farm in Maine. In 1979, FitzGerald located 30 acres of land beside the Ducktrap River and started his enterprise. He built a make-shift smoker and almost immediately he was smoking trout, mainly as gifts for friends. The result was excellent and the response, tremendous.

In 1983, he traveled to Scotland to learn to smoke salmon their way. And today, Ducktrap is unique in that it offers both Western- and Eastern-style smoked salmon. The first is smoked with a combination of oak, maple, cherry, and apple woods so that the fish, still firm and moist, is also delightfully fruity and not salty. The second, a saltier product, is slightly oilier, but wonderfully delicate.

The tables turned quickly for the young entrepreneur and raising trout is now a hobby, and the smoker has become the business. FitzGerald has replaced the ''funky wooden thing'' he once used to smoke fish with a fancy imported smoker, and Ducktrap River Fish Farm smokes some 200,000 pounds of the freshest fish imaginable each year. The product list varies from trout to bluefish, pollock, haddock, mahi mahi, mackerel, scallops, tuna, monkfish, shrimp, and mussels. Many are Maine and New England seafoods; still others are brought in from the far corners of the world.

FitzGerald's secret for success is to produce a light smoky flavor with fruit woods and native hardwoods, while retaining the taste of the fish. ''Otherwise, why fool around with $12-a-pound scallops? You might as well chew on a hickory log,'' says FitzGerald.

HOW TO PURCHASE: Smoked Eastern Salmon sides (2–2½ lbs. sell for $59.50; Smoked Western Salmon sides (same size) are $53.50. A box of six 6-oz. smoked trout costs $29.50 and 1 dozen is $42.50. It's best to check with Ducktrap before ordering as price change seasonally. Costs include shipping and handling which i U.P.S. Second Day Air or Federal Express. Packages arrive packed in branded wooden boxes inside insulated containers. Ducktrap accepts Visa and MasterCard.

Pasta with Smoked Salmon and Cream Sauce

This is a light pasta dish made even more so by adding delicate tasting smoked salmon from Ducktrap. Serve as a main course or an appetizer.

4 cups broccoli florets
2 cups carrots, peeled and cut in julienne strips
2 tablespoons unsalted butter
2 large cloves of garlic, minced
2 cups heavy cream
1 teaspoon black pepper
Juice of ½ lemon
6 oz. Ducktrap Smoked Eastern Salmon, cut into
*   thin strips*
12 oz. fresh fettuccini or linguine, cooked

1. Cook the broccoli for 2½ minutes in lightly salted boiling water Drain and rinse under cold water; then drain and reserve. Repeat with the carrots.

2. In a large sauté pan melt the butter and add the garlic. Sauté for 30 seconds. Add the cream and the pepper and simmer until liquid is reduced by ½ cup. Add the lemon juice and the smoked salmon and simmer 1 minute. Add the vegetables and stir to heat. Add the pasta and stir to coat with sauce. Transfer to a serving platter and serve.

Serves 8.

Smoked Fish

HORTON'S DOWNEAST FOODS, INC. P.O. Box 430, Waterboro, Maine 04087 207/247-6900.

Don and Jean Horton's business is going up in smoke, and they couldn't be happier! The Hortons operate a thriving business that specializes in smoked seafood.

Don Horton, a Rhode Island native with a doctorate in marine biology, moved to Maine with his wife Jean in 1975 so he could take a job as director of the Research Institute of the Gulf of Maine, a consortium of educational institutions devoted to marine research. He had a hand in creating the Portland Aquarium before he decided to give up working as an oceanographer to start his own business.

Given their proximity to some of the world's finest seafood and growing demand for smoked fish in gourmet food circles, the Hortons decided on a fish smoking business. In 1983, they launched Horton's Downeast Foods. Unlike some of the old-fashioned stone smokehouses of yesteryear, the Horton's operation is neither quaint nor antique. The couple built a fancy 7,000-square-foot smokehouse, and Don purchased a $50,000 stainless steel smoker that's the size of two refrigerators.

The idea behind all this state-of-the-art equipment, with a control board that looks like the controls on a spaceship, is to keep the flavor from going up in smoke. The moisture content is perhaps the most vital factor in smoking fish and the temperature must be readjusted for each variety (halibut, for example, requires 3 hours of smoking while shrimp and mussels need less than an hour). Horton determined just the proper amount of brine and smoking for each type of fish through trial and error. He varies the type of wood according to the natural flavor of the fish. The more delicate-tasting fish are smoked with the more fragrant woods such as apple. Stronger flavored fish, such as bluefish, are smoked with hickory.

Although they try to use as much locally caught fish as possible, the year-round supply of Maine seafood hasn't been enough to support what's become a quarter-of-a-million dollar enterprise. Fresh salmon is flown in from Norway, trout from Idaho, and scallops are sometimes flown in from Peru. Items such as bluefish, mussels, and finnan haddie (smoked haddock) are local. The smoking couple have also added a line of fish pâtés—seafood, whitefish, bluefish, trout, mackerel, and tuna.

HOW TO PURCHASE: Boneless smoked trout (6–9 oz.) is $8. Atlantic smoked salmon is $16.50, and Western smoked salmon is $14.50. Smoked bluefish costs $5.25. Finnan haddie is $8. Smoked shrimp and scallops are both $17. Smoked mussels sell for $9.25. Pâtés range from $7.50 to $9.25 and are sold in 3- and 5-oz., 1-, 2-, and 3-lb. containers. All prices are per pound. Shipping is extra based on destination. U.P.S. is used within New England; items are sent Federal Express elsewhere.

Spinach Roulade with Smoked Scallop Mousse

This rich appetizer was created by well-known caterer and cookbook author Francine Scherer, who first introduced it at her New York Soho Charcuterie and now makes it for customers at her new specialty foods shop, FOODWORKS, in New Milford, Connecticut. We're including it here with much thanks.

> ¾ lb. spinach leaves, washed, stems removed
>   (1½ packages of frozen chopped spinach (10 oz.)
>   may be substituted)
> ¼ lb. unsalted butter, in all
> Salt to taste
> Freshly ground pepper to taste
> 3½ tablespoons vegetable oil
> 5 tablespoons unbleached flour
> 2 cups heavy cream
> 1 tablespoon Dijon mustard
> 1 teaspoon fresh thyme leaves, chopped
> ¼ teaspoon freshly grated nutmeg
> 6 extra-large eggs, separated
> 6 tablespoons grated Parmesan cheese, in all

Scallop Mousse

> 8 oz. Horton's smoked scallops, feet removed
> 8 oz. cream cheese, softened to room temperature
> 1½ tablespoons horseradish
> Juice of ½ lemon
> Freshly ground pepper

1. In a large frying pan, sauté the spinach leaves in 3 tablespoons of butter and a dash of salt and pepper, just until wilted but still bright green. Drain and cool; then squeeze out all the liquid. Finely chop and reserve.

2. Preheat oven to 350°F. Grease a jelly roll pan with half the oil. Line with parchment or waxed paper. Grease the paper with the rest of the oil. In a medium saucepan, melt 5 tablespoons of butter. Whisk in the flour and stir constantly to blend. Cook 2 minutes over medium heat. Gradually add the cream, whisking while it's added. Whisk in the mustard and seasonings and cook several minutes. Remove from the heat and whisk in the egg yolks, one at a time. Add 4 tablespoons of cheese and the spinach and mix.

3. Beat the whites until they form soft peaks that hold their shape. Gently fold into the spinach mixture until no white streaks are visible. Pour the roulade mixture into the prepared pan. Spread out evenly with a spatula. Bake 25–30 minutes or until puffed and springy. Remove from oven and immediately turn onto a towel or cloth napkin that's been sprinkled with the remaining 2 tablespoons cheese. Peel away the parchment paper. Fold the edge of the towel over one of the long sides of the roulade and gently roll the roulade in the cloth. Let cool completely at room temperature before unrolling and filling.

4. In a food processor fitted with a steel knife, purée the scallops. Add the remaining mousse ingredients and purée until blended. Unroll the roulade and spread the scallop mixture over it in a thin, even layer. Trim the edges, as they tend to be dry. Reroll as tightly as possible and cut into ½- to ¾-inch slices. If this is not going to be served immediately, rewrap in the towel and cover with plastic wrap. Store in the refrigerator and slice when ready to serve.

Yields 10–15 slices.

KOHN'S SMOKEHOUSE, INC. CR 35, Box 160, Thomaston, Maine 04861. 207/372-8412

Prying off the lid of a well-nailed rectangular wooden box seemed a bit like opening a pirate's treasure. And, indeed, the contents made us feel as if we'd captured a precious cargo. Perched on a long wooden board and encased in yards of plastic wrap was a wonderful reddish brown Maine lobster just smoked by Ute Kohn the night before.

A subtle smoky flavor mingled with the moist, lightly cooked lobster meat so that even a purist would be pleased. Although Maine lobster smoked in the shell may be the *pièce de résistance* in Ute and Dietrich Kohn's smokehouse repertoire, it is only one of a long list of products they make — wursts, local fish, poultry, and cheese among them.

The Kohns emigrated to Maine from Germany in 1975, with "no plans to open a business." But the two missed the smoked foods they had eaten at home, so they made a small wooden smoker and began smoking their own specialties. They followed family recipes from Dietrich's father, who had owned a butcher shop and smokehouse in East Prussia. Soon they were sharing their delicacies with friends and neighbors, who encouraged them to go into business. In 1979, that's exactly what they did.

Today Kohn's Smokehouse, which does not advertise beyond the local area, has a following that extends throughout the United States and some foreign countries. Products are smoked with a variety of hard and fruit woods. (They get the wood chips from nearby boat-building shops.) And they use no preservatives in most items. A light hand on both the salt and the smoke enhances the natural flavor of the products rather than overwhelming it.

But first the meat is soaked in brine (a secret recipe of salt, water, and herbs) or injected with a little salt for better curing. Each type of product requires a different amount of smoking time. Fish take a few hours, but a salami or sausage may hang in one of the three smoking lockers for up to a week. Sometimes it's more than a full-time job. The smoking chambers must be checked regularly, even throughout the night, to make sure the temperature is just right. Everything is federally inspected, and the smoking process must be closely monitored.

Ute's favorite product is the smoked eel, which she says unsuspecting customers usually vote for as well, if they don't know what they are tasting. Her second choice is the chicken, a very juicy, lightly smoked product. But there are so many others, and a list of specials is always posted on the blackboard out by the road. The Kohns will also custom smoke anything. They've even smoked an entire moose from a local hunt.

HOW TO PURCHASE: All Kohn's Smokehouse products are available by mail. A 5-lb. pork and beef salami is $31; smoked Atlantic mussels cost $10.50 for two 8-oz jars; a box of 6 rainbow trout is $21; and smoked chicken is $13.50 per bird. The smoked lobster, eel, and salmon are available at seasonal prices. Items are shipped in pine boxes. Shipping is by U.P.S. and depends on location. To order, call or write for current brochure. Orders must be prepaid with check or money order to Kohn's Smokehouse. MasterCard and Visa are accepted.

Smoked Lobster with Tarragon-Lemon Mayonnaise

This heavenly combo makes an appetizer you won't soon forget.

4 Kohn's Smoked Maine Lobsters

Mayonnaise

1 large egg plus 1 egg yolk
2 teaspoons Dijon mustard
4 tablespoons freshly squeezed lemon juice
Pinch of salt
Freshly ground white pepper
2 ½ cups oil (combine olive and vegetable oils)
⅓ cup fresh tarragon, finely chopped
Lemon slices for garnish

1. In a food processor with a steel blade attached, combine egg, yolk, mustard, half the lemon juice, salt, and pepper. Process 1 minute.
2. With motor running, add ¼ cup of the oil through the feed tube, a drop at a time, until the mixture thickens. Add remaining oil in a thin, steady stream. Add tarragon and remaining lemon juice and pulse to mix.
3. Serve a generous dollop of the mayonnaise with each lobster and garnish plates with lemon slices. Keep leftover mayonnaise in the refrigerator.

Serves 4.

Freshly Killed Rabbits/Rabbit Pot Pies

PINEBROOK RABBIT PROCESSING. Box 2665, Sam Allen Road, Sanford, Maine 04073. 207/324-3390.

Frank and Sally Higgins lived on a 270-acre farm in western Maine where they raised every kind of animal imaginable (and three children, besides). When the children grew up and moved away, the farm seemed too big. So Sally, who had been raising sheep, and Frank, who was in the commercial interior and cabinet-making business, bought a smaller (15-acre) farm.

Sally gave up the sheep when they moved, and soon Frank turned his business over to one of his sons. Then the two joined forces with another couple, Pat and Robert Winslow, and began raising rabbits. They turned the Higgins barn into a rabbitry and a large processing plant. Now they are knee-deep in the bunny business.

Sally says they are easier to raise than sheep. "You don't have to sit up [all night] when they foal," explains the surrogate mother of these many hundred furry creatures and the person who now has complete charge of the rabbitry.

The two couples began with a zero population of bunnies in 1983. And the demand for their product caught them a little by surprise. In 1986 they sold 60,000 pounds of rabbit. By 1987, that figure was well over 100,000, and it continues to "multiply like rabbits" each year.

Perhaps part of the new-found popularity for rabbit meat is its high nutritional value, low level of cholesterol, and significant amounts of vitamin B-12. Unlike wild rabbit, which tends to be tough and stringy, Pinebrook farm-raised, grain-fed rabbits are lean, tender, and more delicate tasting. They should be cooked like veal or chicken instead of being cooked interminably as was done in the past with the strong-flavored wild animals.

Pinebrook Rabbit Processing sells rabbits whole and dressed, or cut into six pieces, much like a frying chicken. They also make and sell frozen Rabbit Pot Pies, a good old Yankee tradition with a new kind of meat. Their primary customers are restaurants and gourmet stores, but a burgeoning mail order business is becoming a large part of the operation. When Pinebrook rabbits appear on the menu of a restaurant or someone buys a Pinebrook Rabbit Pot Pie, the response has been overwhelming.

For one ex-cabinet maker and his former sheep-rearing wife, the rabbit business seems to be one hoppin' success.

HOW TO PURCHASE: Whole or cut-up rabbits (average 2 ½ to 3 lbs.) sell for $2.75 per lb. Rabbits are shipped fresh inside New England and frozen to locations outside the area. Rabbit Pot Pies (13 oz.) are $8.67 for 3 pies and $16.74 for 6. Pies are shipped frozen. Postage is extra and based on destination. Products are sent U.P.S. or Federal Express. To order, write or call Frank and Sally Higgins. Orders must be prepaid with a check or money order made out to Pinebrook Rabbit Processing.

Rabbit in Mustard Sauce

This wonderful rabbit stew makes a hearty winter meal. It is equally tasty with chicken or veal.

> 1 Pinebrook rabbit in 6 pieces (about 2 ½ lbs.)
> 2 tablespoons butter
> 1 tablespoon vegetable oil
> 4 oz. bacon, diced
> 3 medium onions, peeled and cut into thin wedges
> 4 large carrots, peeled and cut into 1-inch pieces
> 1 tablespoon potato starch
> ½ cup Pommery mustard or other whole grain
>   mustard
> 2 cups dry white wine
> ½ teaspoon dried thyme leaves
> 1 bay leaf
> 2 sprigs of parsley
> Salt and freshly ground black pepper
> ½ cup sour cream

1. In a large casserole, brown the rabbit parts in the butter and oil. Remove to a platter and reserve. Add the bacon and cook about 2 minutes. Discard all but 2 tablespoons of fat. Add the onions and brown with the bacon over medium heat about 5 minutes. Add the carrots and sauté for 1 minute. Remove to the platter with a slotted spoon.

2. Return the rabbit to the casserole, sprinkle with potato starch, and mix. Add mustard and stir until rabbit and vegetables are coated. Add wine, herbs, salt, and pepper and cover the casserole. Simmer over medium-low heat for 1 hour or until meat is tender. Stir occasionally to prevent sticking. Remove the bay leaf and the parsley and discard. Mix in sour cream and serve.

Serves 6.

Blackstrap Bacon

SMITH'S LOG SMOKEHOUSE. Back Brooks Road, Brooks, Maine 04921. 207/525-4418.

In a modest log smokehouse in rural Maine, Andy and Kay Smith are making some of the best-tasting bacon this side of heaven. A blackstrap bacon that's slightly sweet and wonderfully smoky, this one's marinated in molasses, spices, and salt for a week before it's smoked with hickory wood and corncobs. The pork slabs are finally taken down and finished off by aging them in a cold drying room for 24 hours.

The Smiths created their bacon almost by accident. They were entered in a fair that prohibited selling products with nitrites and sugar. So the couple developed a bacon that would conform to the fair rules, and in doing so, their blackstrap bacon was born.

The Smith family moved to the Maine woods from Philadelphia in the late 1960s to live off the land. Today the wood for the smoker is still cut on their property and hauled by horse to the smokehouse. Smoke is produced in a wood stove and piped into the rafters of the log building, where hams and sausages hang from the roof.

In addition to blackstrap bacon, the Smiths also make a delicious blackstrap ham that's won them praise and honors from chefs and food critics. They make several delightful sausages, too. Included are some that are unique to the New England smokehouse industry — thuringer and Sheboygan (two soft German sausages) and a spiced ham roll which is a chunky Ukrainian sausage that comes from a recipe given to Andy by a retired butcher. They also make a fine prosciutto that's slowly smoked, then aged for 45 days.

All Smith Log Smokehouse products are made with all-natural ingredients and no chemicals added. Smith uses only Maine hogs and they, too, are "all-natural."

Although pork is their main product, Smith and his family have smoked everything (and we mean *everything*) from goat to moose to bear. Smoked bear spareribs are the ultimate treat, according to Andy Smith. But we'll be sticking to blackstrap bacon, thank you very much!

HOW TO PURCHASE: A 12-oz. package of Blackstrap Bacon is $2.99. Blackstrap Ham, a boneless ham weighing on average 5–8 lbs., is $5 per lb. Sheboygan in a 12-oz. package is $2.90. Thuringer (8 oz.) sells for $1.95. Spiced Ham Roll comes sliced in an 8-oz. package for $2.60. Prosciutto is $6.50 per lb. (5–8 lb. apiece) and must be special ordered. (Allow 1 month preparation time.) Shipping is extra and based on destination. Check, money order, Visa, or MasterCard accepted.

Spicy New England Corn Pudding

This recipe was inspired by a great friend and chef, Steve Kantrowitz who makes the "World's Best Cornbread" (page 28) which is used here.

> ½ recipe World's Best Cornbread, 6 cups of crumbs
> 1 cup chopped Smith's Blackstrap Bacon
> 1 cup diced red pepper
> 1 cup diced onion
> 1½ cups fresh or frozen corn kernels
> 1½ teaspoons dried, crumbled rosemary
> 1½ teaspoons dried thyme leaves
> 1½ teaspoons dried oregano
> 2 cups heavy cream
> 1½ cups chicken stock
> 2 teaspoons Tabasco sauce
> 2 teaspoons freshly ground black pepper
> Salt to taste
> 8 eggs, lightly beaten

1. Grind the cornbread into breadcrumbs in a food processor. Reserve. Sauté the bacon in a large skillet until cooked but not crisp. Remove bacon with a slotted spoon and drain on paper towels. Pour off all but 2 tablespoons of the rendered fat. Sauté the pepper and onion in remaining fat until soft. Add the corn kernels and herbs and sauté 1 minute. Remove from heat.

2. Preheat oven to 325°F. In a medium saucepan, bring the cream and stock to a boil and remove from the heat. In a large mixing bowl, combine cornbread crumbs with the sautéed vegetables and bacon and toss well. Add the hot liquid, Tabasco, pepper, and salt and mix well. Add the eggs and blend.

3. Butter an oven-proof 8-cup shallow baking dish and turn the pudding mixture into it. Set dish in a baking pan and half-fill with hot water. Set in center of the oven and bake 50–60 minutes or until pudding is set. Remove from water bath and serve warm.

Serves 12.

MASSACHUSETTS

Clambakes to Go

CLAMBAKES TO GO!
THE CLAMBAKE COMPANY, INC.
P.O. BOX 1677, ORLEANS, MA. 02653

THE CLAMBAKE COMPANY. P.O. Box 1677, Orleans, Massachusetts 02653. 1/800-423-4038 or 508/255-3289 in Massachusetts.

"Even when New Englanders move away, they never lose their yearning for a clambake," says co-owner of the Clambake Company Juki Ritchie. Thanks to that tie, the Clambake Company has blossomed from a tiny seed into an impressive business that has even been featured on the cover of a Neiman-Marcus Gourmet Gift Catalog.

Started in 1983 by Eric Blomberg, Clambakes to Go was originally founded to satisfy the hankering of summering folks on Cape Cod who would pick up the ready-made clambakes. Blomberg had plenty of previous experience in the clambake business, having learned because "my father did them for people and I was the cheapest labor in town," says the native Cape Codder.

When Federal Express made overnight delivery possible, Ritchie, with partner Blomberg, saw great prospects for a mail order business. Today most of their business is done that way. "The biggest market outside New England is the West Coast," says Ritchie, who surmises that's because so many East Coast people have relocated here.

These seafood feasts arrive as a complete package, in large gold-colored aluminum containers, with directions for cooking and eating. The size of the barrel depends on the number of people it's intended to feed. The container, lid and all, is set over high heat until it begins to steam. The heat is lowered, and about 30 minutes later, these succulent sea morsels are ready to eat.

The clambake contains not only the requisite (per person) lobster and clams, but red potatoes, Italian sausage, mussels, corn on the cob, a huge sweet onion, and a parchment-encased fillet of cod. This massive feast is packed in seaweed. The food is always fresh; if a doubting customer should peek before cooking, he or she would find lively lobsters kicking underneath this web of green.

The perfect gift for someone who has everything, Clambakes to Go are particularly popular for Christmas giving, New Year's Eve parties, or really anytime a New Englander has a yen for one. It's a great idea for a romantic couple, although they are actually more economical for three or more (that's when the price per person drops). Customers choose their own time and place for receiving their clambake. These details are carefully checked with the customer before the product is shipped to make sure there is someone home to receive it.

If this seems like a frivolous, self-indulgent purchase that would appeal only to a few, think again. During the busy seasons (summer and the Christmas holidays), the Clambake Company sells between 300 and 500 clambakes a week!

HOW TO PURCHASE: A clambake for one person is $60. For two, the cost is $100. At three or more people, the clambake is an additional $35 per person. That means for ten persons a clambake costs $38 per person or a total of $380. Prices include packaging and shipping; however, there is an additional charge of $20 for Saturday delivery. All clambakes are shipped Federal Express. The best way to order is by calling the toll-free number. All major credit cards are accepted.

Maine Lobster Stew

Growing up in Maine meant frequent lobster feeds with friends and relatives lined up along plastic-cloth covered tables with stacks of 3- and 4-pound lobsters and a pile of steamed clams in the center. We would eat for hours, then the kids would dissect every morsel of the remaining lobsters for the next day's lobster stew. Today, lobsters are rationed carefully at our clambakes, and there are seldom any leftovers. If, by chance, there are at yours, quickly put them in a stew and eat it up!

> 1¼ lbs. cooked lobster meat, cut into
> bite-size pieces
> 4 tablespoons unsalted butter
> 6 cups whole milk
> 2 cups half and half
> Salt and pepper to taste

In a medium saucepan, sauté the lobster in the butter for 2 to 3 minutes over low heat. Add the remaining ingredients and heat until the mixture is steaming. Serve, or better yet, refrigerate for at least 8 hours and reheat gently before serving. Serve with oyster crackers or warm rolls.

Serves 6.

Linguiça & Chouriço

GASPAR'S SAUSAGE COMPANY. P.O. Box 436, North Dartmouth, Massachusetts 02747. 1/800-542-2038 or 508/998-2012 in Massachusetts.

Over the last century, immigrants from Portugal traveled to this country, settling chiefly in the fishing villages of Rhode Island, southeastern Massachusetts, and parts of Connecticut. With these settlers came cherished memories and customs from their homeland, including the tradition of sausage-making. Each family had its own secret blend of ingredients that gave a personal seal to their epicurean treasures. Not surprisingly, no two family recipes were alike, and the "art" was a fiercely guarded secret. Manuel Gaspar was one of those artists.

He came to this country from Lisbon in 1912 and became a partner in the Hendricks Linguiça Company of East Providence, Rhode Island. In 1927, Gaspar started making his own linguiça and chouriço (pronounced *lin-gwee-sah* and *shoor-reese*) in the garage of his home. Today this family-owned business is the largest manufacturer of Portuguese sausage in the country, and the name Gaspar is synonymous with Portuguese sausage around southern New England.

Three generations of Gaspars have joined the family business, and the company still follows the sausage recipe that originally belonged to the patriarch's wife, Justina—coarsely ground, lean fresh pork, combined with a spice blend that includes vinegar, salt, garlic, and paprika. Left to marinate overnight, the meat is stuffed into natural casings and smoked over a hardwood fire the next day. This is the formula for making linguiça, but the chubbier chouriço follows much the same method, except that hot chili pepper is added.

Gaspar's products are sold primarily in New England. But they also ship to Bermuda (where there is a small Portuguese settlement) and to a growing clientele in south and central Florida, popularized by a homesick New Bedford woman who had moved there. The company mails orders all over the country.

HOW TO PURCHASE: Gaspar's sells a combination of linguiça and chouriço in 3-lb. minimum orders at a cost of $3.75 per pound. A 4-lb. sausage assortment is sold for $14.95. It includes linguiça franks (small links of linguiça) or linguiça slices (patties) in addition to the other two. An 8-lb. assortment of the same is $28.95. Specify how you would like the selections broken down for either. All prices include shipping. Gift packages may be ordered. Payment is by check, money order, Visa, or MasterCard.

Kale & Potato Soup

A Portuguese classic, kale soup would not be the same without slices of linguiça or chouriço to give it an Old World taste.

> ¾ lb. Gaspar's linguiça or chouriço
> 1 lb. beef shank
> 8 cups water
> 1 large onion, peeled and chopped
> 1 teaspoon crushed red pepper
> 1 teaspoon salt
> 1 bunch kale, rinsed, stems removed and discarded, leaves coarsely shredded (2 boxes frozen kale may be substituted)
> 3 large potatoes, peeled and diced

1. Place the linguiça or chouriço in a medium skillet. Prick 2 or 3 times with a fork. Cover with water and simmer 15 minutes. Remove and drain on paper towels until cool. Slice into ¼-inch rounds and reserve. In a large pot, add the meat and the water and bring to a boil. Skim the top and add the onion, pepper, and salt. Cover and simmer until meat is nearly tender (about 1½ hours).

2. Add potatoes and cook until potatoes are tender. Remove the shank bones. Remove the meat and reserve. Discard the bones. Break the potatoes into small pieces with the back of a slotted spoon until they are half-mashed. Add the kale, the sausage, and the meat to the soup. Bring to a boil and simmer 15 minutes. Add more salt and pepper if desired.

Serves 8.

GREEN ACRES TURKEY FARM

ROUTE 121 - WEST STREET
WRENTHAM, MASSACHUSETTS

REEN ACRES TURKEY FARM. 566 West Street, Route
21, Wrentham, Massachusetts 02093. 617/384-2441.

When Dick Boudreau realized that people were paying more
tention to their appetites than to their educations, he resigned as
resident of Fisher College in Boston and bought a working turkey
rm in neighboring Wrentham in 1984. Affectionately dubbed the
Turkey Hilton'' by the former academician, Boudreau began by
st raising turkeys. Soon he saw a demand for other poultry and
ded poussin (young, tiny chickens with almost no fat), geese, and
cks. He has a virtual corner on the market for the first. To date,
reen Acres is one of the few eastern farms to raise poussin.

Boudreau also had a feeling that a market for smoked birds could
e cultivated among the many upscale restaurateurs in the Boston
ea. And smoking seemed like a natural avenue of growth for a busi-
ss that already handled fresh poultry. Boudreau set up a smoke-
ouse where he processes all the types of birds he grows and some
e doesn't raise on the farm—pheasant and duck among them.

His smoked poultry is cured in a light brine and smoked with
ple wood. It produces a sweet and mild flavor that's a perfect
omplement to the delicate taste of poultry. ''The secret is the spices
the brine,'' claims Boudreau. But there may be more to it. All
e birds he raises (some 20,000 each year) are fed a blend of grains
d slaughtered at a young age, when the meat is at its tenderest.
e doesn't believe in using additives or hormones, or injecting water
to smoked products.

Boudreau also operates a barn kitchen on the farm where home-
oked country foods such as turkey pie, apple crisp, and baked
quash are sold. An unfancy cook by his own estimation, he makes
d sells his own very good, fancy pâté. There's also a small petting
o on the farm where goats, ponies, and other animals delight the
ung visitors.

In addition to a mail order business (smoked products only),
oudreau is a major supplier of fresh and smoked poultry to some
f the finest Boston restaurants, including Jasper's, Four Seasons,
ostonian, and Upstairs at the Pudding. So, if you happen to dine
a Boston eatery, and you're served poussin, goose, baby turkey,
smoked duck or pheasant, it just might be one of Boudreau's.

HOW TO PURCHASE: Green Acres Turkey Farm smoked poultry
can be purchased by mail. A smoked turkey (about 12 lbs.) is $21.99;
pheasant (about 4 lbs.) is $19.99; boneless turkey breast is $5.75
per lb.; duck is $9.95 per bird; chicken is $4.99; poussin (about
16 oz. each) costs $2.90; and smoked goose (about 10 lbs.) is
$39.90. Shipping and handling are by Parcel Post and included in
the price. Orders must be paid in advance by check or money order.

Smoked Turkey Pâté

This pâté is one that Dick Boudreau whips up for a crowd. Even
for a small group, we find it disappears quickly.

3 lbs. Green Acres smoked turkey breast
1 lb. boneless pork shoulder
1 lb. salt pork (excess salt washed away)
2 tablespoons unsalted butter
6 large shallots, peeled and chopped
2 carrots, peeled and chopped
6 oz. roasted cashews
1 bunch fresh sage, stemmed and chopped
½ bunch fresh parsley, stemmed and chopped
6 sprigs of fresh thyme, stemmed and chopped
¼ cup Chardonnay or other dry white wine
½ cup heavy cream
3 eggs, lightly beaten
Salt and freshly ground black pepper to taste

1. In a meat grinder, grind the turkey, pork shoulder, and half the
salt pork. In a large sauté pan, melt the butter over medium-low
heat. Add the shallots, the carrots, and the cashews and sauté until
shallots are soft, but not brown. Add the fresh herbs and the wine
and simmer for 2 minutes. Remove from heat and mix with the
ground meat. Put the mixture through the meat grinder again. Add
the cream, eggs, and salt and pepper and mix.
2. Preheat an oven to 350°F. Cut the remaining salt pork into thin
sheets and line an 8-cup mold with it. Pack the meat mixture into
the mold and smooth the top. Set in the center of a roasting pan
that's half filled with hot water and bake 1 hour or until a meat
thermometer inserted in the center reaches 115°F. Remove from oven
and turn onto a serving platter. Chill. Remove the strips of salt pork
just before serving.

*Serves 40–50 as an appetizer with crackers or slices of French
bread.*

Fresh Dressed & Smoked Trout

RED-WING MEADOW FARM, INC. 187 North Main Street, Sunderland, Massachusetts 01375. 413/665-3295.

Ken Bergstrom, a man with marketing savvy and a keen sense of trends in food, had a game plan when he opened Red-Wing Meadow Farm in 1984. He wanted to stock and sell live or very fresh dressed trout to a growing market of individuals who want to eat more fish.

Back then, Bergstrom was doing some part-time farming but had his eye on a 100-acre parcel of land in Sunderland (just next door to Amherst). As a former teacher and environmentalist who had studied wildlife biology as a graduate student, he'd been inching his way toward some kind of farming for a while. He bought the land, which included three ponds, a stream, an artesian well, and plenty of hay fields and started raising trout and hay.

A year later, when a local newspaper reported on Bergstrom and his trout farm, he got a call from a neighbor asking if he'd like to buy the man's trout farm. They met that day. Bergstrom was running the farm by the end of the week and owned the property in Montague 2 weeks later.

Complete with a hatchery, pools where people can catch their own trout, and well-stocked ponds, Bergstrom is supplying some 25,000 pounds of rainbow, brook, and brown trout to restaurants and individuals each year. He anticipates sales will be up to 40,000 pounds very shortly and in the 100,000-pound range by the early 1990s.

But trout is just the beginning for Bergstrom, who also hopes to raise catfish, striped bass, and Koi, a highly prized, oversized Japanese goldfish. His plans include setting up a smokehouse to add smoked trout and striped bass as well as other fish to his product list. He is also planning to add a lobster pool and a farm stand in the very near future.

Even now the catch-your-own fish is catching on. The well-stocked ponds in a tranquil setting complete with picnic benches make for an enjoyable outing and near certain success in the fishing department.

"I always knew I'd end up raising fish," says the naturalist who loves working for himself.

HOW TO PURCHASE: A package of 4 fresh, dressed trout (about 12 oz. each) is $20 plus shipping. A package of 6 smoked trout is mailed for $25 plus shipping. Packages are sent U.P.S. overnight delivery. Orders must be prepaid with check or money order.

TO VISIT: Take exit 24 (Route 116) off Interstate 91. Follow Route 116 toward Amherst. Red-Wing Meadow Farm is at the Sunderland/Amherst town line.

Trout in Orange Herb Sauce

We first encountered the bearded Ken Bergstrom dishing out samples of his trout in this luscious sauce at a local food fair.

4 fresh, dressed Red-Wing trout (about 12 oz. each)
2 tablespoons fresh chopped parsley
2 tablespoons fresh chopped tarragon
2 tablespoons fresh chopped thyme
¼ lb. unsalted butter, melted
1 teaspoon paprika
1 oz. dry sherry
Juice of 1 orange
1 tablespoon orange zest
Extra chopped parsley for garnish

1. Leave trout whole and cut 3 diagonal slices on top side of each fish. Combine the chopped herbs and sprinkle into the slices.
2. Preheat oven to 350°F. Butter a baking dish and set the fish in it. Combine the butter, paprika, sherry, and orange juice. Pour over the fish and bake 20 to 30 minutes or until done.
3. Transfer fish to a serving platter and sprinkle with orange zest and extra chopped parsley.

Serves 4.

Smoked European Wurst & Sausage

SMOKEHOUSE, INC. 15 Coventry Street, Roxbury, Massachusetts 02119. 617/442-6840.

When Victor Nosiglia's son Dave announced that he did not want to go to college, Nosiglia insisted he learn a trade. The young man chose one that doesn't attract many Americans. He learned the art of sausage-making and spent 3 years as an apprentice to a master butcher in Germany perfecting that skill. When he returned, the senior Nosiglia decided to go out of his business as an importer of sausage equipment and team up with his son to make sausages.

The result was Smokehouse, Inc., started in 1982 in Hyannis. The two set out to make top quality European-style wurst and sausages. But the Nosiglias discovered that Cape Cod wasn't their market and moved the small venture to Roxbury in 1985.

The father-son team started with German knockwurst, weisswurst, bauernwurst, and the like. Their first major customer was Jacob Wirth's, a German restaurant and Boston landmark. They've since added many other customers—Commonwealth Brewery in Boston, Panache in Cambridge, and Al Forno's in Providence among them. Since the Smokehouse does not advertise, business began slowly until word of their products got out.

Soon customers were offering suggestions for other types of sausage, and today the Smokehouse offers an international selection from English-style bangers to Italian hot, mild, and garlic sausage to andouille, a Cajun specialty. There's also a jalapeno pepper sausage and a tomato sausage that's 25 percent diced fresh tomato.

In addition to some twenty kinds of wurst and sausage, Nosiglia and his son produce smoked hams, turkey, duck, chicken, pheasant, goose, and several varieties of bacon. Their products can be ordered with or without nitrites.

The Nosiglias use a a light hand on the smoking and brine so that products have a subtle smoky flavor. And customers told them they didn't want too much salt, so the Nosiglias took some out. Spices, too, are nicely blended to let you know they are present but not to overpower the meat.

In addition to sales via mail order and restaurants and other retail sales, the duo operates two of their own retail shops. And before long they hope to open a shop in Faneuil Hall, the restored market area near Boston's North End. About half of the Nosiglia clientele is European-born; the other half are "fairly sophisticated," and most have been abroad.

"The sausage is as authentic as you can get," says the junior partner. "You go towards Milwaukee, and you can get a knockwurst or bratwurst outside any sports event, but here all you get is a pretzel or a hot dog," says Dave Nosiglia. "We want to do something about that."

HOW TO PURCHASE: The wurst (including knockwurst, bauernwurst, and Polish) are all $4.70 per lb. Sausages (including garlic, Italian sweet & hot, tomato, and jalapeno) are $4.20 per lb. Wurst and sausages are sold in 5-lb. units. Canadian bacon (3-lb. unit) is $7.80 per lb. Irish bacon is $5.50 per lb. Regular bacon (a 7-lb. unit) is $3.50 per lb. Smoked pork chops (about 4 oz. each) sell for $6.80 per lb. There is a 20-lb. minimum. Prices include shipping. Nitrite-free products are shipped frozen. A check must accompany the order.

Smoked Pork Chops with Apricots and Raisins

A flavorful combination of tastes, this dish may be served with lightly curried rice for a terrific meal.

> 6 Smokehouse, Inc. smoked pork loin chops (about 1½ lbs.)
> 2 tablespoons unsalted butter
> 1 large onion, chopped
> 1 cup apple juice
> ⅓ cup slivered dried apricots
> ⅓ cup raisins
> 1 cup chicken stock
> 1½ teaspoons curry powder
> ½ cup good quality chutney (best is apricot flavored)
> Salt and pepper to taste

1. In a medium sauté pan, brown the chops on both sides in 1 tablespoon of the butter. Remove and reserve. Melt remaining butter and sauté the onion 2 minutes. Add the apple juice and simmer until reduced by half.

2. Add the apricots, raisins, chicken stock, and curry powder and bring to a simmer. Simmer until liquid is reduced by a third. Return the chops to the pan and spoon sauce over them. Cover and cook over low heat for 15 minutes. Uncover and add the chutney and salt and pepper to taste. Simmer uncovered for 10 minutes. Serve at once.

Serves 3–4.

Beef Jerky & Finnan Haddie

NATURAL STYLE
BEEF JERKY
MADE FROM SOLID PIECES OF BEEF

Watson's Smokehouse

WATSON'S SMOKEHOUSE. 546 John Fitch Highway, Fitchburg, Massachusetts 01420. 1/800-876-BEEF (orders only) or 617/345-7800.

Beef jerky just isn't one of those foods most of us crave. It's certainly nothing like chocolate. It isn't even on a par with carrots, squash, or spinach. But Stan Ferrebee, owner of Watson's Smokehouse, makes a beef jerky that is downright habit-forming. "The business built by jerky" is the slogan at Watson's, and sampling his chewy beef strips, it's easy to understand why.

Ferrebee, who thinks of himself as a good smoker but not much of a cook, whips up a magical marinade of soy sauce, wine, and other ingredients then marinates his beef overnight before smoking it into a moist and tangy product. The jerky loses about 50 percent of its weight in the smoking process, but he's figured out how to avoid that shoe-leather texture that makes most beef jerky so unappealing.

Ferrebee got the idea from his father-in-law, who had a small home smoker and a great recipe. He started to make the hickory-smoked beef jerky to give away for Christmas presents. Before they knew it, the stuff caught on and the demand was big.

Ferrebee looked for someone to smoke the meat for them but couldn't find anyone. So, in 1985, he built his own smokehouse and started doing it himself. It's not the kind of old stone smokehouse that the farmers of the past had out behind the barn to process their own meats and bacon. This one is in the Peerless Plaza shopping center right next to a liquor store. Nevertheless, it has a devoted following.

Today Ferrebee smokes about 30 items, including a delightful light, cold-smoked finnan haddie, a good old Yankee tradition that was once done with haddock but now is done primarily with cod. "It has more flavor," says Ferrebee. He also smokes bluefish, salmon, trout, several kinds of sausage, chickens, turkeys, ducks, and geese. But beef jerky still accounts for much of his business. He uses only natural brines and marinades and uses no nitrites in most of his products.

The industrious Ferrebee juggles his smokehouse schedule with his wife's catering business. The two alternate their schedules so that one is always home with their two young children. "I'm trying to take care of my smokehouse and raise a family, too," says the slightly frantic Ferrebee.

He chuckles when he explains how he had to become an expert cook to operate the fancy smokehouse oven but still can't figure out how to use the family stove. "I'm new at this, but my heart's in it," says the jerky king.

HOW TO PURCHASE: All of Ferrebee's products are available by mail. Beef jerky is $20.99 per lb. A half pound is $11.99, and one-quarter pound costs $6.99. Finnan Haddie is $23.99 for about 3 lbs. of fish. (Ferrebee says it's advertised as 2 lbs., but he always throws in extra.)

Finnan Haddie with Cream Sauce

The name, *finnan haddie*, comes from haddock smoked on the seaside banks of Findon, Scotland. It most likely came to New England through Scottish settlers to the Prince Edward Island and Nova Scotia regions of Canada. The traditional dish was introduced into our family by my grandmother, who soaked the fish for hours before she cooked it. This recipe is far simpler owing to a much more lightly smoked fish.

> 2 lbs. Watson's Smokehouse finnan haddie
> 3 tablespoons butter
> 4 tablespoons flour
> 1½ cups milk
> ½ cup heavy cream
> 2 egg yolks
> Salt and pepper to taste
> 2 tablespoons butter
> 1 tablespoon lemon juice
> 3 large potatoes, peeled and boiled
> 3 tablespoons butter
> ⅔ cup heavy cream or milk

1. Simmer the finnan haddie in water (just enough to cover the fish) for 4 minutes. Remove the fish and drain. Break the fish into pieces and line the bottom of a medium baking dish with the flaked fish.
2. In a medium saucepan, melt 3 tablespoons of butter over moderate heat and add the flour. Whisk for 2 minutes, then add the milk, whisking continually until the mixture has thickened. Beat the ½ cup heavy cream with the egg yolks. Add a ladleful of the hot milk to the cream and yolks, whisking to incorporate. Add this back to the hot liquid, while whisking. Add salt and pepper, 2 tablespoons of butter, and the lemon juice. Pour over the fish.
3. Whip the potatoes with butter, ⅔ cup cream, and salt and pepper. Transfer to a pastry bag and pipe around the outer edge of the finnan haddie casserole. Set under the broiler just until the edges of the potato are browned. Serve hot.

Serves 6.

NEW HAMPSHIRE

Smoked Cheeses

 SMOKEHOUSE

NORTH COUNTRY SMOKEHOUSE. Box 1415, Claremont, New Hampshire 03743. 603/542-8323.

Mike Satzow was minding the store at his family's butcher shop when a lady from New York came in and asked for something to take home to remember New England by. Ironically, Satzow recalls, she bought 30 pounds of Hormel meat that was processed in Minnesota!

Then and there he realized there was a market for New England regional foods, and so he opened a smokehouse to smoke hams, poultry, seafood, and cheeses. Satzow uses a maple syrup brine and corncob smoke to produce some specialties that have been called nothing short of extraordinary by food lovers. Now his products are found at Bloomingdale's, Boston's Ritz Carlton, and L. L. Bean in Freeport, Maine.

Satzow started his smokehouse back in 1973. Today he processes 200,000 pounds of smoked meats and cheeses a year. Turkey, duck, pheasant, quail, salmon, trout, scallops, smoked brisket, lamb, and venison, and Polish and Cajun sausage are among the items on his list. Meats are smoked lightly (just 12 hours for a ham) making for a light, juicy meat that has just the hint of sweetness.

Located near the Sugar River in the Lake Sunapee region of New Hampshire, the smokehouse is just across from Claremont's airport in this sleepy town that sits on the boundary of Vermont and New Hampshire. More than once a traveler has stopped in to pick up a North Country Smokehouse product to take home some remembrance of New England. These days they are buying the genuine article—local regional foods.

HOW TO PURCHASE: All North Country Smoked products may be mail ordered. Prices are whole ham, $65; 4-lb. bacon slab, $19; brace of pheasant, $43; turkey breast (5–6 lbs.), $24; whole turkey (10–12 lbs.), $34; sausage products (4 lbs.), $19–$20. A 2½ lb. smoked Mozzarella cheese is $15; a 3-lb. block of Vermont cheddar is $19; and smoked provolone is $5.99 per lb. Prices include shipping which is via U.P.S. To order, send check, money order, or credit card information. Orders may be placed by telephone, and a phone call will give you the latest order forms and price list.

Bean and Smoked Provolone Salad

This lively salad is also very adaptable. It's at home on a buffet table or at a pool party.

> *1 cup fresh green beans, trimmed*
> *1 cup fresh yellow beans, trimmed*
> *1-lb. can of cannellini beans, rinsed and drained*
> *½ lb. North Country smoked provolone*
> *2 tablespoons chopped green onion*
> *1 tablespoon chopped fresh oregano*
> *Salt and pepper to taste*

1. Steam the green and yellow beans until tender but still slightly crunchy (about 4 minutes). Run under cold water to cool. Drain well and cut into 1-inch pieces. In a large serving bowl, combine the green and yellow beans with the cannellini beans.
2. Remove the rind from the cheese and discard. Cut the cheese into bite-size cubes. Add to the bean mixture. Add the onion, oregano, and salt and pepper and toss.

Vinaigrette

> *2 tablespoons red wine vinegar*
> *2 teaspoons Dijon mustard*
> *2 teaspoons mixed Italian herbs*
> *¼ cup extra virgin olive oil*
> *¼ cup vegetable oil*
> *Salt and pepper to taste*

Whisk the vinegar with the mustard. Add the herbs and salt and pepper. Slowly whisk in the olive and vegetable oil. Pour over the bean and cheese mixture and toss to coat. Refrigerate until ready to serve.

Serves 6.

VERMONT

Corncob Smoked Hams

THE HARRINGTON HAM COMPANY. Main Street, Richmond, Vermont 05477. 802/434-3411 or 4444.

For more than a century, Harrington's has been smoking hams over slow fires of corncobs and maplewood to produce a distinctly flavored ham that's moist, tender, and unique and that many think produces a superior taste to the more traditional hickory smoke. Today Harrington's is one of the largest makers of smoked hams outside of Virginia, and its reputation parallels that of any of the southern smokehouses. Its famous hams have been served at the White House and featured on the menus of many fine restaurants and resorts. Harrington's mail order customer list reads like a celebrity showcase.

Harrington's origins go back to 1873, when it was primarily a meat business. Luke Harrington bought the company in 1937 and gave it his name. In the bargain, he got a recipe for smoking hams with corncobs and maple sawdust. The method was invented by the local Indians and copied by the early Vermont settlers. Now it's a closely guarded secret. In fact, the formula for Harrington's smoked hams is kept locked away in a vault, according to company lore.

Harrington's sells some 750,000 pounds of pork per year, yet each ham is handmade with no automation or shortcuts and plenty of individual attention. Hams are carefully trimmed, then treated in a special cure that includes maple syrup. Then each is smoked anywhere from 10 to 18 hours.

Besides hams, Harrington's also cooks turkeys with the same corncob-smoked flavor. They produce several kinds of bacon, such as Canadian and breakfast, and cold smoked Pacific salmon. All are made under the watchful eye of Harrington's Smokemaster Vern Richburg; nothing leaves Harrington's without Richburg's expert say-so.

Harrington's now has six retail shops throughout Vermont, Massachusetts, and Connecticut. But the smallest and most interesting is the shop located atop the smokehouse in Richmond, Vermont. One step inside, and visitors are sure to catch the sweet, smoky aroma of the smokehouse at work.

HOW TO PURCHASE: A Harrington 6-lb, bone-in, uncooked half ham is $39.95 but is often featured as a special for $29.95. The same, but whole ham (10–12 lbs.) is $69.95. Fully-cooked boneless half hams (4½–5½ lbs.) cost $48.25; a whole ham is sold for $86.50. A whole smoked turkey (9–10 lbs.) is $41.95 or $48.75 when ordered with wild rice. Within the continental United States shipping, except express delivery, is included in the price. Harrington's takes all major credit cards.

Cob-smoked Ham with Dates and Raisins

When we served this ham for a New Year's brunch, every morsel was devoured. It was such a hit, it's likely to become a traditional feast to start every year.

> *½ Harrington's cob-smoked, uncooked ham,*
>   *bone-in (6–7 lbs.)*
> *2 tablespoons Dijon mustard*
> *¼ teaspoon ground cloves*
> *1 cup apple juice*
> *½ cup brown sugar*

Sauce

> *1 cup chopped dates*
> *½ cup raisins*
> *¼ cup Port wine*
> *1 cup apple juice*
> *2 tablespoons of cornstarch mixed*
>   *with 2 tablespoons of water*

1. Preheat the oven to 325 °F. Set the ham on a rack in the middle of a roasting pan. Score the ham. Combine the mustard and cloves and brush over the meat. Coat the top and sides with the brown sugar. Pour 1 cup of apple juice into the bottom of the pan. Make a tent with aluminum foil and cover the roasting pan. Bake 1½ hours.

2. Combine the sauce ingredients (except the cornstarch) in a sauce pan and bring to a simmer. Remove from heat and let sit until ham is cooked. Pour the sauce over the ham, replace the tent, and cook 25 minutes longer.

3. Remove the ham to a carving board and let cool 15 minutes before slicing. Transfer sauce to a saucepan. Skim fat from the sauce then bring mixture to a boil. Add the cornstarch mixture. Stir until sauce has thickened. Remove from heat and serve with the ham.

Serves 12–14.

Smoked Fish, Ham & Turkey

LAWRENCE'S SMOKE HOUSE. R.R. #1, Box 28, Route 30, Newfane, Vermont 05345. 802/365-7751.

In the years since Merril Lawrence founded Lawrence's Smoke House in 1930, Lawrence's smokers have carried on a tradition that began before the colonists arrived, when American Indians were smoking fish and meats with corncob.

When sociologists Bill and Mary Erickson bought Lawrence's in 1981 and moved from Manhattan to Newfane, they were excited about their link with the past. They couldn't have been more pleased with the reputation they had also inherited—an old-fashioned smokehouse that stressed quality.

They continue to smoke with corncob chips, a smoke that results in a delicate tasting, moist product. Unlike in the past, however, the corncobs of today are a bit more sanitized and are bought in 50-pound bags.

Particularly known for their hams, Lawrence's uses only top of the line for smoking—the kind of ham without added water—and these are cooked slowly for about a week, using a cold smoke process. Lawrence's hams have won national recognition, including a gold medal from *Food & Wine* magazine and accolades such as "the country classic: heavenly ham" from *Town & Country* magazine.

In addition to many fine pork products, Canadian and regular bacon among them, the Ericksons are producing several new products in response to customer requests. They feature boneless turkey breast, a delightful boneless trout (served as an appetizer at many local inns), salmon that's smoked in an East Indian spice cure (all nitrite-free), and several corncob-smoked cheeses.

The Ericksons invite customers to come visit their Newfane store and see the smokehouse in operation. For those who can't make it, they have an impressive mail order business that guarantees their products to arrive in perfect condition.

HOW TO PURCHASE: Lawrence's includes shipping costs in all their prices, which vary according to destination and weight of products. Half a bone-in ham is $32.95 to $49.95, and size is 4 to 8 lbs. Whole hams are $58.95 to $104.95; weights are from 9 to 20 lbs. Boneless hams are somewhat more expensive. Three trout (6 fillets) sell for $16.95 to 18.95, depending on destination. The price for salmon ranges from $32.95 to $61.95 for a 1- to 3-lb. fish.

Smoked Trout with English Mustard Sauce

At the Old Newfane Inn in Newfane, Vermont, owner and chef Eric Weindl serves Lawrence's fillets of smoked trout with this tangy sauce. It is with thanks to him that we include his recipe for this popular appetizer.

> *8 fillets of Lawrence's smoked trout (4 fish)*
> *2 tablespoons good quality prepared mayonnaise*
> *1 tablespoon sour cream*
> *1 tablespoon dry English mustard*
> *1 tablespoon horseradish*
> *1–2 teaspoons Worcestershire sauce (to taste)*
> *Salt and freshly ground black pepper to taste*
> *4 leaves of red leaf lettuce, washed and dried*
> *4 thin slices of lemon, for garnish*

1. Place the mayonnaise, sour cream, mustard, and horseradish in a blender and blend for 5 to 10 seconds or until combined. Add 1 teaspoon of the Worcestershire sauce and salt and pepper. Blend to combine. Check for seasonings and add more Worcestershire, salt, and pepper, if desired. Chill until needed.
2. Set a leaf of lettuce on each of 4 small plates. Arrange 2 fillets of trout over the lettuce. Spoon ¼ of the sauce over the fish and next to it. Garnish with lemon slices and serve.

Serves 4.

Smoked Hams and Turkeys

THE PORK SCHOP OF VERMONT, INC. P.O. Box 99, Hinesburg, Vermont 05461. 802/482-3617.

In the early 1980s Martha and Joseph Keenan read an article that said most Vermont smokehouses were not using local meats. In fact, they were importing hogs and other meats from such places as Iowa. It seemed to the Keenans there was a perfect niche for a totally local product. If they could buy meats from small regional producers, smoke them, and market the finished product, they'd have quite a business and be helping Vermont farmers and the New England economy at the same time. So the two set about building a business that would produce some of the best smoked foods in New England.

Although the Keenans were both working in the building industry at the time, meat and smokehouse processing were not totally foreign to the enterprising couple. Martha had majored in agriculture and had spent 8 years working on a hog farm in Virginia. The two met Larry and Kimberly Parker, who had a reputation for raising fine hogs, and the four decided to go into business. They put together a business plan, then found both a site for a smokehouse and financing for their enterprise. In March 1985, they opened the Pork Schop in a 2,500-square-foot facility that includes a processing plant, smokehouse, and retail store.

Today the busy smokehouse processes some twenty hogs a week. They start with choice products from a select group of Vermont farmers who raise their animals only on grains and without hormones or additives. The meats are cured with sea salt and maple sugar and smoked naturally over maple wood and corncobs in a slow-smoke fashion. The Pork Schop uses no nitrites or added water weight.

The Keenans' and Parkers' untiring attention to detail and quality has paid off. Where some smoked products actually taste like the dried-up cobs with which they've been smoked, these hams and turkeys are incredibly moist and tender, with a memorable, delicate smoke taste.

Products range from bone-in and boneless hams to bacon and Canadian-style bacon, the Pork Schop's own special country sausage, hot and mild Italian sausage, and Polish kielbasa. Our favorite, surprisingly, for a chiefly pig business, is the plump, succulent, bone-in (just the wishbone, though) and boneless turkey breast. Juicy and tender, this is a taste that's a little bit like Hog Heaven.

HOW TO PURCHASE: All products at the Pork Schop can be mail ordered. The line includes bone-in smoked turkey breast (4–5 lbs for $24.75; boneless turkey breast (3–4 lbs.) is $25. A bone-in maple cured ham (12-lb. minimum) is $54.25 (a half a ham, about 6 lbs. is $30.25). Shipping is included and is by U.P.S. Visa and MasterCard are accepted. Write or call for the latest price list and order forms.

Smoked Turkey Waldorf Salad

This is from a recipe that well-known caterer and cookbook author Francine Scherer introduced at her Soho Charcuterie Restaurant in Manhattan and now makes at her store called FOODWORK in New Milford, Connecticut. When Scherer has the time, she makes a homemade Madeira mayonnaise, but when she's rushed, she uses a good quality commercial product and "doctors" it as we have.

> 1 lb. Pork Schop smoked boneless turkey breast,
>   cut into 1-inch cubes
> 1 medium endive, cut into julienne strips
> 1 apple, peeled and diced
> ¾ cup diced celery
> 1 cup seedless grapes, halved
> ½ cup currants soaked in ¼ cup Madeira wine
>   for 30 minutes then drained
> ⅓ cup walnut or pecan pieces, lightly toasted
> 1 cup good quality mayonnaise
> 1 tablespoon Dijon mustard
> ⅓ cup chutney

Combine turkey, endive, apple, celery, grapes, currants, and nuts in a large mixing bowl. Mix together the mayonnaise, mustard, and chutney and pour over the turkey. Mix well. Chill before serving.

Serves 6.

Smoked Lamb, Lamb Pâtés, Lamb Sausage

VERMONT COUNTRY LAMB, INC. R.F.D. #1, Route 73, Orwell, Vermont 05760. 1/800-527-5313 or 802/948-2294 in Vermont.

The corporate headquarters for one of Vermont's most creative cottage industries isn't a cottage at all, but rather a pre-fab log cabin. In keeping with the do-it-yourself-style of the entire Vermont Country Lamb enterprise, it was built by Michelle DaVia, co-owner of the upscale specialty food company.

The Wrentham, Massachusetts, native bought the sprawling 70-acre SheepShed farm, nestled in the Champlain Valley of Vermont, in 1975. She assembled the simple cabin on the property during weekends off from a full-time job in Boston. Today, what comes out of that rustic setting is some of the finest lamb pâté, lamb sausage, and smoked lamb that's ever been produced in New England.

While working in Bean Town, DaVia met Susan Munger, a New Jersey native and product development manager for Erewhon Natural Foods. The two talked about raising livestock in Vermont, but when DaVia joined forces with Munger in 1983, there was no do-it-yourself manual to help get them started. They researched the options and decided to raise sheep since they were easier to breed and could be sold for meat in 5 months rather than the 2 years required for cattle.

At first, business was confined to supplying whole lambs to fine area restaurants. But the restaurateurs naturally wanted the prime parts, not the shoulders and shanks. One chef suggested the two women turn the less popular cuts into other products and introduced them to a French country lamb pâté, the likes of which they had never tasted.

The two discovered there were plenty of pork and game pâtés on the market, but no one was making one out of lamb. After about a year of experimenting, the two came up with a lamb pâté flavored with pine nuts and Feta cheese, and one with apricots, prunes, and walnuts. They developed a third, equally delicious mousse pâté made with lamb liver, Cognac, spices, and spinach purée.

At the end of 1987, the two introduced yet another unusual and tasty item, Vermont Country Lamb sausage—one with herbs and garlic, and a milder and sweeter version with apple and mint.

Today, Munger handles most of the sales for their products, which are now shipped to every state in the United States. DaVia continues to wield a mean hammer. She has built two barns for the sheep and does all the repairs, bookkeeping, and midwifing for the livestock.

The products are all made from "the best quality" Vermont lamb. More than 300 are raised on their 70-acre farm, and more are bought from other local sheep farmers. "One of our goals is to become the Perdue of the lamb world," says the self-made DaVia. With sales growing at a rate of 100 percent per year, it's entirely possible they will.

HOW TO PURCHASE: All Vermont Country Lamb products are available by mail. Pâté with Pine Nuts & Feta and Pâté with Fruits & Walnuts (about 3.4 lbs. per loaf) are $7.99 per lb. Mousse of Lamb Liver Pâté with Purée of Spinach is $6.99 per lb. (A loaf averages 2.25 lbs.) Smoked Boneless Half Leg of Lamb is $10.99 per lb., and average weight is 1.85 lbs. Lamb Sausages are $8.50 per lb. Shipping is extra and based on destination. Orders must be prepaid by check, money order, MasterCard, or Visa. Allow 2 weeks for delivery.

Smoked Lamb, Orzo & Feta Salad

We had to be physically restrained to prevent us from devouring an entire bowl of Vermont Country Smoked Lamb before we could incorporate it into this salad. Once made, the salad disappeared faster than we could say, "Yum!"

Salad

4 cups Vermont Country Smoked Lamb in ½-inch cubes (about 1¼ lbs.)
1½ cups cooked orzo (about ½ cup raw orzo)
6 oz. Feta cheese in ¼-inch cubes
15-oz. can artichoke hearts, drained and quartered
3 hearts of palm, thinly sliced
2 tablespoons fresh, chopped mint leaves
2 tablespoons fresh, chopped parsley
2 teaspoons fresh, chopped oregano
Generous sprinkling of freshly ground black pepper
Salt to taste

Vinaigrette

½ cup olive oil
4 teaspoons raspberry vinegar
4 teaspoons freshly squeezed lemon juice
1 teaspoon mustard

1 medium head of radicchio, washed and patted dry (to garnish)
½ medium head of Boston lettuce, washed and patted dry (to garnish)

In a large bowl, combine the salad ingredients. Whisk together the ingredients for the vinaigrette, pour over the salad, and toss gently. Arrange lettuce on a serving platter. Spoon salad over bed of lettuce.

Serves 6.

PASTA, SNACKS, SOUPS & BEVERAGES

Chowder and Bisque Concentrates

ABBOTT'S OF NEW ENGLAND. 12 Methodist Street, P.O. Box 1008, New London, Connecticut 06320. 203/447-8373 or 1/800-HOT-SOUP.

Brisk weather and piping hot chowder go together like baked beans and brown bread. A keeper of this New England tradition is Abbott's of New England. Founder Ernie Abbott's products, rich and creamy New England chowder and bisque concentrates, have been around for some 50 years.

In recent years, this Yankee institution fell on hard times, however. When John Laundon bought the company in November 1979, it was in danger of crumbling. Laundon had no doubt he had bought a fine product—Ernie Abbott had seen to that. His additive- and preservative-free soups were well known to the people around the eastern coast of Connecticut, where his vintage cannery was located. His 40-year reputation had been built on the philosophy that each soup would be chock full of clams, fish, or seafood, and the cook could add fillers such as potatoes at home.

However, the machinery was obsolete, and the company was all but liquidated. When Laundon first took over, he introduced 48-ounce cans to restaurants, schools, and hospitals. The product promptly took off. Then he introduced new products, changed his packaging, and hired a home economist to work on improving the taste of his already good products. He soon bought new machinery and moved the company into bigger quarters in New London, Connecticut. Next he began expanding the retail market for his products.

The soups come in eight varieties of concentrates. Not to be confused with instant soups, however, these concentrates need to be mixed with cream or milk. They should be heated slowly, whisking all the while. They taste just about as good as any homemade chowder, but Abbott's is a whole lot quicker than making it from scratch.

Happily for those of us who are fans of New England clam chowder and lobster bisque, Abbott's soups are now readily available through a number of exclusive stores and a healthy mail order business. For those who are unable to visit New England but have a hankering for hot chowder some brisk autumn or winter day, Abbott's will help fulfill that yen.

HOW TO PURCHASE: Abbott's all-natural seafood concentrates come in packs of six, twelve, or twenty-four 8-oz. cans. Prices are Clam Chowder, $2.75; Chopped Clams, $1.99; Lobster Bisque, $3.49; Seafood Chowder, $2.99; Clam Broth, $1.29; Clam Fritter Mix, $2.75; and Clam Bisque, $2.75. The price per pack is the total of products selected. Shipping is by U.P.S. Add $3.40 for 6 cans, $4.50 for 12, and $6.75 for 24. Orders must be prepaid with check or money order.

Abbott's Bouillabaisse

This tummy-tickling, hearty soup leaves a glow inside and out. It's too good to serve "just for lunch," but whenever you serve it, will become a special occasion.

> *8-oz. can Abbott's Clam Chowder*
> *12 oz. clam broth*
> *1 cup dry white wine*
> *28-oz. can tomatoes*
> *1 lb. cod, cut into serving pieces*
> *12 sea scallops, feet removed*
> *16 large shrimp, shelled and deveined*
> *12 mussels, scrubbed and debearded*
> *Freshly grated black pepper*
> *2 tablespoons chopped fresh parsley*

1. In a medium soup pot, combine the clam chowder, broth, wine, and tomatoes (with juice). Break up the tomatoes with a spoon and mix to blend the chowder concentrate into the other ingredients. Simmer 15 minutes.

2. Add the cod, scallops, shrimp, and mussels. Cover and simmer 5 minutes or until mussels open. Discard any mussels that do not open.

3. Spoon into serving bowls and top with pepper and parsley.

Serves 6.

FOODWORKS Fried Walnuts

FOODWORKS. 35 Park Lane Road (Route 202), New Milford, Connecticut 06755. 203/354-3005.

Francine Scherer, owner of FOODWORKS, was operating her Soho Charcuterie Restaurant in Manhattan, when she began teaching a cooking class in northwestern Connecticut that included visiting several local farms. Soon Scherer realized there was a wealth of small farms nestled in those rolling hills of western Connecticut and the owners were producing some wonderful things.

So Scherer, who was burning out on the long hours of restaurant work, sold her 12-year-old operation in 1986 and moved to Litchfield County, Connecticut, where she opened FOODWORKS, a farm store, bakery, and catering business that specializes in New England–made products.

The store features primarily foods from small farmers and cottage industries—everything from farmstead cheese to local yogurt, freshly made cider, and smoked meats from the nearby Nodine's Smokehouse. (Many are products that are also in this book.)

Although much of Connecticut's farmland is no longer in production, there's been a resurgence in small farms in Connecticut, as there has been elsewhere in New England, and Scherer has "found a farm for just about everything." After all, years ago Connecticut was nicknamed the "Provision State" because it had so many farms, Scherer points out. She hopes her business, too, will help revive that reputation.

Scherer's goal for FOODWORKS is to create a full grocery concept from local and regionally grown products. In addition, an elaborately redone kitchen in the barn-turned-store (due to the capable carpentry work of Scherer's husband Jack Fitzpatrick) is the site for production of a complete line of baked goods, take-out foods, and a catering business.

One of the most popular items, a carry-over from the Soho Charcuterie days, is the Oriental-style Fried Walnuts. Spicy, slightly sweet, and salty snacks, these are packed in printed tins and are sold by mail as well as through the store. Other take-out and mail order items are planned shortly and include Banana Jalapeno Chutney and White Peach Butter. The latter is made from Litchfield County peaches.

Meanwhile Scherer, who spent most of the seventies leading a busy urban life with a successful New York restaurant, has traded all that for something a bit more countrified. Now every chance she gets, she is traveling the countryside visiting new farms. "I pet the pigs; the dogs run after me," she says.

HOW TO PURCHASE: Oriental-style Fried Walnuts are sold in 1- and 3-lb. tins for $10 and $25, respectively. Shipping is by U.P.S. and is an additional charge based on destination. Orders must be prepaid, and checks should be made out to FOODWORKS, Ltd. Scherer also accepts American Express.

Sweet Potato Chips

PILGRIM'S PROGRESS. 485 Main Street, Hartford, Connecticut 06103. 203/278-4210.

"The theory that the potato chip is the center of the universe has long been dismissed by philosophers and scientists alike" reads the star-spangled midnight blue package of Pilgrim's Progress Sweet Potato Chips. But owner and creator David McKay has a different theory. "If not the center of the universe, at least the center of a lot of good times . . ." he promises of his chips. We'd tend to agree. If not a high-brow gourmet treat, they're great fun.

At once irreverant and gracious, McKay waxes philosophical about his mail order food business. His fascination with the Shaker movement, once popular in New England, is quickly apparent. Shaker simplicity is a main theme of the products he makes. His sweet potato chips are just sweet potatoes and a tiny bit of salt. "People have done all the spicy stuff," he says. The honest taste of the product itself is what McKay seeks. Pilgrim's Progress, too, reflects that philosophy, standing for modernization and good old Yankee tradition.

McKay's career is as colorful as he is. His slightly counter-culture style has enabled him to try his hand in many things from Green Beret in Vietnam to promoter of a 60-piece orchestra to restaurateur. In 1982, he acquired his current restaurant, the Municipal Cafeteria, in downtown Hartford, but not before signing on as the dishwasher for a month to check the restaurant's cash flow. At the end of the month, he made an offer to buy the place, a request not often made by dishwashers, he chuckles. Ten days later, he and his brother owned the Municipal. It's here that McKay has been trying out the products for his line of Pilgrim's Progress foods. He calculates that he's eaten nearly 400 pounds of chips in the process of finding the exact formula for making the delectable crunchy sweet chips. (A 15-second window in the cooking time, he says, is the difference between perfection and undercooked or charred chips.)

McKay's latest addition to his business is a dense, custard-based wonderfully spiced bread pudding which is also a top seller in the restaurant. This product keeps alive the theory that New England food is meant to be homey and keep out the cold. And McKay sees it as reflecting old-fashioned Shaker ingenuity to produce hearty, slightly rich foods that would satiate even the appetite of a person who had been working in the fields all day. He's working on a cranberry maple cooking glaze, another product made by the Shakers.

HOW TO PURCHASE: Pilgrim's Progress Sweet Potato Chips are mailed in their aluminum-lined packages which keep them fresh for up to 6 weeks. Chips are $1.69 per bag. The bread puddings come in three flavors: cinnamon & clove, fruit, and chocolate. They are sold in 1-lb. containers for $5, 2 lbs. for $10, and are shipped frozen and packed in ice. Shipping charges are extra and based on destination. Special orders can be placed for any size bread pudding. Orders must be prepaid with check or money order payable to Pilgrim's Progress. McKay also accepts Visa and MasterCard.

Tortilla Chips

SEVERANCE FOODS. 3476 Main Street, Hartford, Connecticut 06120. 203/724-7063.

South of the border—the Windsor-Hartford border, that is—a company is making tortilla chips that equal or surpass anything from the Southwest. The business was started by three men who left their jobs, pooled their severance money, and created an enterprise that they aptly named Severance Foods. Today, partners John Grikis, Richard Stevens, and Richard Dana are giving more established tortilla companies a run for their money.

The trio met while working in quality control for Ortega products, which at the time belonged to the Hartford-based Heublein Corporation. A change in ownership left the three with two options—move to California or leave the company. They opted for the latter.

With plenty of experience in Mexican foods, they decided to go into business making tortilla chips, "the second most popular snack food after potato chips," says Grikis. The partnership was the sum total of the work force when this enterprise began in 1985.

The three men did it all. They mixed the ground cornmeal with water in a large bin. They put doughy masa into a machine that squeezed it into a fine sheet. Then they put the thinly rolled dough through a machine that cut it into neat triangles and spewed them onto a conveyor belt. One of the three would run alongside picking out the inferior chips, just before they fell into a large vat of oil. When the finished chips came out, another would stand ready with a salt shaker. Finally, the free partner would box and weigh the chips.

The process hasn't changed, but the madness has subsided thanks to success. At the second anniversary mark, Severance Foods had passed the $1 million sales mark. Now the flourishing company makes about 6,000 pounds of tortillas each day under the label Pan de Oro, or golden bread, and with the help of twenty employees. Besides tortilla chips, they make fresh and frozen corn tortillas, and they are toying with ideas to broaden their line.

Severance Foods recently received the seal of approval when a member of the Mexican family who makes their equipment came to Hartford for a visit. "He came here thinking we were just gringos," says Stevens. "By the time he left, he was calling us 'crazy tortilla makers.'"

HOW TO PURCHASE: Severance Foods sells a 3-lb. box of tortilla chips for $6. The price includes shipping via U.P.S. or Parcel Post to any destination in the continental United States. Orders must be accompanied by a check or money order payable to Severance Foods, Inc.

North-of-the-Border Seafood Nachos

This is an absolutely divine appetizer that was made even more so by the ingredients we had on hand. We used fresh Maine crabmeat, Vermont mild cheddar cheese, and, of course, tortilla chips from Severance Foods.

1½ cups refried beans
6 cups Severance Foods tortilla chips
8 oz. fresh or frozen crabmeat
2 heaping tablespoons chopped mild chilis
2 heaping tablespoons chopped black olives
2 cups mild cheddar cheese
1 avocado, peeled, pitted, and chopped
Juice of ½ lime
3 medium green onions, chopped
1 cup sour cream

1. Preheat broiler. Spread the refried beans over the surface of a 12-inch round pan. (A pizza pan is ideal.) Spread chips over the beans then sprinkle with crabmeat, chilis, olives, and cheese. Set under the broiler for 4–5 minutes or until cheese is melted.
2. Toss the avocado with lime juice. Sprinkle over nachos, then top with green onions. Serve with sour cream on the side.

Serves 4.

MAINE

Native Popping Corn

Cock Pheasant Farm
Native Popcorn

15 oz.

John Buckland - Corinna, Me. 04928   Tel. 278-4553

COCK PHEASANT FARM. Box 1605, Corinna, Maine 04928. 207/278-4553.

The experts told John Buckland that popcorn couldn't be grown on a commercial scale in Maine's rugged climate. But Buckland proved them wrong. In 1986 he harvested nearly 3 tons of the old-fashioned, snowy-white snack food.

A former inspector for the Maine Department of Agriculture, Buckland had no intention of raising popcorn as a business. In 1965, he acquired an ear of popping corn from an elderly gentleman and decided to plant it and "see what would happen." After a few successful harvests and more popcorn than he and his wife Millie could eat, Buckland began giving corn to friends and neighbors.

Soon folks were appearing at the door to buy popcorn, and then an article picked up by a wire service spread the word about Buckland to the far reaches of the United States. Before long he was receiving orders for his popcorn from almost every state. Buckland still insists that this is "more or less a hobby" with him. But more and more popcorn lovers are being won over to the slightly sweet, slightly nutty taste of freshly popped Cock Pheasant Farm Popcorn. It's so good just by itself that it needs no butter or salt. And now that this reserved Down Easter has fueled a burgeoning popcorn habit, his pastime is looking more like a business.

Buckland's secret to growing his popcorn is "patience." He plants in late April or early May (about 6 weeks early for Maine crops). He precedes the planting with a light dusting of weed killer and follows it with a light coating of natural fertilizer. Then he sits back and waits . . . and waits. The growing time for this particular strain of corn is a lengthy 120 days. It has to reach just the right level of moisture to pop successfully, explains the popcorn expert. While most of the people to whom he's given popcorn seed are out there picking the not-quite-mature ears, Buckland resists. He picks well into October, after three or four frosts have hit the corn. The whole family is involved in harvesting the hand-picked crop. They carefully husk and dry the corn. By the time they have a finished product, the requests start, and by Christmas, most of the crop is gone.

HOW TO PURCHASE: John Buckland sells his popcorn right "at the door." He also mail orders 15-oz. bags. The cost is about $ plus shipping which is via U.P.S. Prices fluctuate seasonally so it' best to contact John Buckland before ordering. Orders must be prepaid, and checks should be made to either John Buckland or Cock Pheasant Farm.

Millie Buckland's Crispy Caramel Popcorn

Although Cock Pheasant Farm Popcorn is best all alone, this recipe is a close second. It brings back memories of my childhood when we would trudge through frost-coated autumn leaves on crispy Halloween evenings to receive special treats like this one.

> *1 cup sugar*
> *¼ lb. butter or margarine*
> *½ cup dark corn syrup*
> *½ teaspoon salt*
> *½ teaspoon vanilla extract*
> *4 quarts cooked Cock Pheasant Farm Popcorn*

1. In a medium saucepan, combine sugar, butter, corn syrup, salt, and vanilla. Bring to a boil over medium heat, stirring constantly Simmer 5 minutes, stirring occasionally.

2. Pop popcorn and transfer to a large mixing bowl or pan. Pour the sugar mixture over the corn, stirring to coat.

3. Preheat oven to 250°F. Spray a cookie sheet with vegetable spray and turn the corn mixture onto the sheet. Spread evenly over the pan. Bake for 1 hour, stirring every 15 minutes to prevent sticking.

4. Remove from oven and stir occasionally while mixture cools. When cool, transfer to a tightly covered plastic container or plastic bags.

Makes 1 lb. popcorn.

MASSACHUSETTS

Fresh Pasta & Pasta Sauces

ABRUZZI FOODS. 18-22 Baystate Road, Cambridge, Massachusetts 02138. 617/547-2821.

The saying goes, "the more things change, the more they stay the same." That certainly holds true for Mario Boccabella, president of Abruzzi Foods. As a young boy growing up in Brooklyn, New York, Boccabella spent every Sunday in the kitchen making pasta for his family.

Thirty years later, he's still making pasta and living with his family. But he's in Boston now, and he's traded the family kitchen for a large plant in Cambridge and a food business that employees a dozen members of his family. The staff includes his wife, three daughters, two sisters and their families, and Boccabella's 75-year-old mother. Even his partner Domenico Nolletti is also his brother-in-law.

Today the Abruzzi Company, named for Boccabella's home region in Italy, includes two restaurants (Cantin Abruzzi and Abruzzi Via), Dom & Mario's Deli, Bread and Chocolate Bakery, Abruzzi Station Marketplace, and Abruzzi Foods. The last, started in 1984, evolved out of a need to make fresh pasta and sauces for the eateries.

Abruzzi Foods now supplies fresh pasta to a varied list of clients—from restaurants and groceries to individuals who request their pasta by mail. They make at least ten varieties of pasta, from egg pasta such as fusilli (spirals), fettuccine, and lasagna sheets to filled pasta such as tortellini and non-egg pasta such as capellini (angel hair) and linguine. All are made by extrusion and taste just like the real homemade thing, perhaps even as good as what Boccabella once made in the kitchen of his parents' Brooklyn home.

Abruzzi Foods recently introduced ready-to-eat sauces to accompany their pasta. A tomato sauce, marinara sauce, pesto, and Alfredo sauce are sold, and the company now features a mail order pack that offers three types of pasta and three sauces.

With sales of fresh pasta reaching 3.5 million pounds a year, you might not consider Abruzzi Foods a "cottage industry." But this business attributes all its success to the fact that it's a family operation. In fact, the entire family lives together in a 21-room house in Needham. "Everything we have or accomplished is the result of our commitment to each other. We rely on each other," says Boccabella.

The same attitude applies to the 150 or so non-family members who work at Abruzzi Foods and the eateries. They are treated as an extension of the family. While they don't live in the Needham homestead, rewards for good grades and good deeds make them all want to pitch in and help the family. Besides, thirteen under one roof is, after all, family enough!

HOW TO PURCHASE: A 6-pack of Abruzzi pasta includes Fettuccine (plain or spinach), tri-colored Fusilli, Linguine, Spaghettini, Ziti, and Cheese Tortellini (plain or spinach). Price is $17.80 and includes packaging and shipping. A 6-pack of 3 types of pasta and 3 sauces includes 1 package of Tortellini and your choice of 2 other unfilled pastas and Tomato Sauce and Marinara Sauce, Pesto, or Alfredo Sauce. Price is $16 and includes shipping (via U.P.S.) and handling. There is an additional charge for shipping to addresses outside New England. Orders must be prepaid with check or money order, but Abruzzi Foods will bill for additional freight charges or special order items. Credit cards are not taken.

Pasta Salad with Fusilli and Pesto Dressing

Great for a summer picnic, tailgate party, or just about any gathering, this hearty salad can be a meal in itself.

Two 12-oz. packages Abruzzi Foods Fusilli
2 teaspoons salt
1 tablespoon olive oil
1 stick pepperoni, thinly sliced
18-oz. can artichoke hearts, quartered
18-oz. can pitted large black olives, halved
1 pint cherry tomatoes, halved

Dressing

½ cup walnut halves, toasted in 350°F. oven
for 15 minutes
2 cloves garlic
2 cups packed fresh basil leaves
½ cup grated fresh Parmesan cheese
3 tablespoons balsamic vinegar
1 cup olive oil
Freshly ground black pepper to taste

1. Bring 2–3 quarts of water to a boil in a very large pot. Add the salt and 1 tablespoon oil. Cook pasta until tender but still chewy (about 2½ minutes). Drain and rinse in cold water to remove starch and stop the cooking process. Reserve.

2. Prepare the pepperoni, olives, and cherry tomatoes and reserve.

3. In a food processor fitted with a steel blade, add walnuts and pulse on and off until coarsely chopped. Remove the walnuts and reserve. With the machine running, drop the garlic cloves through the feed tube and process until minced. Add the basil to the work bowl and pulse to chop. Add the walnuts and the vinegar and pulse to mix. With the machine running, add the olive oil slowly through the feed tube. Stir in the cheese and pepper and transfer to a glass jar. This makes about 1½ cups. Dressing will keep in the refrigerator for 2 weeks.

4. In a large serving bowl, combine the pasta, pepperoni, artichokes, black olives, and tomatoes. Spoon about ½ cup of the dressing over the ingredients and toss to combine. Add more dressing a spoonful at a time until desired taste is reached. Pesto dressing has a very strong flavor and should be used sparingly.

Serves 12.

Imported Teas

BARROWS TEA COMPANY. 142 Arnold Street, New Bedford, Massachusetts 02740. 508/990-2745.

Ever since Sam Barrows was a little kid with his own roadside blackberry jam stand, he's wanted to run his own food company. So, one day, the former trading clerk on the Philadelphia Stock Exchange said farewell to a job he didn't like and moved to Massachusetts to do just that.

Barrows had other motivations for this radical change in his career, as well. A fortune amassed by his great, great grandfather in the iron and steel industry during the last century was nearly gone, and it looked as if Barrows's grandmother's great old house was going to be sold. Barrows thought he might be able to save the family homestead if he could start his own business and make it profitable.

Sadly, the house was sold before he had a chance to rescue it. But Barrows did achieve part of his dream. He's created an impressive business selling fine quality imported teas. Barrows is one of the few to import an unblended Darjeeling tea. While most imported teas come from several tea gardens, his comes from a single estate, and the result is a tea that's smoother and more flavorful to sip.

The tea is imported in tea chests that weigh about 100 pounds, and Barrows, the sum total of the business, repacks it into 4-ounce packages under his label. A bit more expensive than many of his competitors' teas, Barrows's loose tea is one of the best.

''To sell the best tea at the most affordable prices'' is the company motto, and Sam Barrows sticks to that conviction with great gusto.

Started in 1985, Barrows Tea Company now sells its products in at least sixty stores and is included in several mail order catalogs. An American Breakfast tea (a blend of Assam and Ceylon teas) and a Japanese Green Tea, a Sencha tea imported from Japan, have recently been added to the product list.

An estimated 10 million Americans warm up and cool off to a cup of tea on a regular basis, according to Barrows's statistics. And the ebullient young man feels certain that more and more people will be switching to quality tea once they have tasted his.

HOW TO PURCHASE: Barrows Teas all come in 4-oz. packages of loose tea leaves. Darjeeling costs $8.25; American Breakfast sells for $7.75; and Japanese Green Tea is $8.75. Cost includes shipping and handling. Prices are subject to change due to fluctuation in the dollar overseas, so it's best to contact Barrows Tea Company before ordering.

Barrows Best Sun Tea

This is a wonderfully refreshing drink for cooling off.

6–7 heaping teaspoons of loose tea
½ gallon spring or bottled water (not chlorinated)
6–8 mint leaves
Lemon slices
Sugar, if desired
Additional mint leaves for garnish

Fill a half-gallon clear glass or plastic container with the water, tea leaves, and mint. Cover loosely with cap and place in the sun for 4–6 hours. (Even during a partially cloudy day, the ultraviolet rays will be sufficient for the tea to steep.) Refrigerate or serve over ice with lemon slices and fresh mint leaves. Add sugar if desired.

Yields 6–8 glasses of iced tea.

Switchel—a New England Thirst Quencher

NEW ENGLAND SPIRITS, INC. & NEW HAMPSHIRE WINERY. R.F.D. #6, Box 218, Laconia, New Hampshire 03246. 603/524-0174.

When the Howard brothers—Aldie, Roger, and Pete—bought Lakes Region Winery in 1986, they found themselves with 2,000 gallons of apple cider vinegar and nothing to do with it. That is until they decided to make Switchel, a tart-flavored, colonial thirst quencher and energy source.

The drink originally made by New England farmers and maple sugarers combines apple vinegar and water to quench the thirst, and honey, molasses, and maple syrup for energy. Aldie found just the right mixture for their brew after doing extensive research. The brothers affectionately refer to their all-natural and all–New Hampshire product as an "eighteenth-century Gatorade."

The beverage can be served hot or cold. Cross-country skiers can enjoy a warm version with cinnamon sticks to boost their energies. Runners prefer it cold and mixed with seltzer.

The Howard brothers were delighted to find a product that was so well suited to the region. An abundance of apples, local honey, and maple syrup made for a perpetual stock of ingredients. Now hundreds of gallons of Switchel concentrate are produced at the winery each year.

In addition to Switchel, the Howards, who are the third owners of New England's oldest winery (started in 1969), also make, bottle, and sell red and white wines that are distributed exclusively at the winery and outlets in New Hampshire. (The Howards changed the name of their enterprise to New Hampshire Winery shortly after they purchased it, because, after all, it's the only winery in the Granite State.)

New Hampshire Winery's newest product is Rock Maple Liqueur, a liqueur that tastes a little like Kahlua but has a maple rather than coffee flavor. It sells well locally, but the brothers are hoping to find a national market for this product.

There's also a 10,000-gallon-per-month spring on the winery property. In addition to being used in the making of Switchel and a Rock Maple Liqueur, it's also bottled under the "White Ribbon Springs" label.

HOW TO PURCHASE: A 375-ml. bottle of Switchel concentrate or a 750-ml. wine bottle of ready-to-drink Switchel is sold for $3 plus shipping charges, which vary according to destination. Orders must be prepaid, and checks should be made payable to New England Spirits, Inc.

Coffee Syrup

ECLIPSE FOOD PRODUCTS. P.O. Box 7590, Warwick, Rhode Island 02887. 401/739-3600.

This author's first taste of Eclipse's coffee milk came when my brother-in-law entered our family. At every meal, our finicky new family member would pull out the bottle of Eclipse Coffee Syrup and heavily lace a large glass of milk. He quaffed the sweetish stuff at all hours of the day and night, even at the office. It didn't take long before we realized that the only thing this new member of our family drank was coffee-flavored milk!

As Mainers (untrusting of new-fangled products), we always stifled a little smirk as this brother-in-law hauled out the bottle of "Eclipse." We permitted what seemd a silly indulgence, writing it off as "one of Kennedy's food fetishes."

It is to my chagrin that I must now confess we Mainers were the ones to lose out on a delightful elixir. From this author's research, it seems that every Rhode Islander, from infancy on up, drinks coffee syrup in his or her milk. And being from just the other side of the Rhode Island border in Swansea, Massachusetts, my brother-in-law had fallen prey to this life-long, habit-forming substance, it seems.

It's one of life's delightful mysteries why the coffee milk tradition has taken hold in Rhode Island. But it's so much a favorite that Rhode Island dairies carry shelves of coffee-flavored milk in cartons, an abundance of coffee ice cream, and coffee yogurt as well. The syrup was developed as a flavoring for ice cream in 1914 by a food technologist named Alfonse Fiore. Eclipse Foods bought the company in 1963 and continues to be one of the major suppliers of this product.

Letters from people who "can't live without their coffee syrup" flood into Eclipse company offices daily. Sadly, with the exception of a few far-flung Eclipse syrup retailers in Florida and New Jersey, there is not a drop of coffee syrup sold outside southeastern New England. However, Eclipse Food Products will mail order the syrup to out-of-staters.

Made from the extraction of a special blend of roasted coffee beans combined with sugar or corn syrup, this coveted flavoring contains less than 1 percent caffeine. Once diluted in milk, the amount of caffeine is negligible. In addition to warm and cold coffee milk, many home cooks use the syrup in baking.

HOW TO PURCHASE: Eclipse will sell twelve 16-oz. plastic bottles of coffee syrup (a case) for $8.85. Shipping is extra and based on destination. Orders must be prepaid by check or money order.

Coffee Milkshake (called a Frappe in Rhode Island)

My brother-in-law remembers the days when he would go to the local creamery for one of their thick coffee shakes. "They were the kind you wanted to drink so fast they'd give you a headache, and the only thing you could do was go back for another one!" says our coffee frappe expert. Here's a recipe for a supremely decadent drink based on the recollections of one coffee milk lover.

> *3 tablespoons Eclipse Coffee Syrup*
> *2 cups soft vanilla ice cream (purchase at your*
> *   local creamery or dairy bar)*
> *1 cup cold milk*

Combine all ingredients in a blender and mix at high speed for 1 minute. Pour into 2 tall glasses and drink hearty!

Yields two 12-oz. drinks.

Fresh Vegetable Whole Wheat Pasta

PROVIDENCE CHEESE & TAVOLA CALDA. 407 Atwells Avenue, Providence, Rhode Island 02909. 401/421-5653.

Imagine our surprise and delight when a large cardboard box arrived. In it, a white bag (the kind used in bakeries) stuffed with a folded cardboard pizza plate opened to reveal a mound of wonderfully fresh whole wheat-tomato spaghetti, the kind with the nutty taste of freshly milled grain. Providence Cheese & Tavola Calda does not use plastic wrap. "Natural food should breath," is just a part of their creed, established in the mid-sixties when the late owner, Frank Basso, bought the wonderfully jumbled cheese shop.

Basso was committed to producing food that's both enjoyable and healthy, and did so with gusto and a great deal of fanfare right up until his death in 1987. He would tell visitors: "our products are made with no white flour, no rendered animal fats, no sugar or honey. Everything is very fresh. We don't have a freezer or even a can opener." His enthusiasm and his products won Providence Cheese much acclaim in magazines such as *Bon Appetit, Food and Wine,* and *Cuisine.*

In the dimly lit Federal Hill shop (that's the Italian district of Providence) where Signor Basso always greeted customers with a friendly "buon giorno," his daughter Ginny Wheatley and her son Wayne carry on the tradition of providing wholesome ethnic food. "Signor Basso's spirit is felt in every part of the store and his philosophy is very much present in the business," says Wheatley.

The store itself is said to be one of the oldest fresh cheese operations in New England. Providence Cheese still makes ricotta, mozzarella, provolone, and a no-salt pecorino cheese. Pasta is made with organically grown stone ground wheat and very fresh vegetables (whatever is available in the market that day). Sometimes it's carrot pasta, sometimes eggplant. All of the ingredients for everything made at Providence Cheese are locally grown or raised (except the wheat, which comes from Minnesota).

Nearly everything at Providence Cheese can be sent through the mail, but the homemade pasta is truly their trademark. Instructions come with every order to let the home cook preserve the creator's intent. "Take the phone off the hook when the pasta water comes to a boil so as not to be disturbed," the brochure cautions. When the pasta is ready, "Please put the phone back on the hook. Buon Appetito!"

HOW TO PURCHASE: Providence Cheese whole wheat pasta is sold for $1.50 per lb. Angel hair and other specialty pasta is $2 per lb. Vegetable flavors vary, depending on availability of fresh produce at the market. No-salt pecorino is $5 per lb. Shipping is extra and is via U.P.S. In New England, packages are sent Overland Service; outside the area, they are shipped Second Day Air. Orders must be prepaid with check or money order payable to Providence Cheese & Tavola Calda.

Ricotta and Artichoke Pasta Roll

At Providence Cheese & Tavola Calda, this delightful pasta dish is served with a béchamel sauce.

Filling

1½ cups ricotta
⅓ cup pesto sauce
3 teaspoons grated Parmesan cheese
1 clove garlic, crushed

1 fresh Providence Cheese whole wheat pasta sheet
12-oz. jar marinated artichokes, drained and chopped

1. Combine filling ingredients. Spread the pasta sheet over a large piece of cheesecloth. Spread the filling over the pasta to about ¼-inch thick, leaving a ¼-inch edge uncovered all around the sheet. Sprinkle the artichokes over the ricotta mixture and roll the sheet in jelly roll fashion, pressing down as you roll. Wrap tightly in cheesecloth and tie the ends of the cheesecloth with string.
2. Bring a large pot of water to a medium boil and boil the pasta for 15 minutes. Remove from water. Snip off the string and unwrap. Serve at once with warm béchamel sauce.

Serves 6.

VERMONT

Canine Cookies

2.

COSKI'S CHOICE INC. P.O. Box 544, Bellows Falls, Vermont 05101. 802/463-4561.

It's a dog's life for Jim and Carol Coski, who've found success and maybe even fortune in banana-spiced bears, ham hogs, veggie acorns, and liver pâté hydrants. Their market is the canine crowd, and their specialty is gourmet treats for the four-legged bunch.

It all started when the Coskis were looking for a high-quality, nutritious treat for their championship line of pedigreed cocker spaniels. They discovered that it was next to impossible to find a treat that had no preservatives or dyes. So the two began mixing their own. They gave batches of them away for Christmas that year, and friends liked them so much they came back for more. The Coskis soon found there was quite a market for their products.

In 1984, the couple began selling Coski's Choice biscuits commercially. Once they knew they were onto a good thing, Jim and Carol started looking for financing. Because Jim is legally blind, they were able to get some assistance from the local Department of Rehabilitation. Local banks funded the rest with the understanding that Coski's Choice would move into industrial quarters. The two took a 23,000-square-foot space in a nearby industrial park, and they now have twelve employees. Two employees are also handicapped, and Jim hopes that 60 percent of his work force will be from the handicapped employment pool as the business grows.

Coski cookies are made with fresh eggs, garlic, fresh parsley, malt, stone-ground whole wheat, rye, and unbleached white flour, rolled oats, cornmeal, meat broths, cheeses, carrots, and even peanut butter. The treats contain no salt or sugar. The ingenious couple make a Cheese Quacker that's recommended for dogs with wheat allergies. They contain three kinds of cheese and rye flour. And the two make Chocolate Babies that contain unsweetened cocoa (which is not harmful to dogs). If these sound appealing to you, Carol says they're also good for humans.

The Coskis have tried to include the remaining pet community in their marketing. They suggest treats for cats (containing tuna, mackerel, and other fish), bunnies, sheep, gerbils and hamsters, horses, and parrots.

What comes after biscuits for furry gourmands? The Coskis are looking into adding a line of gourmet frozen dinners, nutritionally balanced meals for mutts and pedigrees too, and with a Coski's Choice cookie for dessert. They've also been inspired with the idea for a doggie catering service. (Bow Wow on Wheels, perhaps?) It may be a dog-eat-dog world, but in Bellows Falls, Vermont, dogs eat gourmet treats.

HOW TO PURCHASE: **Coski's Choice Cookies are available several ways. An assortment of 3 dozen cookies in a dog house gift pack is $7.50; a 2-dozen assortment sells for $5.50. Large bones are $1 each, medium bones are 50¢; and mix n' match assortments are $2.40 per dozen. There is a $10 minimum. The Coskis will custom bake a huge party-size bone for special occasions such as birthdays, new litters, and dog show wins. They make a heart-shaped cookie for Valentine's Day and custom cook for special diets. Shipping is extra. Add $2.45 for orders from $10–$15, $2.85 for orders from $15–$20, and $3.40 for orders over $20.**

Specialty Coffee

GREEN MOUNTAIN COFFEE ROASTERS. 33 Coffee Lane, Waterbury, Vermont 05676. 1/800-223-6768 or 1/800-622-6240 in Vermont.

Who would ever imagine "Vermont-roasted" becoming a catch phrase in the coffee trade? Perhaps it seems like a hemisphere's jump from a success story. But Bob Stiller and Dan Cox, owners of Green Mountain Coffee Roasters, never had a doubt that Vermont and New England were prime locations for a local coffee company.

It all started with a small store in Waitsfield that roasted fresh coffee beans for local retail sales and distribution to neighboring ski lodges and inns. While locally roasted coffee had already become a trend on the West Coast, Green Mountain Coffee Roasters was one of the first to introduce this custom process to New England. The cozy coffee shop's caffeine infusion caught on quickly and business took off.

In fact, it's been so successful since the little Waitsfield store opened in 1981 that Stiller and Cox have opened two more retail shops in Vermont and one in Portland, Maine. They've also developed a thriving mail order business by which they send coffee all over the country. By their own estimation, they are now selling more than a million cups of coffee a week.

As more people taste Green Mountain Coffee, the list of clientele grows. "Getting people to taste is by far our best advertising," says Stiller. Every time a customer exclaims, "Wow, that's the best I've ever tasted!" it's money in the bank.

Stiller and Cox buy only the best hand-picked coffee beans from around the world. They blend, roast, grind, and package the coffee in small batches in a plant that's right under the shadow of Camel's Hump Mountain. And it's depicted exactly that way on the logo.

Green Mountain Roasters produce more than forty types of robust brews that run the gamut from exotic beans such as Jamaican Blue Mountain or Yemen Mocha Sanani (that sells for nearly $20 per pound) to more common coffees such as Columbian and Kenyan. Our favorite is Breakfast Blend. It's just about the best eye opener we've tasted.

With the long road to success still only partly traveled, Stiller and Cox are looking to move into the Boston market and, who knows, even New York. "There's nothing like us in New York, even with all the gourmet food shops," says Cox. Green Mountain Coffee Roasters growth has not reached a plateau, according to the Vermont coffee tycoons. "Maybe we'll have 500 shops in 20 years," they laugh.

HOW TO PURCHASE: With 40 types of coffee beans to choose from, it's impossible for a coffee lover to grow tired of GMCR. Varieties range from rare coffees such as Hawaiian Kona for $10.89/lb. and Celebes Kalossi for $12.99/lb. to wonderful blends: Breakfast Blend, $6.89/lb.; Custom Blend, $5.99/lb., and French Blend, $6.39/lb. Shipping is $2.50 for 1–3 lbs. of coffee. Over 4 lbs., the charge is $2.60 plus 20¢ for each lb. over 4. Customers should specify whole bean or grind size and may request standing orders to receive coffee shipments at regular intervals. Payment is by check, money order, Visa, or MasterCard. Use Green Mountain Coffee Roasters toll-free number for assistance and the latest price information.

Maple-coated Nuts ✓

THE MAPLED NUT COMPANY. Box 346, Main Street, Montgomery Center, Vermont 05471. 802/326-4661

Any number of people in New England are "doing" maple syrup. But only Marsha Phillips makes maple sugar–coated nuts—pecans, walnuts, and almonds covered with a granulated powder that produces a subtle maple flavor with every bite. The first mapled nuts were a happy accident. Phillips was trying to duplicate a glazed nut she had tasted. "Since we're in Vermont, I thought I should use maple sugar," Phillips explains. When the heated sugar cooled, instead of becoming shiny as she expected, it crystallized. "Everyone enjoyed them so much that they encouraged me to market them," says the maple nut expert.

Phillips began her business in 1985 as a way to stay home, raise her children (then ages 4 and 5), and still produce an income. Her first full year of business (1986) saw well over 1,000 pounds of nuts produced in her home kitchen.

Phillips buys maple syrup from local sources and makes her own maple sugar. Then she heats the nuts (which she buys strictly fresh from a local distributor) with the sugar in a process that coats each nut. "They're a great snack—high energy, high protein, low cholesterol, and absolutely addictive!" says Phillips.

Along with friends and family, Phillips also has the appreciation of guests at their bed and breakfast, The Seven Bridges Inn, which is also part of their home and the Mapled Nut Company. Bags of maple-coated nuts are put in each guest room, and dishes of nuts are set around the house.

On production days, guests are treated to an extra reminder that they're in Vermont as the aroma of maple sugar leaves a wonderful smell throughout the whole house. If it's ski season, guests have the opportunity to enjoy yet another Vermont specialty. They bring handfuls of snow indoors, pour hot maple sugar over it, and enjoy Sugar on Snow.

Phillips wryly sums up her active family life and business, "I've always wanted to live in a nut house," say this busy entrepreneur.

HOW TO PURCHASE: Maple-coated walnuts, almonds, and pecans are sold by mail in 4-oz. cellophane packages for $3.75 (specify the kind of nuts desired), and 12-oz. gift containers (a mixture of all 3 types of nuts) for $10.95. Minimum order is 3 bags or 1 container. Add $1.75 per order. Shipping is via U.P.S. Orders must be prepaid with check or money order. Drop a line for the latest prices and shipping chart.

Maple Sticky Buns

Serve these right from the oven, if possible, or reheat briefly for the most flavorful sweet roll you'll ever eat.

5½–6 cups of unbleached flour
¾ cup granulated sugar
1 teaspoon salt
3 envelopes active dry yeast (¼ oz. each)
¼ lb. butter, softened and cut into small pieces
½ cup water, warmed to 110°F.
½ cup milk, warmed to 110°F.
3 eggs
½ cup firmly packed dark brown sugar
1 tablespoon cinnamon
4 tablespoons butter
4 tablespoons pure maple syrup
¼ lb. butter
1 cup firmly packed dark brown sugar
½ cup pure maple syrup
1 cup Mapled Nut pecans or walnuts, broken

1. In a large bowl of an electric mixer, combine 1¼ cups flour, granulated sugar, salt, and yeast. Mix ingredients with a spoon. Add the ¼ lb. butter and combine with electric mixer on low speed. With the machine running, slowly add the water and milk. Raise speed to medium and beat 2 minutes. Add the eggs and ¼ cup flour and beat at high speed for 2 minutes. Add remaining flour, 1 cup at a time to produce a soft dough that can be kneaded. Turn dough onto a lightly floured surface and knead 8 to 10 minutes or until smooth and silky.

2. Preheat oven to 375°F. In a small bowl, combine the ½ cup brown sugar and the cinnamon and reserve. In a small saucepan, combine the 4 tablespoons each of butter and maple syrup and heat over medium until the butter has melted. Reserve.

3. In a medium saucepan, combine ¼ lb. butter, 1 cup brown sugar, and ½ cup maple syrup and set over medium heat until the butter and sugar have melted. Add the nuts. Lightly grease two 9x9-inch pans and pour half this mixture into each pan. Turn the pans so the bottoms are coated with the mixture.

4. Cut the dough in half. Roll one piece into a 14x9-inch rectangle. Brush with the melted butter and syrup mixture then sprinkle with half the cinnamon and sugar. Roll the dough up from the short end like a jelly roll and pinch the seam. Cut into nine 1-inch slices and arrange cut side down in one pan. Repeat with the second piece of dough. Cover pans with plastic wrap and let rise until puffed, but not quite doubled in size.

5. Bake 20 minutes. Cool for 15 minutes in the pan, then turn onto a serving plate and serve.

Makes 18 buns.

Upcountry Cocoa

ERMONT COUNTRY SEASONINGS. P.O. Box 46, Belmont, Vermont 05730. 802/259-2359.

John Des Jardins is a seventh-generation Vermonter who traces his ancestry back to 1793 and the village of Belmont. He and his wife Anne decided to return to that countryside and work for themselves. An industrial engineer by training, John had the knack for producing things. He had also studied art in Paris and already had designed just the right logo for the company, a freehand sketch of a quaint Vermont village that's become the company's trademark. Anne was a Paris-trained professional chef and had some terrific recipes and ideas.

They decided to combine their talents and backgrounds to market good Vermont tastes—a dry blend of salad spices and herbs, an all-purpose seasoning mixture, and an instant upcountry cocoa that's ever so chocolatey, but not too sweet. Calling their business Vermont Country Seasonings, the two started in 1982, basing their marketing strategy on "wholesome" Vermont flavorings. What's followed has been a succession of growth spurts with sales tripling one year and doubling the next. Products are now sold in no fewer than twenty states.

The leading seller by a country mile is the Upcountry Cocoa. In 1987 they sold about 50,000 pounds. Made with Vermont whey and milk as well as Dutch cocoa, and about a third of the sugar that major cocoa makers use, the cocoa has become almost a calling card for state events because it speaks of wholesome, old-fashioned Vermont. Cocoa comes in several flavors such as Orange, Mint, Coffee, Cinnamon, and Classic. Upcountry Cocoa is marketed in all the major ski areas as well as about 300 stores in the Northeast. Customers call it "fabulous," and one teacher in an Eskimo village on the Bering Sea in Alaska orders a case each year but cautions, "Don't ship UPS; we have no roads."

While John does most of the marketing and sales for the booming company, Anne is the official taster. She also invented the recipe for their salad dressing. This pungent, flavorful mélange of dried herbs and spices needs only oil and vinegar to be ready for use. It's also a wonderful marinade for chicken, pork, or beef.

HOW TO PURCHASE: A 9-oz. tin of Upcountry Cocoa (any flavor) is $2.50 and makes nine 6-oz. cups of hot chocolate. Better yet, buy a case of 12 tins. It's $30 (weight 9½ lbs.). There is an additional charge for shipping based on destination. A 5-oz. shaker of Country Seasonings and 2-oz. jar of Salad Dressing herbs and spices are $1.50 plus postage. (Cases are available.)

Upcountry Hot Fudge Sundae

What could be simpler or more chocolatey?

> *3 tablespoons Upcountry Cocoa*
> *1 tablespoon heavy cream*
> *1 tablespoon butter*
> *½ pint good quality vanilla or coffee ice cream*
> *2 tablespoons chopped walnuts*
> *½ cup unsweetened whipped cream*

Mix the cocoa and cream together in a small saucepan. Set over very low heat and stir until warm. Add the butter and stir until melted. Scoop ice cream into 2 dishes. Pour sauce over ice cream. Sprinkle with nuts and top with half the whipped cream.

Yields 2 sundaes.

Vermont Common Crackers

THE VERMONT COUNTRY STORE, INC. P.O. Box 3000, Manchester Center, Vermont 05255. 802/362-2400.

Vermont Common Crackers are as indigenous to the rich food lore of Vermont as lobsters are to Maine and baked beans to Boston. Most of the legends center around the cracker barrel that sat in the middle of the nineteenth-century country store heaped with dry, flakey, hollow-centered crackers. The town's folks would sit around the cracker barrel playing checkers or catching up on town politics and gossip and waiting for the two-horse mail stage to deliver the day's letters. Some folks would wager how many free crackers a person would grab from the barrel before he bought a hunk of cheese to go with it. Others would see who could whistle through a mouthful of dry crackers.

The country store and its cracker barrel have all but disappeared into the pages of history. However, a few have been restored so the tradition is not yet completely lost.

Vrest Orton is credited with reviving the country store when he established the Vermont Country Store in 1946. As a native Vermonter, he always had the old stores and the Common Crackers as part of his heritage. Like so many generations of Vermonters, he too had crumbled crackers into a bowl of milk with a hunk of cheese on the side. And it delighted him to be able to preserve part of that childhood memory.

In 1981, the original manufacturer of Vermont Common Crackers went out of business after 153 years of producing these roundish morsels. Orton bought the machinery (itself over 100 years old) and set about reviving the Common Cracker and, with it, the traditional cracker barrel.

The Common Cracker got its start when the Cross brothers, Timothy and Charles, first made the crusty staples in Montpelier in 1828. Charles would make the crackers with his own hands, mixing the dough, forming it into round cracker shapes, then baking the crackers in a hot oven. He would distribute them, first in a one-horse wagon, then with several rigs. Orton continues to make the crackers just the way Charles did.

It's not certain if it was the hard work or the crackers that gave Charles his longevity. Whatever the cause, he ate Common Crackers every day and lived to be 93!

And whatever folklore magic is behind it, Vrest Orton, too, seems to have figured out which way the cracker crumbles.

HOW TO PURCHASE: The Vermont Country Store sells 28-oz bags of Vermont Common Crackers in regular or bite-size, for $4.9 A 28-oz. brightly decorated tin (as close as they come to shippin the whole cracker barrel) is sold for $9.95. Shipping is extra an is based on destination. Credit cards are accepted. Checks shoul be made payable to Vermont Country Store.

Baked Scallops with Common Cracker Crumbs

This traditional Yankee dish can also be made with oysters.

1 quart fresh bay scallops
Juice of 1 lemon
1 cup Vermont Common Cracker Crumbs (crushed
  with a rolling pin)
½ teaspoon salt
Freshly ground pepper
¼ cup chopped parsley
1 cup heavy cream or milk
1 egg, beaten
4 tablespoons unsalted butter

Preheat oven to 350°F. Rinse the scallops and drain them. Toss wi lemon juice. Spread scallops over the bottom of a shallow bakin dish that's large enough to hold them in a double layer. Combir the cracker crumbs with the salt, pepper, and parsley. Sprinkle ov the scallops. Mix the cream with the egg and pour over the casserol Dot with butter and bake 20–30 minutes.

Serves 4.

Champp's Chips

VERMONT OLD FASHIONED POTATO CHIP COMPANY. 66 Pine Street, Burlington, Vermont 05401. 802/863-3203.

Along with maple syrup, apples, and cheddar cheese, Vermont now has its own potato chip company. Champ's Chips are the creation of Bill and Cyndie Reilly. Crispy, thin-sliced chips, these come in cheerful yellow and green foil that boasts a caricature of Champ—nearby Lake Champlain's answer to the Loch Ness Monster.

The two founded Vermont Old Fashioned Potato Chip Company in 1986 with the goal of making the best and crunchiest potato chip ever. The operative word, however, is not *potatoes*, though they certainly are essential, but rather the *oil*—the means of frying these potato wafers. The Reillys use strictly pure, unadulterated peanut oil, which food experts say is the only acceptable way to deep-fry a potato chip.

Peeled potatoes are sliced and cooked in single batches, then drained and dusted with salt. A secret method of slicing and cooking the potatoes produces chips that actually absorb less oil. No matter how they are bagged or sold, "you still begin with potatoes and cooking oil," says Reilly.

The couple became interested in starting a business after they talked with people at the state Department of Agriculture, which has had a hand in the creation of many of Vermont's new cottage industries. They learned what products were already being produced and what foods were marketable. They discovered that no one was making potato chips.

"It seemed to me that if you could develop a food product, market that product, and have the ingredients for the product grown locally, you'd have an ideal situation," explains Reilly of the decision to start their own company.

Potato chips seemed like the way to go for the couple who wanted to be in the food business. Potatoes were already in the Reilly blood. Bill's grandfather had operated a speakeasy in Naugatuck, Connecticut, during prohibition. As a first-generation Irish immigrant, he served potatoes as the daily freebie at his bar. He offered baked potatoes, potato soup, but most importantly, he made potato chips. And they became nearly as well known as Reilly's gin and beer.

Besides already having a recipe, the Reillys liked the idea that if successful, they could develop a large market for Vermont potatoes. The future looks good for the Vermont Old Fashioned Potato Chip Company. In fact, they've just come out with a second product, a ripple cut potato chip, called Peaks 'N' Valleys.

HOW TO PURCHASE: A case of 10 bags is $14.90. A 16-oz. Monster Party Pail is $3.79. Chips are mailed the same day they are cooked. Shipping is via U.P.S. and is an extra charge based on destination. Orders must be prepaid with check or money order. Vermont Old Fashioned Potato Chip Co. will ship C.O.D.

PRODUCE

New England Apples

LYMAN ORCHARDS COUNTRY. P.O. Box 453, Routes 147 and 157, Middlefield, Connecticut 06455. 203/349-9337.

Each fall our family makes an apple-picking pilgrimage to our favorite local orchard, Lyman Orchards. Some years there were only two or three, but more recently we're up to fourteen or fifteen big and small apple pickers. We could easily buy the apples we need at a local farm stand or even at Lyman's Apple Barrel Farm Store. But it's more fun to romp through the rolling tree-lined hills, taking in the fruity fragrance of our surroundings and enjoying the breathtaking scenery. The most difficult decision is whether to pick McIntosh, Cortlands, Empires, Red Delicious, or Macouns. Before we head for home, there's always a stop at the little store at the bottom of the hill for cider and doughnuts.

We're sorry to say that Lyman's doesn't mail order the pastoral setting of its 1,100-acre farm, nor can we ship you the crisp autumn sunshine that's intoxicating to sit in and chilly when one moves into the shadows. But Lyman Orchards does mail order many of its ten varieties of apples so that people all over the United States can enjoy a touch of New England fall.

Lyman Orchards has been in business since 1741. It took 110 years for the first members of the Lyman clan to find Middlefield after landing in Boston in 1631. Once settled, the family never left, and eight generations of Lymans have been farming this land since. In 1917, the family was one of the largest peach producers in the state. However, a killing freeze wiped out all the trees, and the Lymans and other farmers turned to the heartier apple trees, not daring to risk such disaster again. Lyman Orchards began by planting McIntosh apples, a new variety for its time. Today, the farm has 225 acres of apple trees, a few acres of pears and peaches, and plums and fresh berries besides. Lesser known apple varieties such as Tydeman, Paula Red, Milton, Ida Red, and Rome are also cultivated along with the more popular varieties.

A huge apple cider business is also carried out on the property. Some 180,000 gallons of cider are pressed each season using a minimum of five different varieties to give it a rich flavor.

For people who are driving through Connecticut, it's worth a stop at Lyman Orchards for a drink of cider and a bag of apples. Early May is apple blossom time, and mid September to October 25 is the peak apple harvest season. Be assured, for those not traveling to these parts, Lyman's Orchard Country will be happy to provide a little bit of New England with a package of apples by mail.

HOW TO PURCHASE: Lyman's McIntosh, Ida Red, Cortland, Red Delicious, and Empire apples are available by mail in 15-, 30-, and 45-apple boxes. Prices are $16.95, $29.95, and $43.95 respectively and include shipping charges. Lyman's will schedule delivery at a time requested by you (e.g., Thanksgiving or Christmas) and handles a large gift package business. Specify dates to deliver, addresses, and greeting. Orders must be accompanied by check or money order payable to Lyman Orchards, or by credit card information.

German Apple Pancakes

These crepe-like pancakes are not only a wonderful breakfast treat, but also a yummy dessert.

> *6 eggs*
> *¼ cup sugar*
> *¾ cup all-purpose flour*
> *½ teaspoon salt*
> *2 cups milk*
> *2 tablespoons unsalted butter, melted*
> *3 McIntosh, Empire, or other good cooking apple, peeled and thinly sliced*
> *⅓ cup raisins*
> *4 tablespoons butter for cooking the pancakes*
> *2 tablespoons confectioners' sugar for garnish*

1. Beat the eggs with the sugar until foamy. Add the flour and the salt and mix just to moisten. Add the milk and the melted butter and mix. Fold in the apple slices and the raisins.

2. Set a medium crepe or omelette pan over medium heat. Melt a half-tablespoon of the butter. Ladle about ¾ cup of batter into the pan and cook until top is set (about 3–5 minutes). Flip with a spatula and cook 2–3 minutes. Turn onto a warm serving plate. Sprinkle with a teaspoon of confectioners' sugar, roll, and keep warm. Repeat until all the batter has been used.

Yields 6 large pancakes.

Specialty Apples

OLD CIDER MILL. 1287 Main Street, Glastonbury, Connecticut 06033. 203/633-4880.

Patti and Stewart Beckett fell in love with the idea of operating a cider mill that dated back to before the Civil War. They liked the old weathered barn, the streams running through the property, and potential pasture land where they could raise their own sheep, cows, goats, and other grazing animals. They found something romantic in the fact that the long, narrow 22-acre strip was bordered on one end by the main street of this quaint New England town and abutted by the Connecticut River at the other end.

Rumor had it that this property was going to be sold for condominium development, a frequent happening in this Hartford suburb. So, in 1974, the two bought the mill. Later they discovered it was the oldest operating cider mill in this country. After further research, they found records indicating that fruit trees grew on the original land-grant property back in the 1600s and that barrels of cider from that mill had been bequeathed in wills dating back that far.

The Becketts with their four grown children continue to make cider at the Old Cider Mill using an apple press that, in itself, is worthy of a visit. Brought down the Connecticut River by barge around 1930, the press was then hauled by oxen over Main Street (then a dirt road) to its present site. The secret to their wonderful cider is that they blend at least four varieties of apples to produce a robust, fruity taste. During the early part of the apple season, the sugar content of the apples is lower than it is later in the season. To balance the tartness of the cider produced then, the Becketts often add a few pears.

The Becketts started shipping packs of any number of their nineteen kinds of apples around 1977, when customers began asking for apples to be sent to family members who lived out of state or were wintering "down south," and children away at school. (After all, there are some parts of this country where apples just don't taste as good as they do in the heart of New England Apple Country.)

The Old Cider Mill sells and ships brands of apples such as Mutsu, Baldwin, Black Twig, Ida Red, Rome, Winesap, Stayman, Empire, McIntosh, Cortland, Red and Golden Delicious. They also ship jams and jellies, honey, syrup, or any number of the items they sell in the retail store at the cider mill. The Becketts also make a cider mulling mix, a mix of cinnamon, cloves, nutmeg, citrus, and other spices that's the same mix they use in the hot mulled cider served at the Old Cider Mill throughout apple-picking season. This, too, can be mail ordered.

HOW TO PURCHASE: The Old Cider Mill mails out 15-apple flats in single, double, and triple layers for $9.75, $17.95, and $25.75 respectively. Packing is included in that price, but shipping, via U.P.S., is extra and based on destination. They will add jellies and jams (two 8-oz. jars per layer) for $3.50 per layer. Mulled Cider Mix is $.95 per ½-oz. package. The Becketts do custom packing as well. MasterCard and Visa are accepted. Orders must be paid in advance. Checks and money orders should be made out to Old Cider Mill, Inc.

Apple Pineapple Crumb Pie

This recipe represents three generations of cooking. Originally my grandmother made an apple pineapple pie with a lattice crust topping, and my mother made an apple crumb pie that was just as popular. We decided to combine these two family favorites to make one so irresistible that it leaves the taster with fork in hand, looking for another helping.

8 McIntosh or other New England cooking apples
1 cup pineapple juice
½-1 cup sugar (depending on sweetness of apples)
Juice of ½ lemon
1 uncooked 9x13-inch pie shell
2 tablespoons unsalted butter
2 tablespoons cornstarch mixed with 2 tablespoons water

Topping

¾ cup toasted walnuts, coarsely ground
¾ cup sugar
1 cup all-purpose flour
¼ lb. unsalted butter, softened to room temperature

1. Peel the apples and cut into eighths. In a medium saucepan combine the juice, sugar, and lemon juice and heat until the sugar has dissolved. Add the apples and simmer about 2 minutes. Remove the apples with a slotted spoon and arrange in the bottom of a pie shell that has been pricked several times with a fork.
2. Bring the liquid to a boil. Add the 2 tablespoons of butter and allow to melt. Add the cornstarch mixture and mix until thickened. Remove from heat and allow to cool while making the topping.
3. Preheat oven to 425°F. Combine first three topping ingredients. Add the butter and mix with a fork until it forms large crumbs.
4. Pour the juice over the apples. Sprinkle the crumb topping over the top. Set on a baking sheet. Bake 10 minutes. Lower heat to 350°F. and continue baking 35 minutes. Remove from oven. Cool slightly and serve or store in the refrigerator and warm briefly before serving.

Serves 8.

MAINE

Fiddleheads

BELLE OF MAINE PRODUCTS. W. S. Wells & Son, P.O. Box 109, Wilton, Maine 04294. 207/645-3393.

During the month of May, most Mainers engage in a pastime called fiddleheading. They gather up buckets and bags and venture out along the country roads to pick the fiddlehead greens that grow wild by the side of brooks and streams.

In recent years, the rest of the world has come to appreciate this regional and very seasonal delicacy. Thanks to Butch Wells, who cans and pickles fiddleheads under the Belle of Maine label, we are all able to enjoy this gustatory delight anytime and anywhere.

The vitamin-filled fiddlehead greens are actually the young tops of the Ostrich Fern, so named because the furled head resembles a fiddle. They grow in abundance near bodies of water that often flood during the early spring. As the water subsides, the feathery greens appear. When properly cooked, they taste a little like asparagus.

Belle of Maine was founded back in 1896 by Butch's grandfather, Walter Wells. It started as a cannery with a sole product—dandelion greens. A variety of vegetables was canned until the 1950s, but by 1961, the business had declined to its original product. Around 1970, they added fiddleheads, then a few years later, beet greens joined the list of cannery items. The dandelion and beet greens are started from seed, but the fiddleheads are all picked in the wild.

Today, the small cannery processes some 26 tons of fiddleheads each year. These are turned into a canned product with nothing added but water. They are also packaged as pickled fiddleheads, crunchily preserved in a vinegar-based brine. Fresh fiddleheads are sold to restaurants and local grocery stores and can be mail ordered during fiddleheading season. Another product, Dilly Beans—pickled, fresh green beans—are peppery hot and piquant.

The company is the only one in the world that's canning dandelion greens and the only one in the United States that's canning fiddleheads and beet greens. W. S. Wells & Sons purposely picked these items because they are so unique. "To compete with larger canneries, we had to be different," says Butch Wells.

HOW TO PURCHASE: Gift packs of six 15-oz. cans (2 each of Dandelion Greens, Beet Greens, and Fiddleheads) are $11.50; gift packs of 12 (4 of each) are sold for $20. Postage and handling are included. Cases are available. Pickled Fiddleheads and Dilly Beans in cases of 12 jars are $20 and can be broken down according to customer's preference. Shipping is extra for these. Fresh fiddleheads are sold during the month of May and cost about $3.50 per lb. Wells prefers to sell in 5-lb. minimums but will sell less. Shipment is by U.P.S. Overnight Express and is an additional charge. Orders must be prepaid, and checks should be made out to W. S. Wells & Son. Credit cards are not accepted.

Cream of Fiddlehead Soup

There's nothing like a bowl of steamed, just-picked fiddleheads when one has a hankering for them. Belle of Maine canned fiddleheads obviously don't pretend to taste like those. But by adding them to this soup, you could easily fool people into thinking they're eating the freshest young ferns around—if you hide the aluminum container!

> *1 medium leek, chopped and rinsed carefully*
> *3 tablespoons unsalted butter*
> *1 large potato, peeled and diced*
> *4 cups chicken stock*
> *Salt and freshly ground pepper*
> *15-oz. can Belle of Maine Fiddleheads, drained*
> *1 cup heavy cream*
> *1 egg yolk*

1. In a medium saucepan, sauté the leek in the butter over low heat about 3 minutes. Do not brown. Cover and sweat the leek for another 5 minutes. Add the potatoes and sauté 1 minute. Add the chicken stock, salt, and pepper and simmer covered for 30 minutes. Add the fiddleheads and heat.

2. Remove from heat and transfer contents to a food processor or blender. Purée the mixture and return to the pot. Combine the cream and the yolk and beat lightly with a fork to blend. Add a ladleful of the hot liquid to the cream slowly, whisking continuously to prevent the egg from curdling. Pour this mixture back into the soup mixture and warm gently. Serve warm.

Serves 6.

Yankee Olé Mexican Dip

MAINE FLAVOR COMPANY. 24 Chamberlain Avenue, Portland, Maine 04101. 207/773-2772.

When Mary Sottery's family was grown and she was looking for something to do with her time that would also earn her some money, she turned to the one thing she knew best, cooking. She'd always been adventurous in the kitchen so there wasn't much she didn't know about herbs and spices.

It also happened that Sottery, who admits to being a purist when it comes to ingredients, discovered an outstanding local herb farm that agreed to supply her with what she thought to be the best dried herbs money could buy. We thought so, too, and included Ram Island Farm in this book.

She came up with innovative ways to package her seasonings, appealing to ease of preparation as well as taste. Each mix includes a recipe for use with the herbs. Among her best sellers is a hot number, Yankee Olé Mexican Dip, which might be a Tex-Mex specialty if it weren't made in Maine. She also packages a Winter Pesto blend that needs just olive oil, cheese, garlic, and freshly cooked pasta to make it a meal. She makes a blend for a corn and clam casserole, a green mayonnaise mix, one for herb butter, and a fish chowder seasoning pack. Her products appear in specialty stores from Maine to North Carolina. And Sottery, who blends everything by hand and is a one-person operation, also sells her Yankee Olé Mix, Winter Pesto, and a fine catnip by mail order.

Sottery, who started her business in 1983, believes the herbs available in her part of Maine are of superior quality due to being cultivated in well-drained glacial soil and nutured by a constant fine mist that comes off the ocean. This is why, says Sottery, she is able to put together such top notch products.

HOW TO PURCHASE: Packets of Yankee Olé Mexican Dip and Winter Pesto are available by mail order for $2 per package including shipping. For feline gourmets she has a top quality catnip available at the same price. Make check or money order payable to Maine Flavor Company. Sottery does not accept credit cards.

Yankee Olé Layered Salad

This is a favorite in our house for summer parties and picnics. The Yankee Olé Mexican Dip adds an extra punch. Be sure to serve this with plenty of tortilla chips.

The Beans

Two 15-oz. cans pinto beans, drained
3 slices of bacon, cooked, fat reserved
1 jalapeno pepper, minced

The Guacamole

3 ripe avocados, peeled, pitted, and finely chopped
2 tablespoons minced onion
Juice of ½ lime
1 clove garlic, crushed
Salt and pepper to taste

The Vegetables

6 green onions, chopped (use the white and lower half of green)
3 large tomatoes, chopped
12-oz. can pitted black olives, chopped
8 oz. Longhorn cheddar cheese, grated

The Dressing

1 cup sour cream
½ cup mayonnaise
1 package of Maine Flavor Company Yankee Olé Mexican Dip

1. In a skillet, heat the reserved bacon fat and add the beans, mashing them with the back of a spoon as they cook. Cook this way for 5 minutes or until the beans are well mashed, then add the bacon and jalapeno pepper and mix. Cool and reserve.

2. Mash all the guacamole ingredients together and chill. Combine dressing ingredients and reserve.

3. On a large platter, assemble the salad layering ingredients as follows: bean mixture, guacamole, dressing, green onions, tomatoes, and olives. Top with cheese and refrigerate until serving time. Serve with tortilla chips. Garnish with black olive slices, slices of avocado, and tomato, if desired.

Serves 12.

Edible Seaweed

MAINE SEAWEED CO.
ALARIA ✓

MAINE SEAWEED COMPANY. Box 57, Steuben, Maine 04680. 207/546-2875.

Larch Hanson has spent more than 15 years giving attention to the oldest plants on earth. He harvests kelp, alaria, and the like as much by communing with them as by physically gathering the vegetables of the sea.

"You accept the plants, carefully, with gratitude, and pass them on, trusting that they will reach the ones who need them," says Hanson, who started the Maine Seaweed Company in 1974 to share his diet and philosophy with others. The primary objective of his small company is "to bring people to an awareness of gratitude toward the sea plants" says Hanson's brochure.

To that end, Hanson publishes a booklet about the edible sea vegetables of New England. He also offers apprenticeships for those who want to become "immersed" in service to plants and people, and he runs a Harvest Camp in June that affords the opportunity to participate in the sea harvest. The camp is open-ended. People come for a week or two or stay through the fall on a barter basis.

Hanson lives way Down East on a penninsula that juts out between Dyer Bay and Gouldsboro Bay, about 30 miles due east of Bar Harbor. His primary harvest area is in that region. But, according to Hanson, the nori and dulse have become contaminated from petrochemicals.

For a while Hanson imported both from Grand Manan Island in New Brunswick, until he became dissatisfied with the lack of quality control. He's retreated back to his own region of the world and, for the moment, does not carry dulse or nori.

Hanson and his crew harvest by hand and in tiny unpainted boats to avoid toxic paint contaminants. Clothed in wet suits, they farm around the rock clusters of the two bays where the seaweeds tend to collect. They try to limit their exposure to 4 hours a day in the cold salt water and rough winds as excessive exposure to the elements is too taxing.

Maine Seaweed Company products include two forms of green brown kelp and alaria, a very fresh tasting, short-cooking form of seaweed. Plants are dried rapidly, then bundled for sale. Much of Hanson's harvest goes to local health food stores, but he's also built up a considerable mail order business.

Customers say he has the freshest and cleanest sea vegetables around. Hanson thinks that's because he pays such close attention to avoiding pollutants and preservatives.

HOW TO PURCHASE: Larch Hanson sells 1-lb. bags of Kelp, Alaria, and Digitata Kelp (Kelp/Kombu) for $7 per bag. There is a 3-lb. minimum and Hanson pays shipping costs. To order, send check or money order payable to Maine Seaweed Company. His booklet, *Edible Sea Vegetables of the New England Coast*, is sold for $2.50 or $2 with a seaweed order.

Green Beans, Alaria, and Toasted Almonds

Even if you haven't yet tried seaweed, you'll love the refreshing taste of the alaria and green beans in this recipe.

> ⅓ *cup dried Maine Seaweed Company Alaria, cut into ¼-inch sections*
> *1 lb. green beans, trimmed and washed*
> *¼ cup sliced almonds*
> *1 tablespoon unsalted butter*
> *1 clove garlic, minced*
> *Salt and freshly ground pepper to taste*

1. In a large saucepan, soak the alaria in 1 cup hot water for 1 minutes. Bring to a boil and simmer covered for 15 minutes. Cut the beans into 2-inch pieces and add to the pan. Cover and simmer 5 minutes or until cooked, but still slightly crisp.

2. In a small pan, melt the butter and sauté the almonds for minutes or until golden brown. Add the garlic and toss. Sauté 3 seconds.

3. Drain the beans and alaria and toss with the almond mixture. Add salt and pepper to taste. Mix and serve.

Serves 4.

Wild Maine Blueberries

MAINE WILD BLUEBERRY COMPANY. Elm Street, Machias, Maine 04654. 207/255-8364 or 800/243-4005.

Not all blueberries are alike. Ask a Mainer, and you'll get a harangue about the difference between those highbush berries that grow out-of-state and the ''real'' blueberries—lowbush berries—that grow wild all over Maine. Some, like Fred ''Bud'' Kneeland, owner of the Maine Wild Blueberry Company, will also tell you there are no others and to use those big plump blues is nothing short of heresy.

There are two reasons for Kneeland's convictions about berries. First, Maine is the center for these delightfully sweet, juicy little bright purple berries. (About 40 million pounds of them are harvested here each year.) And second, Kneeland's Maine Wild Blueberry Company handles quite a bit of the market share of this industry, about 15 million pounds of the tiny Down East treasures each year.

Kneeland's company sells frozen, canned, and dehydrated wild blueberries to customers ranging from major cake mix companies who buy in bulk to individuals who buy just one can. ''Every customer is important,'' says Kneeland.

A native of Bethel, Maine, Kneeland started working in the blueberry industry more than 20 years ago. Recognizing a market for quality wild blueberries, he started his own company in 1984 when an old woolen mill in Machias became available. He turned the mill into a packing plant, added state-of-the-art cleaning and processing equipment, and instituted a strenuous grading system to make sure that ''only the top quality berries got packed.''

He has a roster of 135 working for him, and that number booms to nearly 500 during the peak harvesting season in the late summer. Harvesting is a labor-intensive business: pickers use hand-held rakes to gently comb the berries from tangled bushes.

The harvest is also occasion for celebration, and each August Machias, home of the Maine Wild Blueberry Company, plays host to one of the biggest blueberry festivals in the United States. Piping hot blueberry pancakes and fresh-baked wild blueberry pies are just a couple of the gastronomical treats that greet visitors to this coastal Down East town. And travelers to the region may also notice a wild field or meadow lined with stakes and string. To be sure, it's a wild blueberry field ready for Kneeland to harvest.

HOW TO PURCHASE: Kneeland will sell as little as 1 can of wild Maine blueberries. A 15-oz. can of berries packed in heavy syrup or water is $1 plus postage (which is based on destination). Send check or money order or call or write to place an order. The Maine Wild Blueberry Company will also bill for orders.

TO VISIT: The Maine Wild Blueberry Company gives ''one tour after another'' during the summer months, according to Kneeland. From the center of Machias, take Route 92 (Elm Street) in the direction of Machiasport and you can't miss it.

Blueberry Orange Crumb Cake

This not-too-sweet cake is perfect for brunch, breakfast, or anytime there's freshly brewed coffee at hand. We've made it with fresh blueberries (highbush or lowbush) and with the canned Maine Wild Blueberry Company berries. Naturally, the fresh berries are best, but the canned berries run a close second, and they are always available.

Crumb Topping

½ cup light brown sugar
¼ cup all-purpose flour
2 tablespoons cold butter cut into small pieces
½ teaspoon cinnamon
Pinch of salt
1 tablespoon grated orange zest
½ cup ground walnuts

Combine sugar, flour, and butter and beat until mixture is crumbly. Add remaining ingredients and beat to combine. Set aside while making the cake batter.

Cake

1½ cups all-purpose flour
2 teaspoons baking powder
½ teaspoon baking soda
¼ teaspoon salt
¼ cup light brown sugar
½ cup granulated sugar
⅓ cup orange juice
⅓ cup milk
2 large eggs, lightly beaten
1 teaspoon cinnamon
1 teaspoon grated orange zest
¼ lb. butter, melted and cooled to room temperature
15-oz. can Maine Wild Blueberry Company
   blueberries (in water), well-drained

1. Preheat oven to 350°F. Grease an 8x8-inch pan.
2. In a large mixing bowl, combine the flour, baking powder and soda, salt, and sugar. In a measuring cup, combine the liquids and the eggs. Add liquid mixture to mixing bowl ingredients while beating with a hand mixer.
3. Add the cinnamon and orange zest. Pour the butter into the mixture and beat.
4. Fold in blueberries and pour into pan. Sprinkle crumb topping evenly over this. Bake 50 minutes or until cake is firm. Remove and allow to cool before cutting.

Serves 8.

Morse's Sauerkraut & Aunt Lydia's Beet Relish

VIRGIL L. MORSE & SON. Morse's Sauerkraut, RFD 2, Waldoboro, Maine 04572. 207/832-5569.

An 8-pound white plastic bucket sitting on our doorstep let us know that the kraut had arrived. A no frills, plain brown mailing label with our address was tied to the metal handle. And inside, padded by sauerkraut, was a pint jar of Aunt Lydia's Beet Relish. That's Yankee ingenuity for you. And that's the way Virgil L. Morse & Son has operated for all of its 70-plus years.

The family-run company produces 70 tons of crisp, not-too-sour sauerkraut and 5,000 jars of beet relish each year. All the cabbage is grown on the Morse farm, as are the beets for the tangy sweet and sour relish.

The company was founded by Virgil Morse, who created the recipe for the sauerkraut in 1917 when a local store asked him to make a barrel of it for their customers. The recipe, a secret blend of cabbage, salt, sugar, and water, has never changed. Morse continued running the business until his death in 1963. Then Virgil Jr. kept it going until he died in 1969. Virgil Jr.'s wife Ethelyn is continuing the family tradition. The septuagenarian operates the company with the help of only two employees.

The trio makes sauerkraut from October to March. In keeping with their Down East, no-nonsense style, Ethelyn alerts locals that the kraut-making season has begun with a two-word ad in the local paper that simply says, "Kraut's Ready." At the signal, cars line up at the Morse farm, many with the buckets from last year's product. (Ethelyn likes to have the empties returned.)

The beet relish recipe comes from Ethelyn's mother-in-law, Aunt Lydia, and her name has become part of the package. A combination of finely diced beets, shredded cabbage, horseradish, sugar, and vinegar, the relish is a must for an old-fashioned coast-of-Maine picnic.

Although Ethelyn's only child has no interest in working in the business, she thinks one of her grandchildren may carry on. Asked if she planned to retire soon, she responded, "I might if I played bridge, but I don't play bridge."

HOW TO PURCHASE: Morse's Sauerkraut is shipped in 8-, 15-, 25-, and 35-lb. buckets. Prices range from $12.85 to $17.50 for an 8-lb. container to $49.50 to $61.50 for the 35-lb. container. Add $2 and Morse's will include a 16-oz. jar of Beet Relish. Otherwise Aunt Lydia's Beet Relish is $10.50 to $13.50 for four 16-oz jars. Price include shipping (via U.P.S. or Parcel Post), depending on destination. Orders must be prepaid with check or money order.

New England Sauerkraut Garni

This dish requires the freshest possible sauerkraut, and Virgil Morse's is just the ticket.

> *3 strips smoked bacon, chopped*
> *1 medium onion, chopped*
> *1 large apple, peeled and chopped*
> *2 meaty country pork ribs*
> *2–3 smoked pork chops*
> *2–3 large garlic sausage (preferably handmade)*
> *4 cups Morse's Sauerkraut*
> *2 cups dry white wine*
> *1 cup water*
> *2 teaspoons juniper berries, crushed*
> *3 large potatoes, quartered*

1. In a flameproof casserole, sauté the bacon over medium heat. Lower the heat and add the onion and apple and sauté until soft but not brown. Blanch the pork ribs in a pot of boiling water to remove extra fat.

2. Add ribs, pork chops, and sausage to the pan. Spread the sauerkraut over the meat and add the wine and water. Add the juniper berries and mix gently to combine. Preheat oven to 350°F. Bring sauerkraut mixture to a simmer. Cover and bake 1¼ hours.

3. Add the potatoes, making sure they are covered by the liquid. Bake another 45 minutes.

Serves 4.

Culinary Herbs & Herb Blends

RAM ISLAND FARM. Cape Elizabeth, Maine 04107. 207/767-5700.

We first learned of the wonderful Ram Island Farm through Mary Lottery of The Maine Flavor Company. She told us that Ram Island's fine organically grown herbs were the inspiration for her business. We, too, find Ram Island inspirational. Not only are their dried herbs more flavorful than most that are right from the garden, but the philosophy here is also refreshing.

Situated on a large, private estate on the Cape Elizabeth coast south of Portland, Ram Island has been in the business of growing organic herbs and everlasting (dried) flowers since 1979. Named for the tiny island that's just off the coast at the estate, the picturesque farm is blessed with rich soil and mild climate (for these parts). Formal gardens, seedling-filled elegant old greenhouses, and wild iris and lupine live harmoniously in this fairyland by the sea.

To mirror the natural beauty of Ram Island and share it with the rest of the world where serenity may have given way to hustle and bustle of modern times is part of the company's tenet. Preservation is another—mainly of the farm that's been a lovely haven in the midst of the amazing growth and development that's overtaken the entire Portland area.

The business started as an experiment in organic herb growing. Today, nearly everything that's sold here is grown on the premises. Products are dried on the premises, producing lucious green, not washed out grey, herbs, a trademark that has made this herb company so successful.

Ram Island sells about fifteen varieties of single herbs, including the not-so-well-known lovage, a sort of cross between celery and parsley, that's delicious in soups and stews. A selection of eight herb blends is also available. Among them are an ambrosial mulled cider mix that is as wonderful to whiff as to drink and a new salad herb blend that contains colorful edible flowers such as pink chive blossoms, nasturtium, and golden calendula. Herb vinegars, herbal teas, potpourris, herbal bath salts and oils, and a host of dried floral arrangements are also sold.

HOW TO PURCHASE: All items are available by mail. Individual herbs are $3.50 per jar. In addition to the more ordinary herbs, they also sell lovage, mint, calendula, and opal basil. Herb Blends: Fish, Soup, Salad, Bouquet Garni, Poultry Seasoning, Italian, Mexican, and Mulled Cider Spices are also $3.50 each. Add $2.50 for shipping for orders under $20, $3.50 for orders between $20 and $40. Orders must be accompanied by check or money order payable to Ram Island Farm Herbs.

Smoked Salmon with Ram Island Farm Fish Sauce

In need of a quick, tasty appetizer for last-minute company, we combed our pantry for ideas and came up with this. Simple, but flavorful thanks to the sauce served with it, no one guessed our cupboard was nearly bare!

½ lb. smoked salmon, thinly sliced
8 lettuce leaves, washed and patted dry
8 thin slices of lemon
Pumpernickel or other bread, thinly sliced
1 cup fish sauce (below)
¼ cup capers, drained

Arrange the salmon slices over the lettuce on 8 small plates. Garnish each with a lemon slice and 1–2 slices of bread. Place a dollop of fish sauce next to the salmon and top with a few of the capers.

Serves 8.

Fish Sauce

1 tablespoon Ram Island Farm Fish Herb Blend
1 tablespoon Ram Island Farm Salad Herbs
½ cup sour cream
½ cup mayonnaise
1 tablespoon fresh lemon juice

Combine all ingredients and mix well. Allow to sit 15 minutes before serving.

Yields 1 cup of sauce.

The United Society of Shakers

SABBATHDAY LAKE • POLAND SPRING, MAINE 04274

THE UNITED SOCIETY OF SHAKERS. Sabbathday Lake, Poland Spring, Maine 04274. 207/926-4597.

For many years, Shakers were among the largest herb growers in the United States. This religious communal sect was long associated with wholesome food flavored with their own home-grown herbs. But today, what's left of the Shaker movement is little more than a mention in history books.

That is, except for one tiny community of the United Society of Shakers, for whom the dried herb and herbal tea business is again flourishing. The Sabbathday Lake Shakers, as this community is called, are spiritual descendents of a small band of religious dissidents who came to this country in 1774. The community was established in 1794 on 1,700 heavily wooded acres of property near Poland Spring in southwest Maine.

For many years the Sabbathday Lake Shakers supported themselves by growing herbs. Early on, the Shakers were known for selling and using herbs for medicinal purposes. The Pure Food and Drug Act of 1906, however, put a stop to selling herbs for healing purposes. The business languished, and their herb gardens began taking a back seat to other industries.

The renewed interest in culinary herbs has revived the business for this community. The Sabbathday Lake Shakers now grow some twenty-one herbs on 10 acres and sell dried, aromatic herbs and herbal mixes in round tins that are packed to overflowing. Their herbal teas, in thirty-four varieties, are not pulverized, but rather a mixture of identifiable flowers and leaves.

The Sabbathday Lake Shakers recently added potpourris, herbal vinegars, and fir balsam pillows to their line of herbal items. In addition, during the Christmas season, the community sells an Alfred fruitcake (named for a former Shaker community in Alfred, Maine) and Shaker stuffed dates.

Known also for their excellent, yet simple style of cooking, Sister Frances A. Carr of the Sabbathday Lake community, has written a cookbook, *Shaker Your Plate*, which is also sold by the community. A museum and a Shaker store are operated on the property from April until early December.

HOW TO PURCHASE: Full-to-brimming canisters of dried herb range from Bouquet Garni ($2) to Marigold ($1.80) and some more traditional herbs such as Oregano ($1.90), Rosemary ($1.70), and Tarragon ($4.15). Herbal Teas range from Wintergreen for $3.25 to Marshmallow Root for $4.40 on the high side. And the least expensive include Angelica Root, Horehound, and Spearmint, all $1.70 for a reusable tin. Shipping is extra. Add $1.75 for orders up to $10; $2.75 for orders between $10 and $20; and $3.75 for orders up to $30. Orders must be accompanied by check or money order payable to the United Society of Shakers.

Shaker Tarragon Chicken

Don't be fooled by the simplicity of this recipe. In true Shaker fashion, it's wonderfully moist and flavorful and the best chicken we've ever had!

> *3–4 lb. whole chicken*
> *Salt to taste*
> *¼ cup Sabbathday Lake Shaker dried tarragon*

1. Preheat the oven to 300°F. Wash the chicken well and remove giblets for another use. Pat dry and sprinkle inside and out with salt.
2. Crumble the tarragon between the fingers and rub over the chicken and inside the cavity. Put any remaining tarragon in the cavity.
3. Place in a roasting pan and cover the chicken. Bake 2 hours or until the leg can be moved in its socket. Baste the chicken every 20 to 30 minutes with the juices in the pan. Remove the cover, raise the heat to 350°F. and roast the chicken for 30 minutes.
4. Remove and let stand for 15 minutes. Carve into serving portions and serve with rendered juices.

Serves 4 to 6.

MASSACHUSETTS

Old New England Apples

BLUEBIRD ACRES. 714-747 Parker Street, East
Longmeadow, Massachusetts 01028. 413/525-6012.

When Kim Wiezbicki took up the reins at Bluebird Acres, she
became the third generation to manage a business that now sells
fifty-seven varieties of apples, other tree fruit, and berries; runs a
major bakery operation; makes convenience foods, fresh cider, and
dried everlasting arrangements. It wasn't that Wiezbicki felt coerced
into sharing that family dream. But her two younger brothers didn't
seem interested in going into farming, and "here was a place that
my father had worked so hard for all his life. I wanted to preserve
the feeling you get here," she says.

Wiezbicki's grandfather, who immigrated from Poland in 1918,
started the farm with 100 acres he bought in 1942. He planted blueberries and started the orchard. However, it was just a hobby for
this pharmacist. When Wiezbicki's father returned from the Korean
War, he decided he liked farming. He stayed on at Bluebird Acres
and started a wholesale and retail operation. He began by selling
his fruit from the back of his truck, serving a route of some 200
stops. The delivery route was eventually exchanged for a store that
he opened in 1962.

Originally named for the large bluebird population on the property, Bluebird Acres is now a sprawling complex with several small
buildings, a large farm stand store, and a miniature zoo complete
with goats, peacocks, and turkeys. Today the farm is also a part of
the Audubon Society's Project Bluebird, aimed at encouraging blue-
birds to nest again in western Massachusetts.

Although Wiezbicki manages the farm, her father still oversees
the farming, and her sister Kathy developed and manages a full-scale
bakery, which she started in 1986. Most of what's sold at Bluebird
Acres grew out of consumer demand, Wiezbicki says of the bakery,
salads, and frozen entrées. It's their answer to many health-conscious
people seeking alternatives to fast food.

The apple selection is a "find" for serious cooks who want that
certain special variety. Aside from the usual—McIntosh, Delicious,
Macouns, Empires, and Cortlands—Bluebird Acres also carries many
old Yankee apples that are rarely seen in markets or most orchards.
The farm grows Tolman Sweets, an apple that was grown by early
settlers because it was such a good keeping apple and a great cooking
apple. They also carry Rhode Island Greenings, Roxbury Russets,
Stayman Winesaps, Baldwins, Kings, and Snows with flavors that are
enough to make an apple lover foresake even the autumn McIntosh.

The orchards, too, are tended in a health-conscious way, using
a pest management program that strives to cut down on the apple
blights without spraying pesticides. It is at least one reason that so
many varieties of apples, and some hard-to-grow varieties, thrive
at Bluebird Acres.

HOW TO PURCHASE: A pack of 16 apples (any variety) is between
$13 and $15, depending on destination. Orders must be prepaid
with check or money order. Bluebird Acres will refund or bill for any
variation in prices or postage. MasterCard and Visa are also accepted.

TO VISIT: From Interstate Highway 91N take exit 2 (Forest Park,
Route 83); from Interstate Highway 91S, take exit 4 (East Longmeadow, Route 83). Go through 13 sets of traffic lights on Sumner
Avenue to Allen Street. At the thirteenth light, bear right onto Parker
Street. Bluebird Acres is 500 yards on left. Hours are 8 A.M.–7 P.M.
daily through the fall months and 8 A.M.–6 P.M. the remainder of
the year.

Apple Pudding with Crème Anglaise Sauce

This is equally a company and a family dessert. It's especially
tasty with one of the special old New England varieties of apples
grown at Bluebird Acres.

> 10 medium-size Bluebird Acres apples (Roxbury
>   Russets or Stayman Winesaps are good)
> 6 tablespoons unsalted butter
> ¼ cup honey
> ¼ cup apricot preserves
> ¼ cup dark rum
> 1 teaspoon cinnamon

Cake

> 6 tablespoons unsalted butter
> ½ cup sugar
> 4 egg yolks
> 1 teaspoon cinnamon
> 1 teaspoon pure vanilla extract
> 1 cup fresh unflavored breadcrumbs
> 1 tablespoon all-purpose flour
> 3 egg whites
> 1 tablespoon sugar

1. Peel apples and cut into thin slices. Melt 6 tablespoons of butter
in a large skillet. Add the apples and sauté 3 minutes or until slightly
soft. Add honey, preserves, rum, and 1 teaspoon cinnamon. Mix to
blend and remove from heat.

2. Preheat oven to 350°F. Butter an 11- or 12-inch quiche pan.
Spread the apple mixture evenly over the pan.

3. Cream the remaining butter with the sugar until smooth. Add
the egg yolks one at a time and beat until fluffy. Add the cinnamon,
vanilla, breadcrumbs, and flour and mix well. In a separate bowl,
beat the egg whites with the 1 tablespoon of sugar until they form
stiff peaks. Spoon a third of the mixture over the breadcrumb mixture and fold well. Add remaining whites and fold in gently. Some
of the whites will still be visible. With a spatula, spread the mixture
over the apples. Set pan on cookie sheet and bake 35 to 40 minutes
or until top is brown. Remove from oven and cool 3 hours at room
temperature before serving. Or refrigerate overnight and serve at
room temperature. Serve with spoonfuls of the Crème Anglaise Sauce
below.

Serves 10.

Crème Anglaise Sauce

> 3 egg yolks
> ⅓ cup sugar
> 1 cup milk
> ½ teaspoon pure vanilla extract
> 2 tablespoons dark rum

In a small saucepan whisk together the yolks and the sugar. Heat
the milk in a separate pan until hot but not scalded, and add slowly
to the yolk mixture, whisking continuously. Set over medium heat
and stir constantly until mixture begins to steam. When mixture
thickens enough to coat a wooden spoon, remove from heat and
add the vanilla and the rum. Cool and serve with the Apple Pudding
above.

Edible Seaweeds

Cape Ann Seaweeds Co.

Alaria ✓

Alaria esculenta

CAPE ANN SEAWEEDS COMPANY. 2 Stage Fort, Gloucester, Massachusetts 01930. 508/283-9308.

Anyone who's ever walked along the Cape Ann shore after a storm or at low tide knows that seaweeds are abundant along this rock-strewn shoreline. Fortunate people such as Linda Parker, creator of Cape Ann Seaweeds Company, know that seaweeds make good eating, too.

Nearly all the North Atlantic seaweeds are quite tasty and supremely nutritious, according to Parker. Among her many products are vitamin-rich kelp, alaria, dulse, and laver. And there are as many ways to prepare them as there are joys of cooking, says the seaweed expert who's whipped up a few of her own tasty recipes: Curried Kelp with Cashews, Raisins, and Red Lentils; Sweet Potato Dulse; and Tiger Moss Chutney among them.

Parker, who is also a polarity therapist, seems to know more about the waters near her home in Gloucester than do the fish who live there. This hearty soul does most of her own harvesting, swimming out in the cold waters to dive for kelp and wading just offshore to collect the varieties of seaweed that drape the shoreline rocks at low tide. She gathers several kinds of seaweed. But she waits until each reaches its peak of growth before it's collected. Products are sun- or air-dried before being packaged for sale.

Parker, who began by collecting seaweeds for her own use, started her business in 1980 when she and a friend discovered a large crop of laver and decided to sell it in a local food coop. Motivated by the knowledge that sea crops are abundant around Cape Ann and that few other dealers were handling seaweed products in Massachusetts, Parker decided to develop her idea into an enterprise.

Part of her business is educating people about these underwater vegetables. She's put together handouts, recipe cards, and demonstrations to help people appreciate ocean vegetables. Parker conducts seaweed identification classes and cooking classes and is writing and photographing a cookbook and handbook about the ocean weeds.

The trick, says Parker, is to treat seaweeds as you would any other vegetable. Each kind has its own properties and characteristics that can be enhanced by cooking it a certain way and with certain ingredients. For instance, she explains, kelp and alaria require more cooking so they are excellent with long-cooking grains and beans. Quick-cooking dulse and laver taste good toasted and stir-fried or mixed with other vegetables.

HOW TO PURCHASE: Cape Ann Seaweed Company sends bags of seaweeds through the mail in large padded envelopes. A 1-lb bag of Alaria is $6, Nori (laver) is $8, Kelp is $5, and Dulse is $6.50. Four-ounce packages are $1.80 for Alaria, $2 for Nori, $1.60 for Kelp, and $2 for Dulse. Shipping is extra and is usually by Parcel Post. That cost is 50¢–$1 per lb. depending on destination. Orders must be prepaid with check or money order to Cape Ann Seaweed Company.

Curried Red Lentils with Cauliflower and Kelp

A tasty vegetarian dish, this one covers all the vital food groups thanks to the addition of Cape Ann Seaweeds kelp. It's quite delicious with steamed rice that's been flavored with turmeric and plumped raisins.

> 1 cup quick cooking red lentils
> 4 cups water
> 1 tablespoon finely chopped fresh ginger
> 1 large clove garlic, minced
> ½ teaspoon cayenne
> ½ teaspoon turmeric
> Four 3-inch pieces Cape Ann Seaweeds dried kelp
> 2 tablespoons vegetable oil
> 1 large onion, chopped
> ½ teaspoon salt
> 1 tablespoon lemon juice
> 1 cup cauliflower florets, steamed 5 minutes

1. Rinse the lentils well and remove any stones. Place lentils and water in a medium saucepan and bring to a boil. Skim the top just as the liquid comes to a boil. Lower the heat and add the ginger, garlic, cayenne, and turmeric. Stir to combine. Top with the pieces of kelp and cover tightly. Simmer 1 hour or until lentils are soft and mixture is the consistency of thick pea soup. Shake the pot occasionally to make sure the lentils are not sticking to the bottom of the pan.

2. In a small frying pan, add the oil and onions and cook until onions are quite brown. Reserve.

3. Remove the kelp with a slotted spoon and cut into 1-inch squares. Add the kelp, salt, lemon juice, cauliflower, and browned onions and mix. Heat gently and serve.

Serves 6.

Fresh Shiitake Mushrooms

DELFTREE CORPORATION. 234 Union Street, North Adams, Massachusetts 01247. 413/664-4907.

"Why in America, land of plenty, have generations been raised with just one fresh mushroom—the common white button mushroom?" queries Peter Duble, vice-president of Delftree Corporation. Duble and his partner Bill Greenwald decided theirs would be the last generation to know only one kind of mushroom. The two have turned that market around by becoming one of the largest growers (and the first year-round commercial producer) of fresh shiitake mushrooms in this country.

In a red brick, turn-of-the-century cotton mill in North Adams, Massachusetts, the two grow nearly 6,000 pounds of these beefy delicacies each week on "logs" made from a secret combination of sawdust and nutrients. A room the size of a football field is crammed with racks that reach up to the top of the 14-foot ceiling and hold about 50,000 of the mottled brown logs that allow the company to produce fresh shiitake mushrooms all year round. Before Delftree, anyone who wanted to grow shiitakes had to do it the Japanese way, by drilling holes in a bunch of oak logs, pouring in the spores, setting them in the backyard, and waiting.

Just how they make their mushrooms grow indoors and in sawdust is a trade secret that the two carefully guard from would-be competitors. It's a process that mycologist Stephen Lundy developed and used to found the Lundy Mushroom Company in 1980. Greenwald joined him as general manager, but in 1984, Lundy was killed in a plane crash. Greenwald and Duble picked up the pieces, acquired many investors, and soon production was soaring.

"Anything you can do with button mushrooms you can do with shiitakes, only better," says Duble, who just might be the world's biggest fan of fresh shiitakes. He likes them just about any way, but marinated and grilled is his favorite.

Indeed, the dense, meaty-textured, dark brown mushrooms have a hearty flavor that makes them far more interesting for cooking than the button variety. They also have a much longer shelf life (about 4 weeks) and twice the protein and fiber of the white mushrooms.

Duble and Greenwald broke into the market primarily as wholesalers and have become major suppliers to fine restaurants, caterers, and specialty stores on the East Coast. Most recently, however, they've made Delftree mushrooms available to individual cooks through mail order. We'd say that's almost as revolutionary as the mushrooms themselves!

HOW TO PURCHASE: Delftree will ship a 3- or 7-lb. ventilated box of mushrooms for $6.50 per pound plus shipping. (These keep up to 4 weeks in the refrigerator or share them with friends.) Orders are mailed U.P.S. Delftree will also accept telephone orders with payment by major credit cards.

Cream of Mushroom Soup

This substantial potage is even heartier when healthy slices of fresh Delftree shiitake mushrooms are added.

1 oz. dried cepes or porcini mushrooms, rinsed well to remove grit
4 cups good quality chicken stock
1 medium onion, chopped
3 tablespoons Madeira or dry sherry
7 tablespoons unsalted butter, in all
4 tablespoons all-purpose flour
½ lb. Delftree shiitake mushrooms, sliced
½ lb. white mushrooms, sliced
2 teaspoons fresh sage leaves, chopped, or 1 teaspoon dried sage leaves
1 teaspoon fresh thyme leaves, chopped, or ½ teaspoon dried thyme
Salt and freshly ground pepper to taste
2 cups half-and-half
½ cup Delftree shiitake mushrooms, sliced, for garnish
¼ cup chopped fresh parsley, for garnish

1. In a medium saucepan combine the dried mushrooms and the chicken stock and simmer covered for 5 minutes. Add the onion and the Madeira and simmer covered until the onion is soft (about 5 minutes). Transfer to a food processor or a blender and blend until smooth.

2. In a large saucepan, melt 5 tablespoons of the butter over medium heat. Add flour and stir with a wooden spoon until blended into a thick paste. Slowly add the purée, stirring constantly until mixture has thickened. Remove from heat and add the sliced shiitake and white mushrooms, the herbs, salt and pepper, and the half-and-half. Heat on low and simmer slowly for 10 minutes. Sauté remaining shiitake mushrooms in 2 tablespoons of butter until golden. Add to soup before serving. Garnish with parsley.

Serves 6–8.

Salt-free Herbal Sprinkles

POTLUCK & THYME. 9 Crescent Street, P.O. Box 1546, Salem, New Hampshire 03079. 603/893-9965.

When her youngest daughter was found to have a dangerously high sodium level, Ursula St. Louis became an instant expert on sodium. At the time, St. Louis was also exploring ways to re-enter the work force without taking on a traditional 9-to-5 job. She wanted to contribute to the family income yet stay home with her children.

The result was a line of salt-free herb and spice blends called Potluck & Thyme. St. Louis began her business in 1983, making three blends: All-purpose Sprinkle has a basil base; Gourmet Sprinkle has plenty of dill; and Seafood Sprinkle combines parsley, lemon peel, and garlic. Her mixes are finely ground rather than the coarse blends that many herb companies offer.

St. Louis first started by buying her herbs and grinding them in coffee grinders. It was a messy job, and she ran the risk of overheating the herbs while they were grinding. So, she found a better, commercial grinding company that would process her herbs in 10 seconds without producing any of the damaging heat that can ruin the fresh taste.

She began marketing her products by telephone and giving demonstrations and lectures. She soon began to feel that her packaging was dull and boring. She exchanged earth tone labels for bright primary colors and added a gift set of all three tastes in tiny wooden crates built by her husband Richard.

By a stroke of luck, a local husband and wife team of physicians, Drs. Gardner and Beatty, moved to California to manage a stress program at the well-known La Costa Health Spa and brought St. Louis's products with them. La Costa started putting the shakers of Pot Luck and Thyme Sprinkles on the dining room tables. "People actually started 'lifting' the shakers, because they didn't know where to find it," says the amazed St. Louis.

Although her customers are chiefly health food mavens and people on salt-free diets, St. Louis encourages everyone to "shake the habit." She now distributes nationwide, and according to her latest sales information, she makes some 2,500 pounds of salt-free sprinkles each year.

HOW TO PURCHASE: Potluck & Thyme products are available by mail. The All-purpose Herbal Sprinkle is $2.89; Gourmet Sprinkle is $2.99; and the Seafood Sprinkle costs $3.09. A gift pack of all 3 comes in a wooden crate for $11.95. All come in 1-oz. jars. Shipping and handling is extra. Add $1.95 for orders between $2.50 and $9.99; $3.25 for orders between $10 and $24.99; and $5.25 for orders from $25 to $49.99. Calculate shipping and handling separately when gift orders are placed. St. Louis does not accept credit cards.

La Costa Spa Chicken with Pommery Mustard Sauce

This recipe is compliments of La Costa Hotel and Spa dining room in Carlsbad, California. It's so rich and delicious, you'd never guess it's also lo-cal and healthy, too.

Eight 3-oz. boneless chicken breasts

Marinade

½ cup rice vinegar
½ cup balsamic vinegar
1 cup unsalted chicken stock, defatted
¼ cup Pommery Mustard (or other whole grain mustard)

Sauce

1 cup low-fat plain yogurt
1 tablespoon Pommery Mustard (or other whole grain mustard)
2 teaspoons Potluck & Thyme Gourmet Sprinkle

1. Marinate chicken in marinade ingredients for 2–4 hours. Spray a sauté pan with vegetable spray and set over medium heat. Sauté chicken breasts until well browned on both sides. Transfer to a serving platter and set in a warm oven while making the sauce.
2. In a double boiler, whisk together sauce ingredients. Continue whisking until sauce is warm. Ladle about 2 oz. of the sauce over each 3-ounce chicken breast and serve. Or spoon sauce over the chicken in a serving platter and serve garnished with fresh dill.

Serves 8 as part of a La Costa diet plan.

RHODE ISLAND

Herbal Teas and Culinary Herbs

MEADOWBROOK HERB GARDEN. Route 138, Wyoming, Rhode Island 02898. 401/539-7603.

Imagine our surprise as, driving along the nearly deserted Route 138, we came upon a brightly lettered sign for Meadowbrook Herb Garden. Picture, too, our delight to discover that the sign led to an impressive herb farm with formal and educational gardens where naturalists Tom and Marjory Fortier produce only the purest organic items.

It's not without painstaking effort, however, that the Fortiers grow and process a complete line of culinary, tea, and potpourri herbs in this setting and also go to great lengths to preserve the environment. Not surprisingly, absolutely everything is done by hand.

All plants are started from seedlings in an organically run greenhouse. A mixture of botanical pesticides, natural fungicides, and sulfur are used, and in combination with the fragrance of the herbs, the greenhouse is always filled with a wonderful ''stink,'' as the owners say.

Seedlings are transplanted into long rows by hand to avoid any chance that farm machinery may leave axle grease, oil, gasoline, or fumes that could contaminate the soil or growing plants. Plants are fertilized with a bio-dynamic compost devised and mixed at Meadowbrook. Herbs are harvested by hand and dried in the Meadowbrook drying houses at very low heat (around 100°F.). Then they are rubbed through steel screening and graded to remove stems and coarse particles. Finally the herbs are shaken in a cloth bag to remove any remaining leaf particles. The herbs are packaged only in glass jars because the Fortiers believe it keeps flavor in and moisture out better than other types of packaging.

Perhaps the two are a bit old-fashioned in their quality control. Certainly, it's challenging not to select easier, more modern technology to do the job. But these botanical perfectionists are not looking for the most economical route. The Fortiers aim to produce the tastiest and purest organic herbs they can while preserving the environment for the next generation of herb growers. That's a tradition that started with the original owner Heinz Grotzke, who began Meadowbrook Herb Garden in 1965. The Fortiers apprenticed under Grotzke, a world-renowned herbalist, before buying the operation from him in 1982. Grotzke trained in traditional, very strict, prechemical herb growing which he passed on to his two protégés.

Approximately 250 varieties of herbs are grown on the farm; other spices, teas, and herbal cosmetics are imported from a trustworthy processing plant in Germany. Teas range from the single flavors such as peppermint and spearmint to the ever-popular House Tea, which blends fourteen herbs (including blackberry leaves, peppermint, woodruff, calendula, and yarrow). Meadowbrook also makes several culinary mixes, including fish herbs and hamburger seasonings.

About 16,000 people use herbs from Meadowbrook Herb Garden. ''Most farmers would have to have massive machinery to feed that many people,'' says Tom Fortier. ''It feels good to have so many beneficiaries of our efforts and we do it all by hand!''

HOW TO PURCHASE: All Meadowbrook Herb Garden products are sold by mail. Tea blends (including the House Tea) are $2.95 per 3-oz. package. Tea and potpourri herbs, chiefly packed in .75-oz. quantities, are $1.90 each. Others, in 1- to 4.5-oz. packages, range in price from $1.50 to $4.50 each. Culinary herbs are $1.45 each. Imported and domestic spices are $1.45 each. There is a $3 shipping and handling charge per order, and a $10 minimum order is required. Orders may be paid with check or money order. MasterCard and Visa are accepted. Write or call for the latest 30-page catalog which is $1 and chocked full of information about herbs.

VERMONT

Apples, Maple Syrup & Preserves

GRAFTON VILLAGE APPLE COMPANY, INC. RR 3, Box 236D, Grafton, Vermont 05146. 802/843-2406; 1/800-843-4822, orders only.

Joe Pollio's secret for success in farming Vermont style is plenty of good old-fashioned hard labor combined with all the high-tech assistance available. A former executive vice-president with Pollio Dairy Products in Manhattan, Joe and his wife Janice fell in love with Vermont more than 20 years ago during a fall vacation. The romance never stopped, and in 1979, they bought a home on the outskirts of Grafton and turned to a life of farming.

Pollio slowly and purposefully worked his first 30 acres into farm and orchard, planting and experimenting with fruit trees as he cultivated the land. He planted about 400 apple trees in those first 3 or 4 years. By 1987, he had 3,800 trees, and the Grafton Village company had reclaimed some 300 acres of land that had been overrun with forest. Pollio hopes to successfully cultivate nearly 6,000 apple trees by 1989.

On the high-tech side, Grafton Village Apple Company uses few pesticides in growing apples. Instead, Pollio runs his orchards under a strict Integrated Pest Management program that studies pest populations and introduces good bugs to gobble up the bad bugs.

The company operates two apple orchards, a country store, an apple storage barn, a sugar bush, and sugar house, a cider pressing facility, and a sizable mail order business. It's all run by a series of five fancy computers that handle everything from accounting to orchard management.

This apple company features seven varieties of McIntosh apples. Pollio is also working to bring back several types of old-time apples that are seldom cultivated anymore.

The company makes its own honey, preserves, maple syrup, and cider, which are all for sale in the country store on the premises as well as through a multi-page mail order catalog that includes a number of made-in-Vermont products from other cottage industries.

HOW TO PURCHASE: An apple mini-crate (12 McIntosh apples in a miniature wooden apple crate) is sold for $16.95. A gift box of 16 crunchy McIntosh apples, picked just after the first frost, is $13.95. Apples are available from September 15 to January 15. Shipping is extra. Add $1.75 for orders up to $10; $2.75 from $10-$14; $3.95 for orders between $14.01 and $25. Credit cards are accepted.

Auntie's Famous Apple Cake

My husband's Aunt Irene is known for making terrific pastries. She's particularly famous for this one. Every time there's a question about what to make for dessert, the response is "Make Auntie's apple cake."

> 3 cups sliced McIntosh apples
> 5 tablespoons sugar
> 5 teaspoons cinnamon
> 3 cups all-purpose flour
> 2 cups sugar
> 3 teaspoons baking powder
> 1 teaspoon salt
> 4 eggs
> 1 cup vegetable oil
> ½ cup orange juice
> Grated rind of ½ orange

1. Grease and flour a tube cake pan. Preheat oven to 375 °F. Toss the apples with the 5 tablespoons of sugar and the cinnamon. In a large mixing bowl, sift together the flour, 2 cups sugar, baking powder, and salt. In a separate bowl, combine the eggs, oil, juice, and rind and mix until blended. Add to the sifted ingredients and mix just until moistened. Do not overmix.
2. Spread a third of the batter over the bottom and slightly up the sides of the prepared pan. Cover with half the apple mixture then cover with a third of the batter. Use a spatula to smooth the batter over the apples. Repeat with remaining apples and batter and smooth the top of the cake so that the batter fills in around the apples. Bake 1 hour. Cover with a tent of aluminum foil and bake 20 minutes longer. Remove from oven. Leave in the pan and cool on a wire rack for 1 hour. Turn onto a serving plate.

Serves 8–10.

Herbal Recipe Kits

RATHDOWNEY LTD. 3 River Street, P.O. Box 357, Bethel, Vermont 05032. 1/800-543-8885 or 802/234-9928 in Vermont.

Louise Downey-Butler is the kind of new-breed entrepreneur one reads about in business magazines; the determined and innovative type who leaves a job as an environmental engineer in Ohio and turns a fantasy into an "overnight success" in small-town Vermont.

It all started when Downey-Butler realized that her hobby was more satisfying than her job. She would work in an office 5 days a week, then go out on weekends begging to help in other people's herb gardens. So she and husband Brendan picked out a Federalist-style farmhouse in Bethel, Vermont, with 3 acres of poison ivy and sumac in the backyard.

The newly landed homesteaders cleared the property and planted pounds of organically grown herbs. In 1981, Rathdowney (named after a town in Brendan's native Ireland) was created. Initially Downey-Butler sold dried herbs, spices, sachets, and some herb mixes. She also sold postcards with recipes done in calligraphy. Her ideas were slow to catch on. Then she had a brainstorm. Why not combine herb blends and recipe cards and call them Recipe Kits? Business grew tenfold.

She started with three mixes: curry powder, chili, and boursin (which transforms cream cheese into a yummy version of the French cheese in seconds). Today more than 30 blends are part of Rathdowney's special packets. There's one for pumpkin pie, spice cookies, winter pesto, a hot, country-style mustard making kit, a salsa blend (just add tomatoes), and a packet that makes "the ultimate garlic bread."

To support their family of five, the Downey-Butlers had started out with other jobs as teachers in private schools. That didn't last long, however. Soon Rathdowney was a flourishing business and included a cafe/gift shop in a nearby shopping mall. By 1985, sales had risen over the $100,000 mark. Expansion came so fast that Downey-Butler had to hire a full-time employee, and the family moved to the upstairs part of the farmhouse.

Today there's a workshop in the Victorian parlor, and a computer adorns the family dining room. The correspondence looks "pretty sophisticated" as a result of the last, but Downey-Butler still does all the letters and bills herself. Her retail catalog and wholesale brochure and an extensive mail-order listing are all done on the computer.

Enthusiasm and commitment aside, Rathdowney offers top quality (no salt or sugar) products that are inexpensive (most are $2 a packet) and can't be beat for convenience and taste. While the Downey-Butlers bask in success, they shrink from being called lucky. Simply put, "work can be your fantasy," says Downey-Butler of their success.

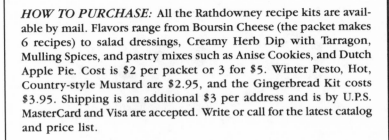

HOW TO PURCHASE: All the Rathdowney recipe kits are available by mail. Flavors range from Boursin Cheese (the packet makes 6 recipes) to salad dressings, Creamy Herb Dip with Tarragon, Mulling Spices, and pastry mixes such as Anise Cookies, and Dutch Apple Pie. Cost is $2 per packet or 3 for $5. Winter Pesto, Hot, Country-style Mustard are $2.95, and the Gingerbread Kit costs $3.95. Shipping is an additional $3 per address and is by U.P.S. MasterCard and Visa are accepted. Write or call for the latest catalog and price list.

Tarragon and Herb Grilled Salmon Steaks

This quick and tasty way to cook salmon is terrific for the barbecue but may also be made under the broiler.

> *¼-oz. package Rathdowney Creamy Herb Dip*
> *with Tarragon*
> *½ cup heavy cream*
> *1 cup mayonnaise*
> *3 tablespoons cider vinegar*
> *6 salmon steaks (about 6 oz. each)*

1. Combine the herb dip with the heavy cream, mayonnaise, and vinegar and let stand 15 minutes.
2. Wash the salmon and pat dry. Spread about 1 tablespoon of the herb mixture over the salmon. Turn each steak and cover with another tablespoon of the dip. Let stand 15 minutes or refrigerate for 1 hour.
3. Heat a charcoal grill and grill the salmon on both sides (about 5 minutes on each side). Serve with remaining sauce.

Serves 6.

Salt for all Seasons

SALT FOR ALL SEASONS. P.O. Box 629, Norwich, Vermont 05055. 802/649-2839.

Barbara von Mettenheim took the scenic route to becoming the owner of the small cottage industry she runs today. Von Mettenheim worked in the restaurant business for 22 years and somewhere during that illustrious career even found time to study at LaVarenne Ecole de Cuisine in Paris, France. Then she retired from restaurants to raise her daughter and get a master's degree in Medieval Manuscripts.

When those last two endeavors were under control, von Mettenheim decided she didn't want to go back to work for someone else. She was always mixing up batches of a salt-garlic-and-herb seasoning that "I discovered to be the best seasoning I have ever used," she says.

"Friends kept bugging me to make 'some of that stuff' for them," says von Mettenheim. With so many requests for the seasoning mix coming in, there was no question but she should market it.

In 1986, von Mettenheim started Salt for all Seasons, an all-natural product that uses aromatic herbs, spices, and fresh garlic. It's a complete seasoning that can be used alone or with other seasonings.

This sprightly salt-plus is at home with soups, fish, poultry, pasta, or even game. It's terrific teamed up with tomato, especially a fresh garden-ripe tomato salad. It's especially useful for busy people, who have found this seasoned salt to be their best ally in the struggle against boring midweek meals.

Herbs and garlic are ground by von Mettenheim, who uses no MSG, sugar, chicken, or beef base in her magical mixture.

HOW TO PURCHASE: A 3-oz. shaker of Salt for all Seasons i $1.79. Case prices are available. Postage is extra and shipment i via U.P.S. To order, send check or money order, payable to Salt fo all Seasons, Ltd.

Tomato and Avocado Salad

This refreshing combination of vegetables and lemon juice i brightened by a sprinkle of Salt for all Seasons. We've used this salad on nachos and over salad greens with equal relish.

> *3 large vine-ripened tomatoes, chopped*
> *2 medium avocados, peeled, pitted, and chopped*
> *½ medium red onion, minced*
> *Juice of 1 lemon*
> *2 tablespoons extra virgin olive oil*
> *¼ cup Italian parsley, finely chopped*
> *¾ teaspoon Salt for all Seasons*
> *Freshly ground black pepper*

Toss the tomatoes, avocado pieces, and the minced red onion in a bowl. Add the remaining ingredients and toss gently to mix. Chill until serving time.

Serves 4.

SWEETS

Chocolate Lace

Chocolate Lace.
the original lace candy by Eugenia Tay

CHOCOLATE LACE. 14 Clark Circle, Bethel, Connecticut 06801. 203/792-8175.

From a sparkling new candy factory in Bethel emerges a one-of-kind chocolate experience that makes even the most jaded chocolate lover feel like Russian royalty. A crunchy marriage of rich, bittersweet chocolate and a web of gossamer caramelized sugar produces the delicate treat called Chocolate Lace.

Behind the distinctive confection is the romantic tale about a young woman named Eugenia Tay, who grew up in a privileged family in Czarist Russia around the turn of the century.

Eugenia and her family celebrated the arrival of the first deep snowfall each year by drizzling molten caramelized sugar onto the newly fallen snow, creating fanciful patterns as it cooled and hardened. Then they would rush inside with their treasures and quickly dip them into a pan of deep, dark chocolate. The result was extraordinary chocolate snowflakes that delighted family and the special friends who were lucky enough to receive them as gifts.

When the Tay family fled Russia and settled in New York, they brought the candy-making tradition with them—only now they used a cold marble slab in place of the New York snow. They continued to bestow friends with chocolate lace presents. Soon the demand for this chocolate treat surpassed the Tays' ability to produce it, causing Eugenia to design a machine that could recreate the lacy patterns in larger quantities.

Today, the candy-making tradition of Eugenia Tay continues on the very machine that she designed in 1917. The only one of its kind, this machine lays down an intricate web of patterns and thus acquired the nickname, "Veronica Lace" after 1940s starlet Veronica Lake.

Tay died in 1979. Eventually the business was bought by Stephen Bray in 1982. Bray, who'd been the marketing director for Warner-Lambert, gladly traded coat and tie for broken-in corduroy pants and a license to work for himself. He moved the machine and the business to Connecticut, where he and his wife Connie continue the tradition.

Bray markets Chocolate Lace as the small company with a very special story and as a candy for those who like to search things out for themselves and discover the very best. The elegant candy comes wrapped in aristocratic red boxes with gold lettering and gold elastic tie and includes the tale of Eugenia Tay and her lace-making machine.

In the style established by the Tays, people are still giving Chocolate Lace when they want to give something special. Just before Connie and Steve were to be married (and before they had any thoughts about buying a chocolate business), their mothers, who had never met, each sent the other a little Christmas gift. It was Chocolate Lace!

HOW TO PURCHASE: Chocolate Lace, in 7- and 14-oz. boxes, may be ordered by mail at a cost of $6.95 and $12.95. Prices include shipping. In addition to dark chocolate, Lace comes coated in mint chocolate or toasted almond chocolate for the same price. Ten-ounce boxes of Lace crumbles are also sold for $6.95 and are the perfect addition to favorite mousse and ice cream desserts. Payment is by check or money order to Chocolate Lace.

Frozen Mocha Mousse Crunch

The smooth, silky texture of this mocha mousse with the added crunch of Chocolate Lace makes for a truly memorable dessert.

> *3 tablespoons instant coffee*
> *½ cup boiling water*
> *1 lb. good quality semisweet chocolate cut into small pieces*
> *6 eggs, separated*
> *½ cup granulated sugar*
> *1 teaspoon vanilla*
> *Pinch of cream of tartar*
> *1½ cups heavy cream*
> *⅔ cup Chocolate Lace candy broken into ¼-inch pieces*

1. Dissolve the coffee in boiling water. Set the chocolate in the top of a double boiler and melt over low heat, stirring occasionally until the chocolate is smooth.

2. Using an electric mixer, beat the yolks with half the sugar at high speed until they reach the ribbon stage. Turn the mixer to the lowest setting. Add the coffee, then the chocolate and the vanilla, and beat to combine. Set the mixture aside.

3. In a clean, dry mixer, beat the egg whites until frothy. Add a pinch of cream of tartar and the remaining sugar and beat until whites form stiff peaks. In a separate bowl, beat the cream until very stiff.

4. Reserve a third of the egg whites and fold the remainder into the chocolate mixture. Then fold in the heavy cream. Add the Chocolate Lace candy to reserved whites and mix gently. Fold into the chocolate mousse and turn the mixture into a 9-inch springform pan. Freeze 4 hours or overnight. Cut a few minutes before serving.

Serves 8–12.

Old-fashioned, Handmade Candies

CRAND'S CANDY CASTLE, INC. Box 3023, Enfield, Connecticut 06082. 203/623-5515.

On the "main road" through Enfield in northern Connecticut is an impressive 1850 Federal-style building. Called "the Chimneys" due to its four massive chimneys, it's both home to the Crand family and to a candy-making tradition known to most throughout this area for nearly 40 years simply as Crand's Candy.

Famous for fine chocolate creations with no additives or stabilizers, the Crand family makes their confections the old-fashioned way. This is a family that uses only top-of-the-line chocolate and is even fussy about the kind of corn syrup it uses, insisting on a difficult-to-obtain "43 Regular" (drawn off the corn syrup at a certain temperature) because it makes the fluffiest centers. And this is the company that hand-pulls its candy canes at Christmas time to produce a dense and substantial stick of candy. The Crands also make a splendid pecan roll, which begins with a thick, handmade piece of nougat, covered with caramel, and rolled in pecan pieces. The nougat, simply egg whites and corn syrup, is not as easy to make as it sounds. Success depends on timing and humidity, explains Thomas Crand, who with brother Robert, runs the business.

Their father, John Crand, was a Greek immigrant who arrived in this country in 1911 and started making candy in the basement of a cousin's ice cream parlor. The persevering man taught himself to make candy by trial and error. During the stock market crash of 1929, he lost everything but made a comeback by starting his own shop in 1935 in Gardner, Massachusetts. In 1952, the Crands moved to Enfield and brought their shop with them.

The patriarch of the Crand operation died in 1966, but not before he'd taught his sons everything he knew about candy-making. Today Crand Candy makes nearly 75,000 pounds of candy a year for sale in the retail shop on the premises and by mail order. This homespun operation sells wonderful items such as cherry cordials, chocolate-covered mints, peanut clusters, dark and light turtles, penuche, and other fudge flavors, bark, and chocolate covered fruits. They make a French roll that's an exclusive for Crands—a cross between fudge and caramel and rolled in nuts.

Crand candy can be mail ordered all year round. In the summer months, they use insulated bags and pack these in insulated boxes to ensure safe arrival. Crand's Candy even makes it intact to the southern states in July or August, promises Thomas Crand.

HOW TO PURCHASE: Crand Candy is $7.50 per lb. for the most expensive assortment (including cherry cordials, pecan roll, French roll, nut cups, and buttercrunch). The regular assortment—chocolate creams, nougats, and fudge—is $7 per lb. There is an additional charge for shipping and it will vary depending on destination. Handling is 50¢. Individual items are available by the pound, and come in milk, white, or dark chocolate. Write or call for a price list and to place an order. Crands bills the customer. They accept MasterCard, Visa, check, or money order.

HAUSER CHOCOLATIER. 18 Taylor Avenue, Bethel, Connecticut 06801. 203/794-1861.

Ruedi Hauser always wanted to make a world-class chocolate in the United States. Now premium chocolate and Hauser Chocolatier are nearly synonymous. Hauser's products have been featured in several food journals including *Bon Appetit* and *Chocolatier*, and his Swiss-style, silky smooth, soft-center truffles and molded chocolate holiday specialties have been pronounced "the best" from professional and amateur chocoholics alike.

But Hauser has not always been in the chocolate business. A culinary wizard who trained as a pastry chef, confectioner, and chef de cuisine, the Swiss-born Ruedi could have picked just about any facet of the food world as his profession. He arrived in this country in 1963 and was working as a pastry chef at the Monmouth Hotel in New Jersey when he met Lucille, his soon-to-be wife and partner in business. Lucille had arrived at the hotel for a summer job and was assigned as Ruedi's pastry assistant.

The two married and moved to Bethel, where they opened the Swiss Pastry Shop in 1973. Although pastry was their drawing card, the two made everything. Soon they had so many special requests, they closed the pastry shop and opened a catering business that they called Edelweiss. The whole time, the two were also making their chocolate specialties. And Ruedi began teaching a chocolate-making class.

By 1983, Ruedi and Lucille decided the chocolate business was the way to go and gave up doing pastries, catering, and all the rest. They built a 10,000-square-foot factory where today they produce more than 100,000 pounds of chocolate products each year. That figure is sure to grow, since the two have just added a wholesale business.

During the busy season, the company becomes a family business with the Hauser's three sons helping out with chocolate dipping, packing, and handling special orders. They also have employees now. But Ruedi still does most of the fillings for the chocolates, and Lucille still does some of the finishing work but concentrates on the publicity and marketing, and the fancy packaging that gives their product the rich glitter of a world-class operation.

Perhaps best known for Swiss-style truffles made with heavy cream, sweet butter, and natural flavorings, the Hauser product list also includes pralines, gingerbread kits, chocolate Easter eggs, Easter bunnies, Christmas ornaments, dark and white chocolate dessert cups, and truffle shells.

HOW TO PURCHASE: Hauser chocolates are sold in a small retail shop on the premises. Hours are 8:30 A.M.–5:30 P.M., Monday through Friday, and 10 A.M.–2 P.M. on Saturday. They are available in fine candy stores, department stores, gourmet shops, and by mail. Prices range from $19.50 for 1 lb. of Swiss-style truffles; old-fashioned almond bark is $12.50 per lb. A box of 12 dessert cups (specify white or dark chocolate) is $11.50. Shipping is via U.P.S. Add $2.50 for orders up to $9.99; $3.25 for orders between $10 and $19.99; and $4 for orders from $20 to $29.99. Shipments to warmer climates are usually sent Second Day Air and an additional charge will be added. The Hausers will send gift boxes. MasterCard and Visa are accepted.

TO VISIT: From Main Street, Danbury, travel east to the intersection with Route 53 (South Street) and take a left. At the intersection with Route 302 (Greenwood Avenue) in Bethel, bear left, then take the third right onto Blackman Avenue. At stop sign take a left and follow to the second right, which is Taylor Avenue. Turn right and cross railroad tracks, and Hauser Chocolatier is on the left.

Cranberry Mousse in Dark Chocolate Cups

This festive and yummy dessert is the perfect ending to a holiday meal. But don't wait for that special occasion. It's wonderful anytime!

Cranberry Mousse

1½ cups cranberries
1 cup water
½ cup granulated sugar
1 envelope unflavored gelatin
2 egg yolks
¼ cup cranberry liqueur
2 tablespoons granulated sugar
1 pint heavy cream

"Frosted" berries

½ cup cranberries
1 egg white
2 tablespoons granulated sugar
12 Hauser Dark Chocolate Cups

1. In a saucepan over medium heat, combine 1½ cups cranberries with 1 cup water and ½ cup sugar. Bring to a boil, reduce heat, and simmer until reduced to about 1 cup. While sauce is hot, add the gelatin and stir thoroughly. Let cool briefly and add the yolks, 2 tablespoons sugar, and the liqueur. Let cool until mixture is just beginning to set.

2. Meanwhile whip cream until very stiff. Spoon out 1 cup of the whipped cream and refrigerate. Gently fold remaining cream into mousse mixture. Spoon mousse into pastry bag fitted with a large tube and pipe a high rounded mound of the mixture into 12 chocolate cups, while cups remain in the tray. Refrigerate.

3. To make the berries, lightly beat the white, and coat ½ cup cranberries with the egg white. Let berries dry briefly then toss gently with granulated sugar for a "frosted" effect.

4. Place the reserved whipped cream in a pastry bag fitted with a star tube and pipe a cream rosette on top of each cranberry mousse cup. Set 3 frosted berries on top. Refrigerate until ready to serve.

Yields 12 desserts.

MAINE

Seavey's Needhams

LOU-ROD CANDY KITCHENS. P.O. Box 258, Lewiston, Maine 04240. 207/784-5822.

For those of us who grew up on Seavey's Needhams, it was shocking to discover, on leaving Maine, that the rest of the world knew nothing about these creamy coconut candies covered in bittersweet chocolate. This author spent her entire childhood hunting down the plain cardboard boxes filled with Needhams and always hidden on top shelves (hidden not so much to keep out the kids, as to save them for the adults!).

Seavey's Needhams, so the story goes, originated in 1872 when a charismatic evangelist, the Reverend George Needham from Needham, Massachusetts, was preaching in Portland, Maine. One Monday morning after an enthusiastic Sunday service, a confectioner named Allen Gow found his candy-maker Mr. Ellsworth making chocolate-coated coconut fondant candies. He asked his young employee what they were, and the man promptly answered, "Needhams." Whether the man was converted or not was never recorded. But there's no question that the inspired candy tasted divine.

Mr. Ellsworth continued to make Needhams until his death in 1937, when the company was bought by John Seavey, who attached his name to the coconut confection. The formula has never changed although Seavey's Needhams was bought in 1962 by its third and current owner Jim Holmes. Holmes merged the Seavey business with his retail candy operation, Lou-Rod Candy Kitchens. In the late sixties, a major fire burned him out of the retail business, and the operation became exclusively wholesale and mail order.

Holmes estimates that his company makes about 30,000 Needhams on a good day or about half a million pounds a year. People who have migrated from Maine or have visited the area are always writing and requesting Needhams. "They send $15, and we send them as many pounds as remain after postage is taken out," explains Holmes. (At about $2 per pound, that leaves a generous quantity for the customer.)

These confections are still pretty much handmade and hand-packaged. But Holmes has had to give up on hand-dipping the coconut squares in chocolate. An enrobing machine now does the job that was once done by people. "We used to have ladies who did that job, but they don't exist anymore," says Holmes. "Hand-dipping is a lost art," he adds with some regret.

HOW TO PURCHASE: Send a $15 check or money order (payable to Lou-Rod Candy Kitchens), and Holmes will subtract postage and send the remainder in Needhams. Since the candy is sold wholesale, it costs about $2 per lb. so that leaves enough for roughly 6 lbs. of Needhams. If you wish to send a larger check, he'll send a larger quantity of candy.

Homemade Chocolates & Needhams

MARY'S CANDY SHOP, INC. 238 Main Street, Lewiston, Maine 04240. 207/783-9824.

"Mary's Candy Store—See Them Made" says the small sign outside this Lewiston candy shop. Inside this neat, no-frills store, the intoxicating aroma of chocolate hits first, followed by the sensation of being surrounded by nearly a hundred shapes and flavors of hand-dipped chocolate confections. Is this a chocolate-lover's paradise, or what?

Lucille Meservier and her husband Armand, a retired loom repairman from a local textile mill, are the third owners of Mary's Candy Shop. Lucille worked for the previous owner for 8 years before buying the business from him in 1979. The Meserviers still make candy the way the original owners did when they started the business in 1933. Everything is handmade from scratch, and even the dipping is done by hand, as it was then.

The Needham, the unofficial state of Maine candy (unless you count Bangor Taffy), reigns supreme at Mary's. An indescribably rich coconut cream center dipped in Van Leer chocolate (the same dipping chocolate used by Godiva Chocolates), Needhams account for one-quarter of the sales.

That's no surprise in Maine. Any local candy store that's worth its salt makes a Needham. All are admittedly slightly different and a source of regional pride. It's a major contest in this northeastern-most state to determine the favorite so, naturally, Mary's Needham recipe is a closely guarded secret.

Besides the Needham, the Meserviers make no less than forty other types of chocolates, including fudge of every flavor, butternut creams, chocolate-dipped nougat rolls, turtles (nuts and caramel covered in milk or dark chocolate) and French truffles.

They also make an entire line of dietetic candies. Mary's is well known for making handmade chocolate baskets, hearts, and other seasonally appropriate shapes and filling them with assorted chocolates.

HOW TO PURCHASE: There's another tradition among the old-time candy shops in Maine. People who have moved "away" but have a hankering for their Needhams, simply mail a check or even cash for $10 or maybe $20. The shop takes out postage and handling and sends them whatever is left in chocolates. During the cooler months (no orders are sent in July or August), Lucille sends Needhams for $6.40 per lb. She will also send a mail order form for customers who want an assortment of chocolates. (Add $2.50 for the first lb. and 75¢ for each thereafter for shipping.)

TO VISIT: The Meserviers invite people to visit their candy-making operation, but it's best to call first and make sure they are making candy when you plan to stop by. To get to Mary's Candy Shop take exit 13 (Route 196, Lisbon Street) off the Maine Turnpike. At the end of the exit ramp, bear right onto Lisbon Street and follow it toward downtown Lewiston and the intersection with Main Street. Bear right onto Main Street, and Mary's is about 2 blocks up on the left, next to the Greyhound Bus Station.

Claudette's Peanut Butter Creations

PEANUT BUTTER & CHOCOLATE CREATIONS BY CLAUDETTE. P.O. Box 622, Benner Hill, Waldoboro, Maine 04572. 207/832-5774.

Claudette Boggs began making peanut butter balls when her sons were young. She was looking for a way to make "lunch money" and turned to an old family recipe that had been a favorite with her boys.

She's been making them so long (since 1972) that she "just knows when they're ready to roll." The business side of her didn't emerge until 1980, however, when she started selling these candies to a local gourmet shop. Now she's handling several local customers and a booming mail order business. She rolls more than a thousand each week during the slow season but makes that many in a single day during the Christmas rush.

It is not necessary to be a peanut butter lover to ooh and ah over the taste of this rich peanut butter crunched with crispy cereal and chocolate chips, and dipped in a deep chocolate coating. But if you have already developed a certain fondness for peanut butter and chocolate, this will help to cultivate the habit.

Boggs makes her standard confection, 1-inch balls. She also makes 1- and 2-pound balls and makes various shapes and 10-pound treats for special occasions. An honest to goodness cottage industry, this one doesn't even have its own company name or logo. But, it's beginning to take over the Boggs's household. Since this little business started, the kitchen has always been a "beehive of activity." Boggs is in the process of taking the first step to separate her candy-making from the rest. She's turning the laundry room into a large kitchen where she can work well out of the way of the regular family goings-on.

In this way, she's not unlike Mrs. Claire Hall, the lady who introduced Boggs to the peanut butter balls. A native of Old Town, Maine (this writer's hometown), Boggs married one of Dr. and Mrs. Hall's sons. We all remember Doc Hall's wife making peanut butter balls by the boxfuls for holidays and gift-giving. Boggs remembers boxes of the sweets lining the hallway all the way up to the attic. Boggs's first husband was killed in Vietnam, and she remarried and moved "away." But she took Mrs. Hall's recipe with her. The good doctor and his wife have both passed away, and Claudette Boggs carries on a longtime legacy making a peanut butter and chocolate confection that's just this side of incredible.

HOW TO PURCHASE: **Claudette Boggs' Peanut Butter Balls can be mail ordered. Cost is 20¢ per ball. She sells a box of 12 balls (about ½ lb.) for $2.40 and a box of 24 (about 1 lb.) for $4.80. Weights may vary since these are handmade. There is an extra charge for postage which is usually via U.P.S. Special packaging and candy designs are available. To order, send check or money order payable to Claudette Boggs. The candy is made to order so allow 2–3 weeks for delivery. Call or write for the latest price list.**

Bangor Taffy

PINE TREE CONFECTIONS, INC. P.O. Box 816, Bangor, Maine 04401. 207/862-2767.

If pigs could fly . . . and Bangor Taffy had no calories . . .

It is just possible that Bangor Taffy is the most unbelievably luscious candy in the world. It's sinfully rich, caramel taste makes it hard to eat just one . . . even two.

Ironically, the little, light-brown cubes dusted with powdered sugar are totally innocuous to look at. There's virtually no resemblance to conventional taffy in its shape. And it's not particularly eye-appealing. But even people who never eat candy fall in love with Bangor Taffy. "People don't trust me when I tell them it's a difficult item," says the vice-president and marketing director, Philip Brady. "People will kill for it. They can't stop eating it," he says.

Bangor Taffy is one of the best and oldest traditions the state of Maine has to offer. It's origin goes back at least to Civil War days making it a contender for the role that's usually saved for the Maine lobster.

The packaging is simple—a gold and black box with sailing ships on the cover. And it doesn't come close to conveying the aristocratic roots of this confection. Bangor taffy became well known during the early railroad days when it was sold car to car with newspapers and tobacco on the Maine Central and the Bangor and Aroostook railroads.

Bangor Taffy is still made in exactly the same way it was back then with heavy cream, corn syrup, and sweetened condensed milk. Much of the trick behind its ambrosial taste is the cooking process. The mixture is cooked in copper kettles over a slow fire until it caramelizes.

Bangor Taffy is a protected recipe that was first made by the Pine Tree Taffy Company. Then, for many years, it was made for them by Colonial Candy Company. Recently the recipe was returned to Pine Tree Confections, and its owner Edward King continues to make the confection under the Bangor Taffy label.

Brady says an imposter is making a product that is called by the same name. "It's supposed to be like Bangor Taffy, but it's God-awful or we'd have prosecuted," says Brady, who thinks they may have to ask them to at least change the name of the candy.

Pine Tree Confections makes a Blueberry Salt Water Taffy that comes close to its caramel cousin in addictiveness. The confectioners also make Bangor Gold, a molasses candy, and several kinds of fudge.

Bangor Taffy doesn't come with a warning, but if it did, it might say, "Try at your own risk. We are not responsible if you get hooked."

HOW TO PURCHASE: **A 12-oz. gold and black box of Bangor Taffy is sold for $4. An 8-oz. bag of Blueberry Taffy is $2.25. Postage and handling are included in the price. To order, send check or money order payable to Pine Tree Confections.**

MASSACHUSETTS

Hand-dipped Chocolates

CATHERINE'S CHOCOLATES

CATHERINE'S CHOCOLATE SHOP. R.D. #2, Box 32, Great Barrington, Massachusetts 01230. 1/800-345-2462 or 413/528-2510 in Massachusetts.

Catherine's hand-dipped chocolates are the kind that grandmothers in New England have been setting out in ornate china candy dishes for generations. Each is beautifully sculptured in shiny chocolate with a mystery filling that could only be discerned by taking a bite. (We never realized that the little curlicue of chocolate on the top was a cryptic message about the flavor in the center.)

You might say that Catherine Keresztes has been in the candy-making business all her life. Catherine is the third generation of confectioners. Uncle Emile's family opened the first of the homemade candy shops around the turn of the century in Savannah, Georgia. Emile moved north and opened one shop, then another, until his business multiplied into seven stores in the New York–New Jersey area. Despite the rapid growth, the chocolates were all hand-dipped, a trademark that has remained consistent.

Catherine practically grew up in the kitchen of one of those shops and learned all about hand-dipping chocolates and packing candy boxes. When she and her family moved to Great Barrington in 1958, Catherine opened her own shop following the recipes that Emile had acquired from the generation before him. Transplanted New Englander, after all, Catherine runs as caring a Yankee company as we've found.

House specialties are stemmed cherry cordials, butter krunch, caramel nut delights, chocolate nut bark, pecan rolls (chewy nougat-caramel center rolled in pecan halves), dipped fruits (orange slices, apricots, orange peel, and crystallized ginger), honeycomb sponge chips, and coconut snow caps. Miniatures, about 60 to 70 per pound, are also dipped by hand with the same pride. No two chocolates are alike, owing to the hand-dipping, but each still bears an identifying mark to tell which center is hidden inside the luscious chocolate.

Catherine's chocolates have been shipped all over the world to places as far away as New Zealand and as exotic as Singapore. The Berkshire-based candy-makers have received every special request imaginable and try to accommodate them all. They've made candy bar corporate logos, chocolate violins, and even computers.

HOW TO PURCHASE: Catherine's Chocolates are available in several assortments. One-pound boxes are $12.95 or $14.95, depending on contents. One-pound of Colonial Creams (all cream centers) is $12.95. Dipped Fruits are $14.95 per 1-lb. box (cordial cherries, orange slices, apricots, orange peel, and ginger). Roasted Nuts, Old Fashioned Finger Crackers, and Dietetic Chocolates are available. Postage is extra and depends on destination. Visa, Master-Card, American Express, and checks are accepted.

World-class Chocolates

HARBOR SWEETS, INC. Box 150, Marblehead, Massachusetts 01945. 617/745-7648.

At roughly $30 per pound, you might expect Harbor Sweets to be the best chocolate you've ever eaten. And you wouldn't be the slightest bit disappointed!

Reputed to be the most expensive chocolates in this country, Ben Strohecker's world-class confections were first created on the stove in his kitchen in 1976. His goal was to prove he could make the world's best chocolates by simply using the finest and freshest ingredients and plenty of time. Since then, many chocolate experts have confirmed that he has achieved that goal.

The grandson of the man who cofounded Luden's (of cough drop fame) and fashioned the first chocolate bunny, Strohecker grew up in Pennsylvania Dutch country with candy-making in his blood.

He founded Harbor Sweets, partly in defiance of decades of working in the corporate food world. The last straw was as marketing director for a prominent candy company where his job was as much puff as product. The company wouldn't listen to their candy experts, says Strohecker, but he did. He asked each one, "If you could just eat one piece of chocolate before you died, what would it be?"

He took their answers and his convictions and proceeded to launch Harbor Sweets. He gave his candies nautical shapes and names, owing to his Boston North Shore location. His first and still most popular was Sweet Sloops, almond butter crunch covered with decadent dark chocolate and white chocolate sails.

Soon his venture took over the basement of his Marblehead home. He added a luscious Sand Dollar turtle of caramel and pecan; Marblehead Mints, dark chocolate with a hint of peppermint crunch; and Sweet Shells, an exotic orange crunch in dark chocolate.

He quickly outgrew that space and moved Harbor Sweets to its present quarters in a colonial brick building in historic Salem, at the same time adding a toasted almond bark that he named "Barque Sarah" for an 1850s sailing ship.

After spending 30-something years working for other companie Strohecker now works only with "people I like." He's turned down some big accounts (Neiman-Marcus) simply because he didn't like their buyer. But he has allowed Gumps of San Francisco and Sak Fifth Avenue to carry Harbor Sweets.

He feels the same way about his employees. A spiritual man who is active in the Episcopal church, Strohecker believes Harbor Sweet has yet another mission. He hires mainly people who would have difficulty in more conventional jobs—the retarded, recent immi grants, the handicapped. They work alongside the police chief's wife, students, and moms.

His employees number 150 during peak production, but Harbor Sweets is more like Willi Wonka's chocolate factory than an automat ed assembly line. They work in irregularly subdivided sections o one large immaculate room decorated in red and white. Until 1980 all the cooking was done on one Prizer Painter gas stove. Quite by chance, Strohecker found a duplicate recently, installed it, and dou bled Harbor Sweets' production. With the growing demand for Har bor Sweets, no doubt, Strohecker will be looking for a third stove before long.

HOW TO PURCHASE: Gift boxes of 30 Sweet Sloops are $16. A box of 60 candies sells for $30.50. A box of 15 Sand Dollars is $14.50. A gift assortment of 44 chocolates is $25. Assortments for special occasions are available. Strohecker has recently introduced the Robert L. Strohecker Assorted Rabbit (named for his grandfather) for Easter gifts. All of the Harbor Sweets tastes are anatomically dispersed throughout this unique bunny. (Cost is $11.50.) Prices include postage and handling. Major credit cards and checks are accepted.

Butter Nut Munch

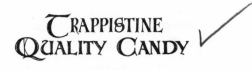

TRAPPISTINE QUALITY CANDY. Mount Saint Mary's Abbey, 300 Arnold Street, Wrentham, Massachusetts 02093. 508/528-1282.

"Candy is made to share—make it into a bond of laughter & exchange. Candy is made for remembrance—give it with love and thoughtfulness." When ordering candy from the sisters of Mount Saint Mary's Abbey, this inspirational message about the importance of giving is enclosed.

Committed to a life of self-support, the 58 sisters of this contemplative community produce 40,000 pounds of spirit-lifting candy a year. This includes their well-known Butter Nut Munch that tastes like twice the butter and triple the "munch," rich penuche (maple fudge), and chocolate fudge that will send taste buds into the stratosphere. The candy line also offers a divine bark and butter-laced chewy caramels.

The Butter Nut Munch is by far the best seller, about 15,000 pounds worth each year. It starts with a crisp toffee center made of butter, sugar, and cream. To that, the sisters add ground almonds. The mixture is cooked, then spread on a marble table to cool. It's scored and coated with a rich milk chocolate. The finished pieces are sprinkled with roasted hazelnuts that are imported from Turkey because they have the best flavor, says Sister Veronica, who's in charge of the candy-making operation.

The sisters of Mount Saint Mary's Abbey have been making their candy since 1956, and even Pope John Paul II sampled the Munch on his trip to the United States in 1979. The sisters started this business after they realized that bread baking was too demanding and not profitable. Chocolate seemed lke a logical extension of their small dairy business and a popular choice.

Although their candy sold well locally, the mail order aspect was slow at first. Then each sister asked her family for the names and addresses on their Christmas list. It must have worked! Today most of their business is done by mail.

The abbey, founded in 1949 by the late Cardinal Cushing, is located in a wooded setting near the Rhode Island border. The convent is chiefly self-sufficient. The sisters maintain and milk a herd of ninety dairy cows, put up hay, sew their own clothes, repair their own shoes, and even print the flyers for their mail order candy business.

They sell bread (but most is for their own use) and candy at the abbey. Visitors are welcome in the chapel on the property but cannot enter the convent itself.

HOW TO PURCHASE: A 1¼-lb. box of Butter Nut Munch is $10.25; the same size box of Caramels is $7.95. The fudge comes in 1½-lb. boxes and costs $8.15 for penuche (maple fudge with walnuts) and $8.95 for chocolate fudge with walnuts. Shipping is included in the price. There is a 2-box minimum, and chocolates are not available during the months of July and August. (Fudge is available year round.)

Old Fashioned Barley Candies

The Handmade
Barley Candy Specialist
Since 1971

DOROTHY TIMBERLAKE
❧ CANDIES ❧

DOROTHY TIMBERLAKE CANDIES. Main Street, Eaton Center, New Hampshire 03849. 603/447-2221.

A vibrant rainbow of colors with flavors numbering in the 150s and more than twice that many shapes sums up a display of Dorothy Timberlake's Old Fashioned Barley candy lollipops and toy candies at a recent food show. But they don't come close to telling the whole story of this grandmother's impressive confection business that started when she was fifty-five.

Fond recollections of watching a friend's mother make barley candy lollipops in her Cambridge kitchen during her childhood helped launch Timberlake's company. Then, during the summer of 1971, she and her husband found three cast-iron clear toy molds and an original recipe for barley candy. That was all she needed to get started in the delightful business of making old-fashioned barley candy.

All summer Timberlake made and sold pops to shops in the White Mountains, where their summer home was located. Since then, the Timberlakes have collected more than 6,000 different shapes. Many are pewter which can produce toxic amounts of lead, so Timberlake has them reproduced in aluminum for candy-making. The originals line the walls of her four candy rooms in the Eaton Center house, an old inn that had been in the family for eight generations and was the house in which she was born.

Timberlake moved the candy-making operation to the property in New Hampshire after it outgrew the Timberlake home kitchen in Belmont, Massachusetts. Two of her five children, a daughter and a son, along with a neighbor, help in the company and fifteen grandchildren are her "best testers."

Timberlake makes her candies by boiling pearl barley in water from her artesian well. To this thick water base, she adds sugar and corn syrup and flavorings as ordinary as lemon and as exotic as fig, cantaloupe, guava, and pomegranate. The result is a strong, not-too-sweet flavored hard candy. Sizes range from very large to very small, but even the smallest Timberlake treats take at least 20 minutes to eat. Shapes vary from Charlie Chaplin, to thirty-six animals in Noah's Ark, to Hamlet holding the skull of Yorick. She also makes special shapes for holidays, clear three-dimensional toys, candy lithopanes (molded pictures), and Christmas ornaments from barley candy.

Most recently, Timberlake spent several days in Paris studying the art of blowing hard candy, a technique that's very similar to glass blowing, and so has recently added hand-blown candy to her list of products.

Timberlake's multi-page catalog (for which she charges $1.50) reads like the menu in a Chinese restaurant with many columns and choices!

HOW TO PURCHASE: Timberlake's Old Fashioned Barley Candies are available by mail in several assortments (your choice). Twenty-five 20-gm. pops are $1.10 each; twelve 40-gm. pops sell for $1.60 each, and six 70-gm. pops are $2.20 each. Orders may be mixed to yield about 3 lbs. of candy, and shipping for that quantity is an additional $1.50. Relief pops (40 gm.) are $1.40 each, and the large (100 gm.) pops sell for $2 each. Everything is made to order. Timberlake will also make up special requests of any size (even 2–3 feet) if the customer provides a model from which to make a mold. All items are shipped U.P.S. and must be prepaid with check or money order or shipped C.O.D.

RHODE ISLAND

Truffles and Truffle Sauces

NEW ENGLAND TRUFFLE COMPANY. 29 Okie Street, Providence, Rhode Island 02908. 401/831-0890.

Tasting truffles made by the New England Truffle Company is enough to produce an endorphin-like high that usually accompanies endurance jogging. One needs only to read the list of flavors to incite an urge for chocolate: Passion Fruit, Zinfandel Port Wine, American Chèvre (white chocolate and Massachusetts goat cheese that's pure heaven), Maple Black Walnut (made with Rhode Island maple syrup), Caramel Crunch (milk chocolate with a nut mix), and Peach Melba made with Rhode Island peach wine and raspberry extract). Add to that seasonal flavors such as an outrageous Cranberry Truffle made with white chocolate; a Wassail Truffle with mulled wine; Gingerbread; and a white chocolate Candy Cane confection.

Now you have a picture of what the New England Truffle Company is all about. All their luscious confections are made with rich Belgian chocolate, their own homemade crème fraîche, and sweet cream butter.

The New England Truffle Company started in 1985 in the kitchen of the café in the Barn Restaurant in Seekonk, Massachusetts. Holly Trinkuth-Bradford, a graduate of the Johnson Wales Pastry school, hooked up with the restaurant's chef, John Elkhay, and owner Guy Abelson.

John began to realize there was a need for a good American truffle. He was buying truffles for the restaurant but couldn't find a product that satisfied him. The three put their heads together and decided to go into business. Abelson had the financial backing. Elkhay and Trinkuth-Bradford had the recipes and the know-how. And Drinkuth-Bradford was willing to manage the company, which also meant doing most of the truffle-making at first.

They quickly outgrew the tiny restaurant kitchen and moved into a former machine shop in nearby Providence. A kitchen and a small office were installed, and soon they had 1,800 square feet of usable space.

The company, which started with only a few flavors, now has sixteen-plus seasonal specials. Several of the best-sellers have been turned into intensely flavored truffle sauces: Peach Melba, Chocolate-Chocolate, Gold Rush, Caramel Crunch, and Champagne Cassis. And these are as versatile as they are delicious.

In their first full year of operation, New England Truffle Company made more than 2,000 pounds of truffles and about 8,000 jars of truffle sauce. In case there was any question in any of the three partners' minds about the need for an American truffle, the company tripled its Christmas orders from 1986 to 1987. In the truffles-for-all spirit, the group is now experimenting with a "blue collar" truffle that would retail for less than half the cost of their blue blood line of sweets.

HOW TO PURCHASE: Truffles are sold by mail. A 4-piece box is $6.50; 9-piece boxes are $14; and 16 pieces cost $25. Truffle Sauces are $6.50 per 9-oz. jar, except Champagne Cassis which is $7 per jar. Add $1.50 per package being shipped within New England and $2.50 per shipment to the rest of the country. Orders are shipped via U.P.S. Payment is by check, money order, Visa, or MasterCard.

Holly's Peach Melba Mousse Cake

Combine New England Truffle Company's Peach Melba Truffle Sauce and whipped cream, and you'll have a mousse in a minute. Spread it over layers of pound cake, and you've got an elegant dessert in 5 minutes!

> *9-oz. jar New England Truffle Company Peach*
>   *Melba Truffle Sauce*
> *2 cups cold heavy whipping cream*
> *16-oz. plain pound cake*
> *¼ cup peach jam or peach conserves*
> *2 ripe peaches, peeled and thinly sliced*
> *Fresh raspberries and shaved chocolate for*
>   *garnish (optional)*

1. Warm the truffle sauce and let stand. Whip the cream until it forms stiff peaks. Pour the truffle sauce into a medium bowl. Top with a quarter of the cream and mix into the sauce. Add the remaining cream and fold gently until blended. Chill for 1 hour.
2. Meanwhile, cut the cake into 3 equal slices through the center. Chill the cake. Melt the peach jam.
3. Spoon out ½ cup of the mousse mixture and reserve. To assemble, place the bottom layer of the cake on a serving plate. Spread with half the jam and a third of the mousse. Top with half the peaches. Center the middle slice of cake over this and spread with remaining jam. Add a third of the mousse and remaining peaches. Top with final layer of cake and frost with remaining mousse. Fill a pastry bag with reserved mousse and decorate with rosettes or stars. Garnish with raspberries and shaved chocolate if desired.

Serves 8.

Deluxe Chocolate Sauces

Tel (802) 222-9352

Bread & Chocolate
INC.

WHOLESALE GOURMET FOODS
Box 623 · Bradford, Vt. 05033

BREAD & CHOCOLATE, INC. Box 623, Main Street, Bradford, Vermont 05033. 802/222-9352.

Caterer and restaurateur Phyllis Perry experienced the proverbial burn out, but she couldn't seem to get the commercial food business out of her blood. Having been in one aspect of food production or another since 1972, the energetic Perry started yet another edible enterprise in 1983 and called it Bread & Chocolate.

Operating out of the renovated barn adjacent to their historical Main Street home in Bradford, she runs a self-styled wholesale bakery and makes wickedly-rich chocolate sauces.

Her menu of sauces reads like a fantasy for chocolate lovers— White Chocolate Hazelnut, Chocolate Espresso, Chocolate Almond, and Chocolate Mint. All are made with Belgian chocolate, fresh cream, and sweet butter. Sauces are elegantly packaged in jars boasting gilded labels and hand-decorated brown paper tops.

She also makes jars of intensely flavored jams made with local fruits and puts together chocolate raspberry cakes and seasonal cakes in hand-painted gift boxes. But so far the last two are a local secret, unattainable via the U.S. mail.

Perry started in the food business when she was 21. Her first ventures were in Manhattan where she grew up. A health food store called Down to Earth was her first project. The store was successful, but Perry became more interested in French cooking. She sold Down to Earth and opened a restaurant called Up the Beanstalk, which received two stars from the *New York Times* restaurant reviewers. In 1977, Perry married and moved to Vermont, where she opened the Paradise Café in Bradford. Then there was a lengthy stint as a chef in a Norwich, Vermont, restaurant and an impressive catering career. The last two and raising a couple of daughters sent Perry into temporary retirement.

Now Perry, who admits that she's never really lost her love for cooking, is working at her own pace and enjoying it. But why did she pick bread and chocolate? Simple. They are two of her favorite foods. She loves making her breads and working with chocolate and looks forward to the time when she can bring her daughters into her business.

HOW TO PURCHASE: Perry's chocolate sauces can be purchase by mail. Flavors are White Chocolate Hazelnut, Chocolate Almon Chocolate Mint, or Chocolate Espresso. A 7-oz. jar is $5, and a ca of 12 jars is $60. Shipping is an additional $3 for up to 12 jars. Ma checks or money orders payable to Bread & Chocolate, Inc.

Flourless Chocolate Torte with Coffee Whipped Cream

In some of our recipes there are obvious substitutes. This dens rich chocolate cake would not be the same, however, without Brea & Chocolate's Chocolate Espresso Sauce.

*Two 7-oz. jars Bread & Chocolate's Chocolate
Espresso Sauce
¾ cup sugar
5 eggs*

1. Butter an 8-inch round cake pan and line the bottom with parc ment paper. Butter the paper and reserve. Preheat the oven to 350° In the top of a large double boiler, melt the chocolate sauce ov medium heat. When melted, add the sugar and whisk for 1 minu Remove from heat and whisk another minute or until chocola cools and thickens slightly.

2. In a separate bowl, whisk the eggs until foamy. Pour into th chocolate mixture, whisking continuously until combined. Pour in the prepared cake pan and set the pan in the middle of a 9x13-inc baking pan. Add enough hot water to come halfway up the side of the cake pan. Bake 90 minutes.

3. Remove from the water bath and allow to cool at room temper ture for 1 hour. Refrigerate for at least 2 hours. Run a knife aroun the edges of the cake and turn onto a serving plate. Peel off the parc ment paper and discard. Serve with spoonfuls of whipped crean below.

Serves 8.

Coffee Whipped Cream

*1 cup heavy cream
2 tablespoons confectioners' sugar
2 tablespoons strong coffee, cooled*

Whip the cream and the sugar together until it forms stiff peak Add the coffee and beat briefly to combine. Chill until serving.

Vermont Chocolate Apples

Vermont Chocolate Apples
by Ivydaro

IVYDARO. P.O. Box 369, Putney, Vermont 05346.
802/387-5597.

After years of doing the bookkeeping for the family orchard, Green Mountain Orchards, in Putney, Vermont, Ivy Darrow decided she wanted to do something on her own and pick up a little extra income in the process. Combining a taste of life in Vermont and her sons' and husband's livelihood in apples, she came up with Vermont Chocolate Apples.

Miniature, one-ounce apples in two halves, fitted together, wrapped in gleaming red foil, and topped with green silk leaves, then packaged in sturdy-handled baskets of twelve or six, these look as tantalizing as a basket of just-picked Vermont apples.

"It was a flash of inspiration . . . the light bulb effect," she says of her idea. It came together for the senior citizen and mother of three grown sons when Darrow met a man who specialized in chocolate-making. The two developed a mold together. Then, for an outrageous price, he offered to make the candy for her. That's when Darrow decided to make the candy apples herself. She takes the finest semisweet and bittersweet Belgian chocolate, melts it, and molds it, then imbeds toasted hazelnuts in the chocolate.

Darrow actually started selling her candy apples in 1986 after many experiments and trial balloons and lots of feedback from friends. Her first year in business was a resounding success, as she sold nearly 1,000 pounds of these little apples. She continues to reassess her product and is always coming up with new ways to make and market her chocolates. Just recently she added whole hazelnuts instead of sprinkling chopped nuts over the molded chocolate. And this candy creator is at work on a new product, a mint-flavored apple that will be wrapped in green foil.

Much of the Ivydaro's (Darrow combined her two names for her company title) product is sold in Vermont stores, inns, and ski resorts. However, a growing mail order business is also becoming a bona fide side of her operation.

HOW TO PURCHASE: Ivydaro's gift-giving basket of twelve 1-oz. chocolate apples will be sent anywhere in the United States for $18 including postage and handling. Orders must be prepaid. Make check or money order payable to Ivydaro.

*Vermont Chocolates &
American Truffles*

LAKE CHAMPLAIN CHOCOLATE COMPANY. 431 Pine Street, Burlington, Vermont 05401. 1/800-634-8105 or 802/864-1808 in Vermont.

If you've ever seen the milk and white chocolate Vermont cows packaged in truck-shaped boxes, then you've seen Lake Champlain Chocolate's trademark—or at least one of them.

The burgeoning Vermont chocolate company is at once upscale and down home with items as slick as American truffles and a line of grass roots products. The latter includes the funky brown cow and Chocolates of Vermont, so named because it features candies such as snow-capped peaks of almonds, raisins, and chocolate.

Lake Champlain Chocolate Company began in 1983 almost on a dare. Jim Lampman, owner of the Ice House Restaurant on Burlington's waterfront, was challenging his pastry chef Tad Spurgeon to make a better chocolate than the expensive confections they were sampling. With a little experimentation, Spurgeon did just that. "A good chocolate should be made so you can taste everything at once . . . like a symphony in your mouth," says Spurgeon, who applied his philosophy to making the line of glitzy, glittery American truffles.

Like their European cousins, Champlain Truffles have ganache centers of butter, chocolate, and a liqueur flavor. They are hand rolled, then coated with chocolate, unlike most truffles, says Lampman, which have their ganache poured into stamped-out chocolate shells. The Champlain truffles are much larger than the European varieties (nearly an ounce), "glorious and big like America," says the company's literature. And the tops of these mellifluous treats are zigzagged with colorful lines. The only thing that's not American is the chocolate. It comes from Belgium.

Lampman and his illustrious chef came up with recipes for several distinctive flavors such as French Roast, Amaretto Praline, Raspberry, Bourbon Pecan, Cappuccino, and Champagne. For months these were served to the restaurant's Sunday brunch patrons, who were unknowingly taking part in the truffle experiment. Then Lampman leased and renovated space behind Floyd's lawnmower service on Pine Street and started a wholesale candy business. The company has since moved across the street to a shop with a storefront where visitors can see the chocolate being made and drink in the wonderful aromas.

After 18 years of ownership, Lampman recently sold his restaurant to "just make chocolates." The chocolate visionary is always up new ideas. Lake Champlain Chocolate has introduced a line of Tropical Fantasies and Exotic Chocolates with butter creams of passion fruit, coconut cream, and guava cream and centers of nuts and fruit such as Diamond Head, a solid dark chocolate filled with butter macadamia nuts.

Although aimed at an upscale audience, this chocolate busines still has a kind of New England appeal. The brown Vermont Co and the truffles run neck and neck as the most popular items f a company that makes more than 75,000 pounds of chocolate eac year. Indeed, this new breed of chocolatier has found that Yanke "moo" and fancy foods do mix.

HOW TO PURCHASE: Lake Champlain Chocolate's America Truffles (15 pieces) is $24; a box of 8 is $13. The Brown Cow-milk and white chocolate, bittersweet chocolate and white choco late, and white chocolate with bittersweet spots—arrives in its ow truck for $7.50. Chocolates of Vermont, including Green Mountai Evergreen Mint, Honey Caramel (with Vermont honey), and Map Crunch (made with Vermont maple toffee and syrup), are sold boxes of 24 for $13.50. A box of 20 Tropical Fantasies is $12.5 Add $3 for postage and handling per destination. Gift boxes an special gift assortments are available for special occasions. Maj credit cards, checks, or money orders are accepted.

TO VISIT: Lake Champlain Chocolates operates a shop that's ope from 9:30 A.M.–5:30 P.M., Monday through Saturday. To get ther take exit 14W from Interstate 89 and continue west on Main Stre past the University of Vermont and the city of Burlington until yo reach Pine Street (3 streets east of Lake Champlain). Turn left an continue ¾ of a mile. The store is on the right.

The World's Best Fudge Sauce

MOTHER MYRICK'S CONFECTIONERY & ICE CREAM PARLOR. P.O. Box 1142, Manchester Center, Vermont 05255. 802/362-1560.

Under the shadow of Mother Myrick's Mountain (named for an eighteenth-century midwife who lived there), Ron Mancini and his wife Jackie Baker are making a chocolate fudge sauce that's possibly better than the best (Blanchard & Blanchard's). It's a sauce that's s-o-o-o good, it's a shame to waste it on ice cream. Instead, it's the kind that requires burying inhibitions, putting diet aside, and eating right out of the jar.

Mancini and Baker's "Fudge Factory" has been turning out this heavenly sauce along with fudge candies since 1978. "I selected the most intense bittersweet chocolate I could find," says Mancini of his secret to success. "I needed a chocolate that would get my attention," he explains.

Mancini came to Vermont on what he calls an "emotional sabbatical" from life in New York City. He arrived with his clothes, car, and very little else. The next thing he knew, he was standing in a storefront selling fudge made by local women. Prompted by a friend to start his own fudge business, Mancini began doing some research.

On a mission to Boston in search of recipes and chocolate, he stumbled on a Greek candy maker's ancient shop. For 7 weeks he worked there, trading labor for recipes. Next he approached a retired candy maker to buy his equipment, and his purchase came with a recipe for buttercrunch and a promise that it could make a million dollars for its owner. That buttercrunch, a sort of Heath Bar with just the right amount of chocolate and dusted with nuts, is now Mother's best-selling candy.

Ironically, when Mother's opened, it nearly went bankrupt. It was Baker who came to the rescue. An ebullient former school teacher, she met Mancini at his shop (and later married him), repaid his loan, bought out Mancini's former partner, and rolled up her sleeves.

Manchester Center has taken warmly to the "factory" that's really a cottage industry. The friendly couple greet customers almost as they would family. And they invite customers to have a hot cup of coffee in the morning and to watch the candy-making process.

Although best known for their Buttercrunch and Ron's Hot Fudge Sauce, Mother Myrick's also makes a full line of handmade and hand-dipped chocolates (every bit from scratch). With the addition of these candies, they changed the company from "Fudge Factory" to "Confectionery." Mother's also makes award-winning cakes and pastries. And, oh yes, there's ice cream.

While everyone is combining the same ingredients—sugar, butter, and chocolate—what make's them all taste so different? "Spiritual essence," answers Mancini. Perhaps what he's really saying is that it's Mother's fudge factor.

HOW TO PURCHASE: All but Mother Myrick's ice cream are available by mail. Ron's Hot Fudge Sauce is $15 for two 15-oz. jars. Buttercrunch Mother's Way is sold in 1-lb. boxes for $16; 2-lb. boxes for $28; and a 4-pack of ½-lb. gift boxes is $28. Postage and handling is $3.50 per destination.

Royal Chocolates of Vermont

ROYAL CHOCOLATES OF VERMONT. Irasville Common, Route 100, Waitsfield, Vermont 05673. 802/496-2144.

What started as a way to use up leftover cake trimmings has become a business that warns, "Bon Bons move over!" A glitzy gold and bronze cover declares, "Chocolat Royal du Vermont," and inside, truffle-like rum and kirsch-soaked rounds of deep, rich chocolate cake coated with nuts and a thick exterior of dark semisweet Belgian chocolate beckon. One is a meal, and two are a sin. But not to worry—no one ever stops at either.

Karin and Arno Noack had been in the food business for many years. Arno was a graduate of the Culinary Institute of America when it was in New Haven. He had been a chef in country clubs in Connecticut and New Jersey. Then in 1977, while searching for a healthier environment, they arrived in the Sugarbush, in the Mad River Valley region of Vermont. Within 2 hours they had picked the Green Mountain State as home. In 1977, they opened a European-style bakery and called it the Bread Basket where the two specialized in wonderful breads and pastries from their native Germany and surrounding countries.

One of their most popular items was a dense chocolate cake, but straightening the layer cakes yielded multitudes of trimmings that were going to waste. So the Noacks created rum balls, soaking the cuttings from the cakes in rum and dipping them in melted chocolate. They bought "a bunch of little boxes" and packaged their intoxicating treats. Soon customers were asking for boxes of rum balls for gifts.

Today the ingenious pair make special cakes just for this business. In addition to rum balls, they have created a Black Forest ball that's flavored with cherries and kirsch. In addition, the two are working on a raspberry almond ball. The flavorings are actually essences imported from Europe and with less than 1 percent alcohol. They've turned one room of the bakery into a chocolate room where they make just the rum balls and other ambrosial flavors of this chocolate confection. Chocolate lovers be warned, these little temptations are not to be trifled—or truffled—with.

HOW TO PURCHASE: **A box of 12 rum balls or Black Forest balls is mailed anywhere in the United States for $18.95 including shipping and handling. Packaging is in an elegant gold box, making them ideal for gift-giving. Just include each name and address. Payment is by check, Visa, or MasterCard.**

Cranberry Chicken, 42
Honey-Mustard Glazed Cornish Hens, 48
La Costa Spa Chicken with Pommery Mustard Sauce, 144
Lamb Curry with Dr. Shah's Indian Spice Concentrate, 63
New England Sauerkraut Garni, 138
Norwegian-style Meat Pie, 87
Putney Chutney Chicken, 62
Rabbit in Mustard Sauce, 99
Roast Stuffed Chicken Thigh with Goat Blue Cheese Sauce, 79
Sautéed Duck Breast with Peach Chutney, 52
Shaker Tarragon Chicken, 140
Smoked Pork Chops with Apricots and Raisins, 105
Spruce Mountain Blueberry Chutney Chicken, 39
Stewart's Maple Barbecue Ribs, 40

Pasta and Light Dishes

Chicken, Broccoli, and Cheese Quiche, 85
Chinese Noodles with Taste Matters Peanut Sauce, 64
Fettucine with Maine Chèvre and Scallops, 71
Leek and Gouda Cheese Quiche, 78
Pasta Salad with Fusilli and Pesto Dressing, 119
Pasta with Smoked Salmon and Cream Sauce, 96
Ricotta and Artichoke Pasta Roll, 123
White Pizza with Broccoli and Farmstead Gouda, 70
Whole Wheat Pizza with Caramelized Onions and Gorgonzola
   Cheese, 21

Salads

Bean and Smoked Provolone Salad, 107
Beef and Green Bean Salad, 38
Citrus Salad with Raspberry Honey Dressing, 4
Goat Cheese Salad with Walnuts and Raspberry Vinaigrette, 73
Joel's Greek Salad, 43
Pasta Salad with Fusilli and Pesto Dressing, 119
Smoked Lamb, Orzo & Feta Salad, 111
Smoked Turkey Waldorf Salad, 110
Tarragon Pepper Jelly Aspic with Shrimp, 50
Tomato and Avocado Salad, 148
Yankee Olé Layered Salad, 135

Sandwiches

Chicken in Pita Pockets with Cochon Mustard, 47
Tuna Pockets with Peach Chutney, 35
Turkey Club Sandwich with Cranberry Russian Dressing, 41

Soups

Abbott's Bouillabaisse, 114
Cold Broccoli Soup with Curry and Crème Fraîche, 89
Cream of Fiddlehead Soup, 134
Cream of Mushroom Soup, 143
Kale and Potato Soup, 102
Smoky Vermont Cheddar Cauliflower Soup, 83
Victoria Scott Spear's French Market Soup, 92

Vegetables

Baked Butternut Squash and Apples with Apple Cranberry
   Conserve, 67
Carrots Au Gratin with Mother's Mustard, 36
Cheddar-stuffed Baked Potato, 72
Curried Red Lentils with Cauliflower and Kelp, 142
Filomena's Zucchini, 57
Green Beans, Alaria, and Toasted Almonds, 136
Kathryn Palmer's Vermont Baked Beans, 11
Mousse of Summer Squash with Salsa, 60
Risotto with Porcini Mushrooms and York Hill Cheese, 74
Spicy New England Corn Pudding, 100
Summer Squash and Cheddar Cheese, 76

Jeffrey Sobiech

Salsa from Vermont, sauerkraut from Maine, johnny cake from Rhode Island—mail-order New England cuisine from the traditional to the unexpected

The new Yankee cuisine is exciting and delicious, and much of it is available by mail order. Detailed here are 150 of the best products and suppliers—all of whom will ship anywhere from Portland, Maine to Portland, Oregon.

Accompanying the entries are complete mail order instructions, a mouthwatering recipe, and a lively profile of the personality behind the product—from the General Electric scion who makes maple sugar to the ex-oceanographer who makes some of the best spice pastes in the United States. Grains and baked goods, honey and maple syrup, condiments, dairy products, meats, fish and poultry, pasta, soups, beverages, produce—and of course, sweets—are all included, making *The Tasty Side of New England* a veritable feast in an armchair.

"A trove of fine treats to the stay-at-home, or a delicious itinerary to the traveler." —Janet Greene, author of *Putting Food By*

"Using her guide not only gives our cooking better flavor and quality, but also reminds us of the dedicated efforts of individuals to produce the best." —Marion Cunningham, author of the revised *Fanny Farmer Cookbook*

BETH HILLSON, a journalist and a food enthusiast, has studied cooking in the United States and Europe. A native New Englander, she began this book while researching local products to use in her cooking classes. Food Editor for the *Hartford Courant*'s "Northeast Magazine," she lives in Connecticut.

Cover design by Neil Stuart
Cover photograph by Thomas Lindley

The Stephen Greene Press
Distributed by Viking Penguin Inc.
Cooking

AUST. $19.99
(recommended)
CAN. $17.95
U.S.A. $12.95

ISBN 0-8289-0664-5

90000

9 780828 906647